Drive Around DATE [

Thomas Cook

Canadian Rockies
Alberta and British Columbia

YOUR GUIDE TO GREAT DRIVES

Titles in this series include:

For further information about these and other Thomas Cook publications, write to Thomas Cook Publishing, PO Box 227, The Thomas Cook Business Park, 9 Coningsby Road, Peterborough PE3 8SB, United Kingdom.

Drive Around

Thomas Cook

Canadian Rockies
Alberta and British Columbia

A journey into the wilderness and
majesty of Canada's great Rocky
Mountains taking in the cultural and
historical highlights of Alberta and
British Columbia

Donald L Telfer and Helena Zukowski

Thomas Cook
Publishing

www.thomascookpublishing.com

Written by Donald L Telfer and Helena Zukowski, updated by Helena Zukowski
Original photography by Donald L Telfer and Helena Zukowski

Published by Thomas Cook Publishing,
A division of Thomas Cook Tour Operations Limited.
Company registration no. 1450464 England
The Thomas Cook Business Park, 9 Coningsby Road,
Peterborough PE3 8SB, United Kingdom
E-mail: sales@thomascook.com, Tel: + 44 (0) 1733 416477
www.thomascookpublishing.com

Produced by Cambridge Publishing Management Limited
Burr Elm Court, Main Street, Caldecote CB23 7NU

ISBN: 978-1-84157-865-1

First edition © 2006 Thomas Cook Publishing
This second edition © 2008
Text © Thomas Cook Publishing
Maps © Thomas Cook Publishing/PCGraphics (UK) Limited

Series Editor: Linda Bass
Production/DTP: Steven Collins

Printed and bound in India by Replika Press Pvt Ltd

Cover photography: Front: Banff National Park © Damm Stefan/SIME;
Back: Brown bear © Erwin & Peggy Bauer/zefa/Corbis

About the authors

A writer, photographer and editor for the past 40 years, **Donald L Telfer** contributes to newspapers and magazines in Canada, the US and abroad such as the Toronto *Sun*, Vancouver *Province*, Edmonton *Journal*, Dallas *Morning News*, San Jose *Mercury News*, Hackensack *Record*, New York *Post*, *CNN Traveler*, *Going Places*, *Passport Newsletter* and *The Peak*, which is circulated in first and business class of Air France, Cathay Pacific and Lufthansa German Airlines. Prior to entering the exotic world of freelance travel journalism, Don was editor and publisher of the Humboldt (Sask.) *Journal*, a weekly newspaper founded in 1905 by his grandfather. He has travelled extensively around the world and throughout the neighbouring provinces of Alberta and British Columbia, though, like many Canadians, this was his first visit to the remote and spectacular Cariboo Country. Between research trips, Don and his wife Mary Anne raised a family of two daughters and a son, the youngest two now studying to become teachers at the University of Saskatchewan in Saskatoon. They were inspired by visions of palm trees and lying on golden beaches but the fantasies evaporated quickly when they realised that teaching provided the opportunity for real vacations.

Helena Zukowski has logged more than 75 countries in her travelling career and has written about and photographed these for magazines and newspapers in Canada, the US and abroad. She has won numerous awards for her travel features and has had large cover stories in major newspapers all over the world. She is a member of The Travel Journalists Guild based in Chicago and served as president of that organisation for two years. Born in Edmonton on a February day that was –47°C, she now makes her home in Vancouver where the temperature is much more agreeable. Her interests are broad and range from caring lovingly for a vast flower and vegetable garden to learning to make a perfect *oeuf en meurette* at La Varenne cooking school in Burgundy to scuba diving in Palau, one of the world's best underwater destinations. Her current project is to explore every part of Canada in addition to visiting exotic countries. She has lived in Toronto, Borneo, Montserrat and in Palm Springs where for six years she edited a glossy magazine called *Palm Springs Life*. 'In many ways, Palm Springs was the strangest and most exotic of them all,' she says.

Contents

About Drive Around Guides

Thomas Cook's Drive Around Guides are designed to provide you with a comprehensive but flexible reference source to guide you as you tour a country or region by car. This guide divides the Canadian Rockies into 25 touring areas – one per chapter. Major cultural centres or cities form chapters in their own right. Each chapter contains enough attractions to provide at least a day's worth of activities – often more.

Ratings
To make it easier for you to plan your time and decide what to see, every area is rated according to its attractions in categories such as Architecture, Entertainment and Children.

Chapter contents
Every chapter has an introduction summing up the main attractions of the area or town, and a ratings box, which will highlight its appeal – some places may be more attractive to families travelling with children, others to wine-lovers visiting vineyards, and others to people interested in finding historical sites, great restaurants, or viewing wildlife.

Each chapter is then divided into an alphabetical gazetteer, and a suggested tour or walk. You can select whether you just want to visit a particular sight or attraction, choosing from those described in the gazetteer, or whether you want to tour the area comprehensively. If the latter, you can construct your own itinerary, or follow the authors' suggested tour, which comes at the end of every area chapter.

The gazetteer
The gazetteer section describes all the major attractions in the area – the ranches, towns, historic forts, national parks or museums that you are most likely to want to see. Maps of the area highlight all the places mentioned in the text. Using this comprehensive overview of the area, you may choose just to visit one or two sights.

One way to use the guide is to find individual sights that interest you, using the index or overview map and read what our authors have to say about them. This will help you decide whether to visit the sight. If you do, you will find practical information, such as the address and telephone number for enquiries and opening times.

Alternatively, you can choose a hotel, with the help of the accommodation recommendations contained in this guide. You can

Symbol Key

ⓘ Tourist Information Centre

🔄 Advice on arriving or departing

🔁 Advice on getting around

↪ Directions

🔟 Sights and attractions

◑ Accommodation

⬭ Shopping

🅿 Sport

◒ Entertainment

Practical information

The practical information in the page margins, or sidebar, will help you locate the services you need as an independent traveller – including the tourist information centre, car parks and public transport facilities. You will also find the opening times of sights, museums, churches and other attractions, as well as useful tips on shopping, market days, cultural events, entertainment, festivals and sports facilities.

then turn to the overall map on pages 10–11 to help you work out which chapters in the book describe the cities and regions closest to your touring base.

Driving tours

The suggested tour is just that – a suggestion, with plenty of optional detours and one or two ideas for making your own discoveries, under the heading *Also worth exploring*. The routes are designed to link the attractions described in the gazetteer section, and to cover outstandingly scenic coastal, mountain and rural landscapes. The total distance is given for each tour, and the time it will take you to drive the complete route, but bear in mind that this indication is just for driving time: you will need to add on extra time for visiting attractions along the way.

Many of the routes are circular, so that you can join them at any point. Where the nature of the terrain dictates that the route has to be linear, the route can either be followed out and back, or you can use it as a link route, to get from one area in the book to another.

As you follow the route descriptions, you will find names picked out in bold capital letters – this means that the place is described fully in the gazetteer. Other names picked out in bold indicate additional villages or attractions worth a brief stop along the route.

Accommodation and food

In every chapter you will find lodging and eating recommendations for individual towns, or for the area as a whole. These are designed to cover a range of price brackets and concentrate on more characterful small or individualistic hotels and restaurants. In addition, you will find information in the 'Travel facts' chapter on chain hotels, with an address to which you can write for a guide, map or directory.

The price indications used in the guide have the following meanings:

$ budget level
$$ typical/average prices
$$$ de luxe

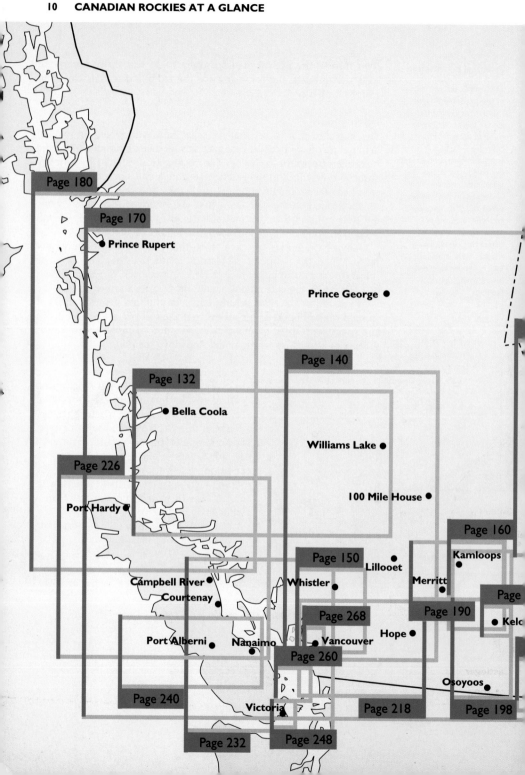

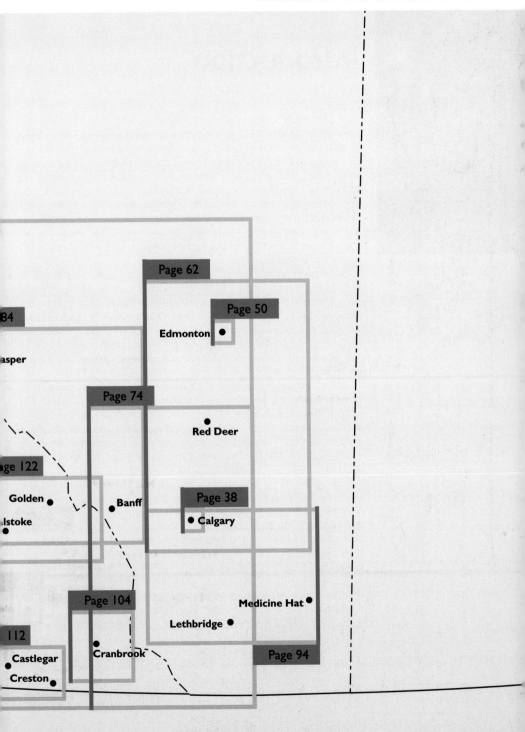

Page 62

Page 50

Edmonton •

84

asper

Page 74

Red Deer

ge 122

Golden •

Banff •

Page 38

lstoke

• Calgary

Page 104

Medicine Hat •

Lethbridge •

112

Castlegar

Cranbrook

Page 94

Creston •

Above
Canadian Mountie

Introduction

One of Canada's more prolific authors, the late Pierre Berton, who once defined a Canadian as someone who could make love in a canoe, couldn't have come up with a more apt phrase to describe western Canadians. Albertans and the 'Lotus Landers' of British Columbia see their chunk of Canada as a large slice of paradise and will bore the knickers off anyone even *vaguely* hinting he might like to come and visit. Westerners firmly believe they live in the only part of Canada worth having and spend a good portion of their lives indulging in all the scenic splendour around them. Beauty, they argue, makes up for any economic rapids or recessionary waterfalls that swirl occasionally around their canoes.

Westerners have a lot of territory to brag about. You could fit Germany, France, Italy, The Netherlands and all of the United Kingdom into the two provinces and still have more than 9,000sq km left over. Mind you, most of this immense territory is unadulterated wilderness, a vast expanse of trees, mountains, canyons, gorges, lakes and rivers, but according to British Columbians (who own the bulk of the wilderness) it's all just one massive virginal playground for nature-loving ecotourists.

Because of geography and climate, the bulk of the population of both provinces lives in a narrow band near the US border. The 4.2 million fun-loving BC citizens are concentrated into the southwestern corner of the province, almost half of them in Vancouver. Step just feet beyond the city's most northerly fringe and you are immediately immersed in mountains and wilderness. Albertans tend to be spread out a bit more through the prairies that occupy about 90 per cent of the province, but Edmonton and Calgary still account for more than half of Alberta's entire population.

While BC is largely trees and mountains and Alberta is prairie, the two provinces do have something in common: the Rocky Mountains that reach 12,000km northwards from the US border and form a divider between the two provinces. For two million years, glaciers, cataracts, streams and winds have sliced and sculpted the upthrust mountain range into an expanse of peaks, alpine lakes and meadows of such beauty they set up double-decker lumps in the throat. The mountains hold many surprises: high-mountain hikers have actually found tiny marine fossils at altitudes of more than 3,000m above sea level. These witnesses to yesterday are evidence that Alberta once sat at the bottom of a warm shallow sea that stretched from the Arctic Ocean to the Gulf of Mexico. As millennia passed, layer upon layer of shale, limestone and sandstone accumulated, creating deposits of what would one day become a fortune in coal, oil and natural gas. Then, about 75 million years ago, tectonic plates clashed and the earth's crust buckled. At the point of collision, the young Rockies were pushed up, lifting the sedimentary layers embedded with the shells of tiny marine creatures from the great sea.

The mountains have meant different things to different people. For the early explorers seeking a Northwest passage, they were a challenge placed on earth by a legion of vengeful devils. For the aboriginals who had lived for thousands of years in undisturbed peace, the mountains were a greater protection than the most fortified castle built by European kings. When engineers finally broke through the barrier and newcomers began to pour through the mountain passes, prospectors rubbed their hands with glee. High-grade copper and silver deposits had been found and dreams of endless riches danced in their heads like sugar plums. So much of the beauty that still exists could have been lost forever to loggers and miners out to drain the resources if it hadn't been for a handful of greedy politicians and businessmen who saw a different kind of gold in 'them thar hills'.

The Rockies, with their emerald-tinted lakes and natural hot springs, were a perfect holiday spot for rich Easterners. They could travel out via the recently built railroad and stay in large hotels built by enterprising businessmen. To ensure that this natural beauty would remain unadulterated, politicians were pressured to create a park preserve in 1885, and two years later Canada's first national park, Rocky Mountain Park (later Banff National Park), was officially established.

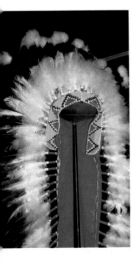

Below
Stony Indian headdress,
Glenbow Museum

It was just the beginning. Small wooden hotels grew into immense chateaux and tourists came in ever-increasing numbers to walk on the glaciers, visit the high alpine meadows, wallow in the hot springs and eventually ski the slopes of numerous great peaks. Not only the Rockies but BC as well would find itself plunged constantly into contradiction: for every government official or entrepreneur anxious to exploit a wealth of natural resources, there was a counter-balancing preservationist or environmentalist to stop him. The tug-of-war continues to this day and often spills out way beyond Canada as members of the international press and celebrities come to champion one environmental cause after another. The most memorable one was in Clayoquot Sound when loggers declared they intended to cut down old-growth trees that had been around since the Roman Empire. The response was explosive as more than 800 protesters were arrested for chaining themselves to trees and throwing themselves in front of logging trucks.

More than anything, people come to the West to experience its stunning beauty. They sample the 'good life' – the pure fresh cuisine, the produce from orchards and the wines from vineyards – but they take home something they didn't expect. The passion Westerners have for their land is contagious and visitors often go home forever infected by a need to return.

Travel facts

Above
Sinclair Canyon,
Radium Hot Springs

Accommodation

In most larger locations, there's a wide spread of accommodation available from hostels to hotels, B&Bs, resorts, lodges, inns and motels. In smaller areas or more remote locations, the best bet will usually turn out to be one of the chain hotels and motels. In the large cities, you definitely need a reservation during the peak seasons and prices can be high. Expect to pay from $70–$200 in BC and $50–$150 in the Rockies and Alberta.

To book accommodation in BC, go directly to the tourism websites or contact **Super, Natural British Columbia**, *tel (tollfree): (800) 435-5622* or *(250) 800-HELLOBC; www.hellobc.com.* **Travel Alberta**, *tel (tollfree): (800) 252-3782 (Alberta)* or *(780) 427-4321; www.travelalberta.com*, has lodging information but does not make bookings. Local tourist offices can provide lists of their area's accommodation.

Because of high demand during peak seasons, hotels in the cities and major tourist resorts are often booked out months in advance so reservations as early as possible are advised. Cost of accommodation can vary as much as 60 per cent from low and shoulder seasons to high season, usually mid-May–late-September and for the winter months at ski resorts.

Airports

Below
First Nations artist in Vancouver

For the Rockies, most international visitors fly into Calgary International Airport (YYC) *www.calgaryairport.com* for the major Rocky Mountain national parks and into Vancouver International Airport (YVR) *www.yvr.ca* for West Coast destinations. Both airports have recently undergone massive facelifting and are almost destinations in themselves with expanded facilities, shops and beautiful art work everywhere. For information on flights and bookings, contact individual airlines at local numbers or on the web, not the airports. Trolleys are available free in the baggage area upon arrival for international passengers; smaller airports usually have pay trolleys for around $1–$2. Major airports have currency counters for exchange and banking services, as well as a range of major car hire/rental counters. Vancouver airport no longer charges an airport-improvement tax, opting to have the fee incorporated into the ticket instead. Both Calgary and Edmonton airports have airport-improvement fees of $15.

Children

Because of reported child abductions, immigration officials will be sure to check a child's passport or ask for a birth certificate. A child travelling with a solo parent may be asked for a letter of permission from the absent parent. Divorced parents with shared custody should carry legal documents establishing their status.

Climate

International visitors are often surprised at the range of temperatures in Alberta and BC and the many microclimates. Summers in BC are warm and dry, with rain confined mostly to the winter months; Vancouver Island is milder with less rain, while the Gulf Islands and the Sunshine Coast have the least rain of all. In the interior, the Okanagan Valley has hot summers and cooler winters. The Rocky Mountain areas tend to have pleasant summers and abundant snowfall in the winter, while Calgary frequently experiences warm winds called chinooks as a break from heavy snowfalls. Edmonton is hot in the summer and extremely cold in the winter with lots of snow.

Currency

Even though rumour circulates about Canadians adopting the US 'greenback', it's unlikely to happen soon. Current Canadian bills come in denominations of $1 coins (called Loonies) and two-colour $2 coins (sometimes called Toonies), as well as $5, $10, $20, $50 and $100 notes (bills). These vary in colour but are a uniform size. There are 100 cents (¢) to the dollar and the coins are: 1¢ (penny), 5¢ (nickel), 10¢ (dime), 25¢ (quarter), $1 and $2.

As travellers are advised anywhere, it's best to carry traveller's cheques and debit and credit cards. Since many smaller businesses may only accept one or two credit cards, it's best to carry several, with the most popular ones being: **Visa**, **MasterCard** and **American Express**. Usually hotels and car hire companies will ask for a credit card upon registration even if payment has been in advance or is to be settled in cash: for hotels, this is usually to cover minibar purchases and for security.

ATMs (automated teller machines) offer the best currency exchange rates and never close. Star and Cirrus are the most common international ATM networks, but check with your card issuer before

Electricity

Canada uses 110v 60Hz current with two- or three-prong plugs. Power and plug converters are seldom available in Canada so buy them before you leave home. Beware of buying electrical equipment: while some are dual voltage many won't operate on the 220v 50Hz power elsewhere. Exceptions are battery-operated items such as radios, cameras and portable computers. Be equally wary of pre-recorded videotapes since Canada uses the NTSC format while other countries are on the PAL or SECAM. When buying pre-recorded videos, check the box for compatibility. If no system is listed, it's probably NTSC.

Festivals

Each community has a long list of festivals that range from autumn fairs and harvest events to wine festivals and stampedes. Numerous cultural festivals are devoted to music and there are many First Nations events visitors can attend. Some of the festivals are just downright silly (but fun), like the annual bathtub race from Vancouver Island. For a full list, check with the local tourism office.

leaving home to ensure that you have the proper four-digit PIN (personal identification number) for Canadian outlets. International airports have currency exchange facilities in the international terminal that are open long hours. Domestic terminals and smaller airports have no exchange facilities at all. US dollar and pound sterling traveller's cheques from Thomas Cook and other major issuers are accepted almost everywhere, but traveller's cheques in other currencies must generally be cashed at a bank. Personal cheques drawn on banks outside Canada are generally not accepted.

Bank opening hours vary widely depending on the location. Some are open as early as 0700 and stay open until 1800.

Customs allowances

Visitors to Canada may bring 1.14 litres of spirits or 1.5 litres of wine, 24 355ml cans of beer or ale, 200 cigarettes, 50 cigars and 200g of loose tobacco. Any alcohol or tobacco in excess of this is subject to duty, provincial fees and taxes.

Drinking laws

The minimum drinking age is 19 in British Columbia and 18 in Alberta; this is strictly enforced and youthful looking visitors may be asked for identification. Unlike the US, beer, wine and spirits are only available in BC Government Liquor Stores or in some places at special beer and wine stores. Alberta also has provincially licensed Liquor Stores for the sale of beer, wine and spirits. Opening hours vary.

Eating out

A few decades ago, western Canadians rarely dined out but today they love their many restaurants, bistros and ethnic specialities as much as anyone. West Coast cuisine concentrates on fresh fish and seafood (particularly salmon, Pacific halibut and Dungeness crab), distinctive local produce and 'fusion' dishes that marry the many ethnic influences in the two provinces, such as presenting wild game with an Asian flair. In better restaurants, you will see exotic meats and often rare regional specialities such as barnacles and sea asparagus.

Prices tend to vary from the super-budget chain restaurants to ultra-expensive fine dining with portions from lumberjack-hearty to minuscule and artfully arranged. Many restaurants have menus posted outside so you can avoid finding yourself in a champagne eatery with a beer wallet.

The coffee house is a recent phenomenon and particularly popular out west since the craze started in Seattle. Chains such as Starbucks and Second Cup are everywhere and feature a wide range of speciality

General Tourism Information

Tourism British Columbia *PO Box 9830, Stn Prov Govt, Victoria, BC V8W 9W5; tel: (800) 435-5622 (HELLOBC) or 3 Regent St, London, England, UK SW1Y 4NS; tel: (020) 7930 6857; www.HelloBC.com*

Travel Alberta *PO Box 2500, Edmonton, Alberta T5J 2Z4; tel: (780) 427-4321; tollfree (NA)* 1-800-ALBERTA (252-3782); e-mail: travelinfo@travelalberta.com; www.travelalberta.com *North America*

Parks Canada National Office: *25 Eddy St, Gatineau, Quebec K1A 0M5; tel: (800) 748-7275; e-mail: information@pc.qc.ca; www.parkscanada.ca*

BC Parks (Provincial) *800 Johnson St, Victoria, BC V8V 1X4; tel: (250) 387-4550; www.env.gov.bc.ca/bcparks*

Below
Freeloader in Stanley Park, Vancouver

coffees (at hefty prices). Coffee served in restaurants is closer to the American style (that is, weaker than in Europe) but most will serve espresso, cappuccino and similar brews.

Entry formalities

Except for US citizens, whose proof of citizenship can currently be a birth certificate, voter registration, baptismal certificate or a passport (although this may change soon), non-Canadian citizens require a passport, visa (if stated) and proof of return travel before departing for Canada.

Canada's firearms laws are considerably stricter than the US so all handguns, semi-automatic or fully automatic weapons and self-defence sprays such as mace or pepper spray are prohibited. Hunters bringing in rifles and shotguns must declare these upon entry. Failure to declare firearms will result in their seizure and criminal charges. Since 1 January 2001, new regulations require visitors to have a confirmed 'Firearms Declaration' to bring any guns into Canada. A fee of $50 will apply and be good for one year.

Narcotics and certain pharmaceutical products may not be imported. Carry documentation such as a doctor's prescription to prove that medications are legitimate.

Food

Alberta beef is quite famous (and Albertans will tell you this proudly) but the province also serves buffalo and wild meats such as venison, caribou, wapiti (elk), moose and quail. Portions are usually hearty. On the West Coast, salmon comes in many species with the best being sockeye and coho served barbecued, grilled or raw. Shellfish here is the best with excellent mussels, clams, geoducks and oysters served steamed or baked. Sushi has become a huge favourite with restaurants everywhere on the coast, where fish comes straight from the ocean. BC particularly promotes organic and healthy food so that even chain supermarkets have sections with everything from soya milk to goat feta cheese. On Vancouver Island and in the Gulf Islands, small boutique farms have sprung up everywhere, each farm specialising in some quality product such as sheep cheeses or fine balsamic vinegar aged in the Modena process.

Health and insurance

The main number to remember in case of a medical emergency is 911: this will bring the police, fire engines or an ambulance. If a life is at stake, treatment is swift and professional as government-run health programmes cover everyone. Non-Canadians will be expected to pay

Language

Canada is officially bilingual in English and French; all public signage and documents will be in both languages.

Maps

The Canadian Automobile Association (CAA or BCAA in BC) prints useful road maps in conjunction with the **American Automobile Association** (AAA) free to members at CAA offices. **MapArt** *70 Bloor St East, Oshawa, Ontario LIH 3M2; tel: (905) 436-2525 or tollfree (877) 281-6277; e-mail: info@mapart.com; www.mapart.com* produce easy-to-use regional and city maps. Detailed, 3-D maps of Rocky Mountain national parks are designed by **Gem Trek Publishing** *#301, 2614 Bridge St, Victoria; tel: (250) 380-0100; e-mail: maps@gemtrek.com; www.gemtrek.com*

Museums

Most museums charge an entrance fee and are closed one day a week. Entrance fees are generally low with discounted prices for children, students and seniors. In tourist areas, museums have seasonal times for opening with many open all week in peak season.

for treatment in both emergencies and non-emergencies; as in most countries, the former can be costly so travellers are highly advised to carry good medical insurance. Most travel agents selling international travel offer travel insurance policies.

Be sure to bring all prescription medications for the entire trip plus a few extra days. Carry a copy of the prescription showing the generic (chemical) name and formulation, not just a brand name since these differ widely from country to country.

Canada is basically a healthy place with no inoculations required. Visitors should eat sensibly and avoid drinking from mountain streams no matter how clear they look since they may be infected with *Giardia lamblia*, an intestinal bacteria that causes severe infection of the gut. Water served in restaurants is completely safe but in rural areas and some small towns it is wiser to stick to bottled water. Drink lots of water or non-alcoholic liquids, especially in warm weather.

Since parts of BC and Alberta can become very hot in the summer, sunglasses, wide-brimmed hats and good sunscreen will prevent burns, sunstroke and heat prostration. Insect spray is advised when travelling in parks.

National parks

National parks and historic heritage sites charge daily entry fees per person, with camping fees extra. If you plan to visit several parks in a region, you can save on park fees by buying a multi-park pass. The **Great Western Annual Pass** ($35) allows entry to 11 parks (excluding Gwaii Haanas National Park). BC provincial parks' fees vary depending on the park and season. Alberta has the **Alberta Federal and Provincial Historic Sites Pass** ($30 adult/$75 family).

Opening times

Standard office and business hours are Monday–Friday 0830/0900–1640/1700. Banks are open Monday–Friday 1000–1500/1700 and Saturday mornings. ATMs are open 24 hours but doors may require a bank card to open. Shops are generally open Monday–Wednesday and Saturday 0900/1000–1800 and Thursday and Friday until 2100, but this may vary (many large discount stores such as Wal-Mart are open until 2200). Sunday hours are 1100/1200–1700. Convenience stores are generally open 24 hours a day.

Some tourist offices outside Vancouver and Victoria have limited hours or are closed from mid-September–mid-May. Petrol (gas) stations are open long hours but may close between 2200–0630. Pub, saloon and restaurant hours vary widely depending on the season and location. For services at churches, synagogues, temples or mosques, check local phone directories for numbers.

Public holidays

The following public holidays are observed in British Columbia and Alberta: New Year's Day (1 Jan); Good Friday (Mar/Apr); Victoria Day (Monday on or prior to 24 May); Canada Day (1 July); BC Day and Alberta Heritage Day (first Mon in Aug); Labour Day (first Mon in Sept); Thanksgiving Day (second Mon in Oct); Remembrance Day (11 Nov); Christmas Day (25 Dec) and Boxing Day (26 Dec). Post offices and government offices close on public holidays.

Packing

With the exception of luxury resorts and 5-star hotels in cities that require at least business attire, dress in the West is casual and practical. Since rain can fall at any time in BC, some kind of coat or fold-up plastic cover is recommended along with a good fold-up umbrella. At higher altitudes even in the summer the weather can turn cold suddenly so at least one change of warm clothing is important (sweater/pullover and jacket). For any kind of hiking, sturdy weatherproof shoes are important: and throw in some bug repellent for wilderness walks. A backpack, essential for trips involving hiking, can be brought or purchased at excellent Western outdoor stores for reasonable prices. Stock this with a hat, sunscreen (at least SPF 15), insect repellent and sunglasses.

Postal services

There are **Canada Post/Postes Canada** buildings usually centrally located in all cities and towns, but many chemists (pharmacy/drug stores) will also have small postal counters at the back of the store (post offices are listed in the phone directory blue pages). Most post offices are open Monday–Friday 0900–1700 but drug store outlets will sell stamps after hours. Hotel concierges, tourist shops and some markets also sell stamps.

Letters or parcels sent abroad should go airmail to avoid delays, but for guaranteed fast service it's best to send by courier. Check the yellow pages under 'courier'. Rates for first class stamps are 52¢ per 30g within Canada; 93¢ per 30g to the US for letters and postcards; $1.55 per 30g internationally for letters and postcards.

Below
Vancouver trolley bus

Public transport

Most large towns and cities have a local bus system; contact numbers can be found in the local phone directory. For transit between towns check under the **Greyhound Bus** (coach) listing. Vancouver also has a quick and efficient SkyTrain that links Surrey, Coquitlam and Vancouver. For local transit information in BC contact **BC Transit**, *www.transitbc.com; tel: (604) 953-3333*. Adult bus rates begin at $2.25; day pass is $8. In Calgary contact **Calgary Transit**, *tel: (403) 262-1000; www.calgarytransit.com*. Adult bus rates begin at $2.25, day pass is $6.75, which is good on all buses and the LRT. In Edmonton contact **Edmonton Transit Service**, *tel: (780) 496-1600; www.edmontontransit.com*. Adult bus charges start at $2.50; day pass is $7.50, valid on all buses and the LRT.

Seniors

Canada has a considerable number of discounts for seniors (over 65) but to qualify you must mention your senior-citizen status up front when booking hotel reservations and before you are seated in a restaurant. Car hire agencies also have special rates for seniors, but often current value promotions may be less.

Taxes

BC has a 7 per cent provincial sales tax; Alberta has none. Most goods and services are subject to a Canadian Goods and Services tax (GST) of 7 per cent, although purchases of goods, including accommodation over $50 per transaction, will be rebated upon application to *Revenue Canada Visitor Rebate Program, Summerside Tax Centre, Suite 104, 275 Pope Rd, Summerside, Prince Edward Island C1N 6C6; tel: (800) 668-4748 or (902) 432-5608. Both provinces charge a room tax.*

Time

Most of British Columbia is on Pacific Standard Time (PST), GMT-8. Alberta and the Rocky Mountain section of BC are on Mountain Standard Time (MST). Both provinces jump ahead to Daylight Time (PDT) GMT-7/ (MDT) GST-6, from the first Sun in Apr until the last Sun in Oct.

For **BC Ferries**, *tel: (250) 381-1401* or *(888) 223-3779; www.bcferries.bc.ca*

Reading

- *Best Places Vancouver*, Kasey Wilson, Sasquatch, Seattle, US, 2000.
- *The Big New Beautiful British Columbia Travel Guide*, Bryan McGill et al, Beautiful British Columbia, Vancouver, 1999.
- *The Canadian Rockies Guide to Wildlife Watching: The Best Places to See and Appreciate Animals in their Natural Habitat*, Michael Kerr, Fifth House, Toronto, 2000.
- *Day Trips from Vancouver*, Jack Christie, Douglas & McIntyre, Vancouver, 1997.
- *Gardens of Vancouver*, Christine Allen and Collin Varner, Raincoast, Vancouver, 2000.
- *Handbook of the Canadian Rockies*, Ben Gadd, Corax, Jasper, Alberta, 1995.
- *Outlaws and Lawmen of Western Canada*, Heritage House, Surrey, BC, 1999.
- *Switchbacks: True Stories from the Canadian Rockies*, McClelland & Stewart, Toronto, 2001.
- *Tell Me a Good Lie: Tales from the Chilcotin Country*, Paul St Pierre, Douglas & McIntyre, Vancouver, 2001.
- *A Traveler's Guide to Aboriginal BC*, Cheryl Coull, Whitecap, Vancouver, 1996.
- *A Traveler's Guide to Historic British Columbia*, Rosemary Neering, Whitecap, Vancouver, 1993.
- *The Way We Were: BC's Amazing Journey to the Millennium*, staff of the Vancouver Province, Harbour, Vancouver, 2000.
- *West by Northwest: BC Short Stories*, David Stouck and Myer Wilkinson, eds, Raincoast, Vancouver, 1998.

Safety and security

- Dial 911 on any telephone for free emergency assistance from police, fire and medical authorities.
- Never discuss travel plans or valuables in public. Walk with assurance in well-lit places and give the impression that you are not worth robbing; for example, don't wear costly jewellery or have expensive cameras hanging around your neck. A wallet in a back pocket or an open handbag is an invitation to theft. Report incidents to local police immediately and get a report for your insurance company.
- Unwatched luggage can vanish in an instant. Most airports and bus or train stations have lockers; guard the key and memorise the locker number. Hotel bell staff may keep guest luggage for a few days, but always get receipts.

Tipping

Tips and service charges are not usually added to a bill in Canada. In general, 15 per cent of the total bill (or more for exceptional service) is recommended to restaurant servers, taxi drivers and beauty salon and spa personnel. Bar tenders get 50¢ per drink. Porters usually get $1 a bag (or more if he shows you your room) and maids $2–$3 per day. Tips for valet parking vary depending on how expensive the restaurant, hotel etc.

Toilets

Canadians refer to them as washrooms; restroom, bathroom and toilet are also used. Men's and women's facilities will usually be differentiated by a symbol of a man and a woman. Parks and recreational areas plus some ultra-trendy bars may have unisex washrooms.

Above
An RV is an alternative, for a holiday on the move

- If your car breaks down, turn on the flashing emergency lights, raise the bonnet (hood) and wait inside the vehicle. Have your keys out to unlock car doors before entering a car park on foot, and check around and inside the vehicle before entering. Don't pick up hitchhikers and never leave the car with the engine running.
- Lock room doors, windows and sliding glass doors from the inside. Ground-floor rooms are convenient but easier to break into. When leaving the room at night, leave a light on. When someone knocks at the door, use the peephole to see who it is. If someone claims to be on the hotel staff, check with the front desk. Money, cheques, credit cards, passports and keys should be with you or in the hotel safety deposit box. Photocopy the important pages of your passport and visas. Carry the copies and extra passport photos separately from the documents themselves.
- When hiking or camping in the back country, you must register with the nearest park warden's office to ensure that if you need help it will come. Be wary of natural hazards and avalanche conditions in the winter. Pay attention to warnings about aggressive animals and follow instructions issued by park authorities.

Telephones

Public telephones (pay phones) are marked by a white telephone on a blue background. Dialling instructions are posted on the telephone or in the local telephone directory white pages. Local calls cost 25¢ (35¢ in Alberta); tollfree (800, 877 and 888 area codes) and 911 emergency calls are free. To talk to an operator, dial 0. To locate local numbers, dial 411. For long-distance information, dial 1 + area code + 555-1212. There is a charge for information calls; there is no charge for local information from pay phones.

Talking Yellow Pages, *www.yellowpages.ca* in both provinces, has free information on time, road conditions, weather, news and entertainment.

Many hotels and motels add steep surcharges to the cost of phone calls, even calling tollfree (freephone) numbers from rooms. Use a pay phone in the lobby; prepaid phonecards are available at many local outfits. The costs for phoning overseas on these cards can vary widely so ask about the most economical.

For international enquiries or assistance dial 00. For international calls, dial 011 (access code) + country code + city code (omit the first zero if there is one) + local number.

Driver's guide

Automobile clubs

There are no reciprocal agreements between the AA and RAC, and the equivalent CAA in Canada. You should ensure that you purchase sufficient insurance when you hire a car.

Autoroutes

The Coquihalla Highway between Hope and Kamloops is BC's only toll road, with a standard $10 toll for a car or RV. The tollbooth accepts some credit cards as well as cash.

Car hire

Car categories vary, but most hire companies offer a range of vehicles. Reserve well in advance to ensure getting the type and size vehicle you need. Some hire companies restrict travel east of Saskatchewan or into the US, and/or charge beyond a certain number of kms. Check the contract carefully. It's usually cheaper to pick up a vehicle at an airport than in the city centre. A surcharge or one-way drop fee, may be levied for leaving the vehicle in another city. All drivers must be listed on the hire contract. If an unlisted driver has an accident, you will probably be required to pay for repairs yourself. Most car-hire companies require a credit card deposit, even if the hire has been prepaid. Before leaving, be sure you have all necessary documents and that you know how to operate the vehicle.

Accidents

Legally, you must STOP if involved in a collision or accident and call the local police or Royal Canadian Mounted Police (RCMP). For most areas in BC, the emergency number is 911 to alert the police or emergency medical services. You can also dial 0 to be directed to the authorities. Emergency service numbers are listed inside the phone directory front cover. Call your own insurance company and, if in a hired car, your car rental company. Collisions in BC resulting in death, injury or property damage apparently exceeding $1,000 are the responsibility of the driver, who is personally responsible for alerting police and, within 24–48 hours depending on the jurisdiction, the Insurance Corporation of British Columbia (ICBC): *tel: (800) 663-3051 (BC)* or *(604) 661-2800; www.icbc.com.* ICBC, whose offices are listed in the telephone directory, is the province's issuer of driving licences as well as the provider of accident insurance. If you are involved in an accident, British Columbia and Alberta require you to produce your driving licence, vehicle licence number, vehicle registration number, insurance carrier and cover policy number along with your contact information to police and other parties to the incident. Exchange your information with the other driver(s) and get the names and contact information of any witnesses. Note as many details as you can, such as the time, location and weather. Photographs can be helpful later. You should remain at the accident site until police arrive and the law requires you to render all reasonable assistance. Pull over to the side of the roadway if possible and set out emergency triangles to warn other drivers.

Documents

Your home-country driving licence is valid in British Columbia and Alberta. You should always carry it while driving and have your picture identification with you at all times.

The vehicle registration, proof of liability and collision insurance coverage, with any rental car contract, must be in the car and accessible at all times.

The minimum driving age is 16 in British Columbia and 18 years of age in Alberta. Provisional licences are not valid. Car rental companies require that all drivers be at least age 25.

Drinking and driving

Driving while impaired (DWI), often called DUI (driving under the influence of alcohol or drugs) is illegal. The criminal blood alcohol limit is .08 mg. Strict enforcement permits a breath sample to be taken by a police officer; a blood sample may be required later. Police and the RCMP establish random checkpoints and may be particularly attentive near winery tasting rooms and entertainment venues. Penalties include fines, imprisonment and loss of licence.

Opposite
Old-style trucking at the Ukrainian Cultural Heritage Village

If your vehicle collides with a parked vehicle, leave a note with your name, address, licence plate number and insurance information securely affixed to the other vehicle. For a collision with an animal – 10 per cent of all BC accidents are with animals – do not try to move it but call the nearest humane society or authorities.

Breakdowns

If you have a breakdown, stop your vehicle on the hard shoulder, getting it as far to the right as possible. On ordinary roads, consider using the verge but beware of roadside ditches. Turn hazard lights on and raise the bonnet. If it's dark or visibility is limited, place flares and reflective warning triangles where they can be seen by other drivers. (Remember, it can be very dangerous to walk on the hard shoulder of any freeway or highway.) Place an SOS note on the windscreen. You and your passengers may be safer out of the vehicle and well up the verge away from the traffic, but for security, stay in the locked car if you are in an isolated area, it is night-time, or it is hard to see for any reason.

You may call for a breakdown lorry, called a tow truck, usually dispatched from a local petrol (gas) station. Breakdown insurance is strongly recommended and one phone call is all it takes to hand the whole problem over to an operator who is expert in sorting things out. Your insurance company may call a towing service it has under contract for emergency roadside assistance repairs or towing to a repair garage. You are responsible for payment or for signing the form that affirms to your insurance company that you have had the service. Most car-hire companies either pay for repairs directly or reimburse the cost shown on repair receipts. If a hire car is going to be out of service for more than a few hours, ask the hire company for a replacement vehicle.

Caravans and camper vans (trailers and RVs)

Recreational vehicles or RVs, often called motorhomes, are a popular way to travel in Western Canada, though hire companies restrict access to some highways and may limit cross-border travel to the USA. Hire options include a choice of daily kilometre limits and seasons; high season is July–August.

The higher cost of hiring and operating an RV is offset by savings on accommodation and meals, and the convenience of not packing and unpacking at each stop.

Maintenance takes time and attention away from touring. Check the vehicle inside and out for its condition. Get operating manuals and a full demonstration for all systems before leaving with a hired RV. Buy a pair of sturdy rubber gloves to handle emptying the waste holding tanks and wear old clothes for the task. For sanitary and

Essentials

You should travel with three red, reflective warning triangles, road flares, a torch, a first aid kit and a jack for tyre repair. If the vehicle has a spare tyre, make sure that it is properly inflated. Have chains for snow season travel.

Fines

Drivers can be fined for moving violations like speeding, illegal turns or other infractions, for parking violations, and for DWI, driving while impaired under the influence of alcohol or illegal drugs. Police authorities will issue a citation, often called a ticket, on the spot. The citation specifies the police authority, jurisdiction (city, town), legal code reference number, a short description of the violation, the vehicle reference, the police officer's identification, your information if it is a moving violation, and where and how the ticket can be paid or challenged.

On-the-spot fine payments are *never* made, and anyone offering to pay a fine when cited may be assumed to be offering a bribe to a police officer, an extremely serious offence.

Citations are registered in a computer database by car licence that is linked to the vehicle identification number. The car or RV rental company will be notified of any citations issued to its vehicles.

environmental reasons, sewage system disposal must be done at authorised dump stations.

The size of an RV or trailer cannot exceed 12.5 metres (41 feet) in length. These vehicles drive more like lorries than cars and are generally treated as lorries by traffic laws. They are blown about more by the wind than cars and are more subject to rollover and drift. Taller and wider dimensions can create hazards at gas stations, tollbooths, parkades and with low-hanging trees and signs. On BC Ferries, the cost of passage for RVs is based on vehicle length.

Woodall's (*www.woodalls.com*) is a fine reference for 14,000 camping spots in North America; the Canada listings are also in *Woodall's Canadian Campground Guide*. There are private RV parks and camping in some National Parks and BC (provincial) Parks during the summer, generally April to September. To book a BC Parks camping pitch, *tel: (604) 689-9025; www.discovercamping.ca.* Travel Alberta handles camping information requests; *www1.travelalberta.com/content/camping.*

Wherever you park along the side of a road or on city streets, the vehicle must always be pulled off the roadway and should only be parked in a safe, well-lit place in view of passers-by. Always lock the vehicle. Canada's wonderful outdoors presents the challenge of bears searching for easy food supplies. Observe all provincial and park recommendations for storing and carrying food to avoid temptation for the bear and an unpleasant confrontation.

Driving in British Columbia and Alberta

Major roads across Canada are superbly maintained and most signs are in both in English and French, with distances in kilometres. The greatest challenge, other than winter driving, is that pedestrians always have the right-of-way at zebra crossings (crosswalks) and intersections.

Away from the coast in winter, blowing snow can reduce visibility to zero and snow, ice and wet roadways slow or halt traffic for hours. Highways require mandatory use of chains (traction devices) between 1 November and 30 April and the speed limit lowers to 40–50kph. It's wise to keep the petrol (gas) tank at least half full at all times. Carry extra water, food, warm clothing and a torch if driving in winter or marginal weather conditions outside of urban areas. Useful snow country equipment includes an ice scraper and small shovel. Parked cars should be equipped with a front engine compartment plug, plugged into an electrical source and the engine block heater turned on when temperatures fall to –10°C.

The green sign with a white maple leaf marks the Trans-Canada Highway (Highway 1) that runs 7,821km from Victoria on Vancouver Island to Kamloops, Golden, Banff National Park, Calgary, and on to St John's, Newfoundland in the east. The Yellowhead Highway, with its road sign of a silhouette of the Iroquois fur trapper, Tête Jaune

Lights

It is recommended that headlights be on at all times. (Note: not mandatory.) Driving only with parking lights is illegal.

Mobile phones

Mobile or cell(ular) phone use while driving is not illegal, but a hands-free device is recommended over one that requires dialling and distracts attention from the road. A cell phone can be useful to call 911 in an emergency or for breakdown assistance.

Road information

British Columbia Ministry of Transport and Highways InfoLine; tel: (900) 451-4997 (75 cents); www.bchighway.com/report/, and in Alberta, on the Internet, www.tu.gov.ab.ca/Roads/RoadConditions.asp, has road condition information. Local radio stations also broadcast weather and driving information. In urban areas, most stations have regular traffic reports during morning and evening rush hours.

Government of Canada Weather Information numbers are in the telephone directory blue pages. Check weather online for British Columbia or Alberta: www.weatheroffice.com or www.weathernetwork.com

(Yellow Head), is a northern alternative to some of the Trans-Canada Highway. The Yellowhead (Highway 16) leaves Highway 1 west of Winnipeg, and is the main route through Edmonton, Jasper, Prince George and ends at Prince Rupert. Highway 3, the Crowsnest Highway, is marked with a black crow on a white signpost and crosses the BC–Alberta boundary in the south. The Icefields Parkway, with hanging and walk-on glaciers, alpine lakes, waterfalls and river vistas between Lake Louise and Jasper, is one of Canada's most scenic drives. Vancouver, Whistler and Victoria are the principal venues for the 2010 Winter Olympics and Paralympic Winter Games and drivers will encounter road construction on the Sea-to-Sky Highway between Horseshoe Bay (Vancouver) and Whistler up till 2009.

Driving rules

Traffic drives on the right in Canada. It is recommended that car headlights be on at all times while driving, even in daylight. Horns are seldom used.

When cars arrive at an intersection at nearly the same moment, the vehicle to the right proceeds first. Unless otherwise posted, a vehicle can turn right from the right-hand lane after a full stop. Before turning, drivers should, but don't always, signal the direction of the intended turn. Buses stopping at the right side of the road and pulling out into traffic proceed first, and bicycles, like pedestrians, should generally be yielded the right of way. Roadways are marked with a solid white line for 'do not pass', and with a broken line on the side where vehicles may pass. In mountainous areas, curves are not infrequent, dictating slower speeds and no passing. Oncoming traffic on narrow roads is required to let the uphill driver proceed. If stuck in mud or snow, gently rock the vehicle by changing from forward to reverse gears. Beware of agricultural vehicles moving more slowly than regular traffic, which will be marked with a reflector, but may scatter hay or splash snow or slush across the windscreen. Stop when a school bus lowers its red and white STOP sign or flashes its lights – and do not pass.

Fuel

Petrol (gas, gasoline) and diesel are sold at gas stations in litres. For drivers from the USA, who are used to gas sold in US gallons (3.78 litres), pump prices may be bewildering. There are several major gas companies, but prices vary only minimally, and can be higher outside of cities and major towns. Most vehicles take unleaded petrol that comes in regular, premium and super grades. Buy regular unless the car hire company or vehicle operations manual specifies otherwise. Most stations are self-service although some offer a high-priced, full-service alternative. Pump prices include all taxes. Cash and credit

Seat belts

The driver and all passengers must wear seat belts. A child under the age of 6 must ride in a British Columbia Motor Vehicle Act-compliant child safety restraint that has a CMVSS National Safety label as complying with Canadian Motor Vehicle Safety Standards. Infants up to 9kg must be in a rear-facing restraint seat. Toddlers from 9kg to 18kg must have a child restraint with an adult seat belt and top tether strap. Safety seats can be hired with the car or purchased for under $100 at a discount store. In an RV, passengers riding behind the driver's seat need not wear belts, but should be safely seated when the vehicle is in motion.

cards are accepted, though for safety, most stations will not accept bills over $20. Try to keep the tank at least half-full at all times and fill up in the daytime when you can be sure stations are open.

Information

Both Tourism British Columbia and Travel Alberta and their Visitor InfoCentres provide fine free provincial maps. The six Canadian Rockies National Parks have maps and visitor information in *The Mountain Guide*, a free brochure that is available at the parks or online at *www.pc.gc.ca/docs*. Auto club maps are useful for specific areas and many area or district chambers of commerce have local maps.

Parking

Parking garages, parking lots and parkades (car parks) are indicated by a white P on a blue background. Prices are posted at the entrance and many urban parkades accept credit cards. Kerbside parking is usually limited, either by posted signs or by coin-operated parking meters, where the per-hour rate may be higher than in lots and parkades.

Kerbs may be colour-coded: red is no stopping or parking at any time; white is for passenger loading/unloading only; green is limited time parking (usually 10 minutes); yellow is a commercial loading zone; blue is special permit handicapped parking. Parking is not permitted within 5 metres of a fire hydrant; near a disabled kerb ramp; at bus stops, intersections or zebra crossings (crosswalks); blocking a driveway; on pavements (sidewalks), or on highways.

Security

Lock the vehicle when you're inside as well as when you leave it. Always park in well-lit areas at night, in the open and within view of passers-by. Check for intruders before getting in your vehicle at night – and an RV any time. Never leave the engine running when the driver is not behind the wheel. The RCMP can always render assistance. Should you have the misfortune to become a victim of crime, your insurers will require you to report the circumstances to the police and obtain a police report that you have done so.

Speed limits

The highway speed limit is 80–100kph for cars, posted less for trucks and RVs (some highways such as the Coquihalla post 110kph). Slow down in towns and cities, where the speed limit is 50kph or lower. If driving conditions are poor, drivers are required to keep to a safe speed, no matter how slow. Police use radar and aircraft to track, stop and ticket (cite) speeders, but be alert – you could be stopped – even when traffic normally flows at least 10kph above the posted limit.

CANADIAN ROAD SIGNS

Yield (Give Way)

No Entry

Curve (bend)

No Left Turn

No U-turn

Divided highway (dual carriageway)

Stop sign ahead

Signs unique to the British Columbia area

Logging trucks use or cross the road

Deer or elk cross the road

Moose cross the road

This sign denotes a severe road condition such as a turn which requires drivers to slow down

Freeway sign showing distance to exit

Rural road destinations are shown with finger boards

B.C. Provincial

Trans-Canada (Highway 1 and Highway 16)

Thanks to the following website for its kind permission to reproduce the B.C. signs: www.bchwys.ca

Getting to the Rockies and British Columbia

Travellers with disabilities

While federal and provincial laws require that public business and services be readily accessible by people with a disability, not all are. For specific information, contact **SATH** (Society for the Advancement of Travel for the Handicapped), 347 5th Ave, Suite 605, New York USA NY 10016; tel: (212) 447-7284; www.sath.org; e-mail: sathtravel@aol.com. **RADAR** 12 City Forum, 250 City Rd, London EC1V 8AF; tel: (020) 7250 3222, publishes a useful annual guide, Holidays and Travel Abroad, with details of facilities for travellers with a disability in different countries www.radar.org.uk

Wheelchair accessibility information is free from the **Canadian Paraplegic Association** 780 Southwest Marine Dr., Vancouver, BC V6P 5Y7; tel: (604) 324-3611; fax: (604) 326-1229; tollfree: (877) 324-3611; e-mail: vancouver@bcpara.org; www.bcpara.org. **Access Canada** Tourism BC, Box 9830, Stn Prov Govt, 300 1803 Douglas St, Victoria, BC V8W 9W5; tel: (250) 387-3023; www.accesscanada.ca, certifies agility, mobility, vision and hearing-impaired,

Unless you live within driving distance of Alberta and British Columbia, flying is the most practical way to get there, with rail a close second. **VIA Rail,** tel: 888 VIA RAIL (842-7245), and **Rocky Mountain Railtours,** tel: (877) 460-3200, have had a recent 'rebirth' and now offer a number of different routes from major centres into tourism areas on both luxury and economy trains. These sightseeing trains operate during the summer months and usually involve stops at night to ensure the best possible views of dramatic mountain scenery during the day. Contact the railroads for specific routes (see also pages 170–9). There is also a ferry service from Seattle and other cities in Washington State to Vancouver and Victoria as well as a rail service from the US via **AMTRAK**. Motor coach travel is possible, though slow and cramped. Air travel is actually even more cramped since airlines try to squeeze in as many passengers as possible into economy; the trade-off is a major time saving.

To reach the Rocky Mountains first, the best airport is Calgary, Alberta with Edmonton second. Banff is two hours by car from Calgary compared to 12–14 hours of driving from Vancouver via Hwy 1, the Trans-Canada Highway. If you choose to drive from Vancouver, consider overnighting in Revelstoke, about halfway to Banff. Some Rockies resorts such as Kananaskis are a one-hour drive from Calgary.

No matter whether you're flying to Vancouver or Calgary, don't let airline flight schedules mislead you into a full first day of touring. Vancouver may be only 10–12 air hours from much of Europe or Asia, but jet lag intensifies the effects of long-distance air travel. Expect to arrive fatigued, disorientated, short-tempered and otherwise not ready to drive.

Overnight flights are attractive because they seem to offer an extra day of sightseeing upon arrival. Resist the temptation. Most travellers do better by timing their flights to arrive in the late afternoon or early evening, then getting a good night's sleep before tackling the sights. Since many airport-area hotels and motels offer a free shuttle service to and from the airport, you can take a shuttle to the hotel, sleep off the flight, shuttle back to the airport the next morning and pick up the rental car at no additional cost.

Jet lag cures are legion but the most effective seems to be to expose your body to as much light as possible as soon as you arrive in order to adjust to the new time zone. Experts suggest drinking as much water as possible on the flight over and avoiding alcohol and overeating.

Above
Heading home to Nimmo Bay
via kayak

disabled-designated
accommodation, Canada-
wide. **SPARC**, *201-221
E. 10th Ave, Vancouver V5T
4V3; tel: (604) 718-7733;
fax: (604) 736-8697;
www.sparc.bc.ca; e-mail:
info@sparc.bc.ca* provide
disabled parking permits
for visitors. Bring a
photocopy of your home
parking permit or mail in
advance to above address.

There are also medications available such as Melatonin that seem to help some people.

Many fly-drive programmes offer what looks like an easy first-day drive such as Vancouver International Airport to Whistler resort, north of Vancouver. It looks easy on the map but in reality two hours of driving time can stretch into half a day if traffic is bad or if there is an accident on the 2-lane highway. Also, on your return to the airport, allow extra time beyond the recommended two hours before an international departure. Unexpected traffic or bad driving conditions can leave you stranded on a freeway as your plane takes off overhead. Allow a safety margin by spending your last night in Canada near the departure airport, or at least in the same city.

Try to arrive with a few dollars in Canadian currency and coins. Luggage trolleys are free at larger airports such as Vancouver International but must be paid for in some domestic airports. Some trolley stands accept credit cards, usually Visa or MasterCard, but other stands require cash and currency exchange facilities are located outside the arrivals area. Tips for porters may also be necessary.

Canadian airports do not have duty-free shopping for incoming travellers, but it's no great loss. Prices for alcohol and other duty-free items are almost always lower in Liquor Stores, supermarkets and discount stores than in duty-free shops.

Car-hire companies usually have cars at the major airports or nearby, but others require that you take a coach to an off-airport facility to pick up your hire car. Be sure to ask when making your reservation.

If hiring an RV ask the hire company about airport pickup and drop-off when making your booking. Most hire companies provide free transport to and from their offices, which are usually located some distance from the airport.

Setting the scene

The land

While the nature of many European countries is shaped largely by their history, for Canada, and especially the West, the defining force is geography. Because most of the northern parts of Alberta and British Columbia are wild, hostile, unforgiving and brutally cold in the winter, European explorers were defeated by the landscape so aboriginal people retained control of the land much longer than elsewhere. Most of today's cities are less than 150 years old: photographs of Edmonton, for example, taken in 1871 show the town as a trading post surrounded by a palisade.

The south coast of BC on the other hand is warmed by benign currents and fertile soil piled up over aeons by the Fraser River, so living for the First Nations people was easy. For coastal tribes such as the Haida fish were so abundant and food so easily grown that there was time to develop a complex and richly artistic culture. East of the Rockies, great plains provided grazing for millions of buffalo so that Plains tribes, when they needed meat, had simply to stampede the herds over cliffs. This would provide enough meat to keep the tribe fed over the long winter.

Today, the two provinces claim perhaps the most diverse geography on earth: mountains, valleys, sea coast, plateaux, glaciers, tundra, prairie and even a desert. During the Pleistocene Age, nearly the entire area was blanketed in ice and from that time thousands of glaciers still remain. In the northern part of BC these run side by side, separated only by rivers, while those in the Rockies now form one of the area's most popular tourist attractions. Most of BC is ribbed by parallel ranges that are considered one of the world's major mountain systems. The Rocky Mountain Trench is North America's longest valley, extending 1,600km from BC's northern border to Montana in the US. This is the birthplace of BC's most important rivers including the Peace, Columbia and Fraser.

While cities were springing up in the East as early as the 17th century, the West remained *terra incognita*, a place where 'there be dragons'. The forbidding Rocky Mountain range was an impenetrable obstacle that challenged and usually defeated those seeking a passageway to the western ocean. The most romantic events in Canadian history come from the explorers who fought enormous obstacles to find that passage.

The history of the West

While anthropologists now believe that wandering Asians migrated here as far back as 60,000 years ago, European settlement is barely a hiccup in the span of history. As one English visitor commented on viewing BC's historic buildings, 'I've got moss on my roof older than that'. Little more than 50 years ago, when officials had to take the census in northern Alberta, they went in with trains of mules, killing their own food as they went along. Vancouver, 150 years ago, was wilderness.

Alberta, named after a daughter of Queen Victoria, became a province in 1905 but remained a rugged place where bushy buffalo roamed freely through vast rolling grasslands. Homesteaders from Europe began trickling in to tame the prairies and turn them into wheat fields, in the process enduring unbelievably harsh conditions. The glaciers had left a landscape of muskeg bogs and bug-laden swamps so that these early pioneers, living in sod houses, broke both the land and their backs at the same time. Alberta's future changed one blustery February afternoon in 1947 when a crowd gathered in a field near Edmonton and shouted 'Here she comes!' As oil gushed from the ground everyone knew that something very big, very important had happened. Today Alberta is Canada's *wunderkind*, a province that seems to be able to do no wrong, economically speaking at least. Calgary, Canada's energy capital, continues to be a boom town.

There are tales of exploration along the BC coast that go back to an early Chinese manuscript dated 220 BC, and Asian shipwrecks dating back to the 5th century AD seem to confirm this. Sir Francis Drake was thought to have visited the coast on his 1579 voyage as well, but Juan de Fuca, a Greek sailing from Spain in 1592, is credited as the first outsider to officially visit BC. It was the search for the Northwest passage to China (and a prize of £20,000 to the discoverer) that lured explorers to challenge the mountains and rivers. Alexander Mackenzie was the first White to cross the continent north of Mexico, making his way to the mouth of the Bella Coola River in 1793. David Thompson, in trying to open trade with the Indians west of the Rockies, created the first comprehensive maps of the West as a result of his explorations, and Simon Fraser in 1808 struggled through the perilous canyons and rapids on to the mouth of the river that would be named after him.

The course of BC's history was changed by two things: gold and the railroad. During the first half of the 19th century, development was slow, consisting primarily of fur trading at various Hudson's Bay Company posts such as Fort Langley, Kamloops and Fort George. Just as the California goldfields were trickling out, vast quantities of the precious substance were found in the sandbars along the lower Fraser River in 1857. Thousands of fortune hunters flooded in from all over the world, crowding into a wholly inadequate Victoria demanding picks and shovels and permits. With wagon trains and on foot, the gold seekers walked the tributaries of the Fraser, striking major finds of gold. Barkerville became a gold boom town with a population of 25,000, making it the largest town west of Chicago and north of San Francisco. With greed the motivating factor, chaos ensued. In order to maintain some order, the British established the mainland colony of

British Columbia in 1858 under James Douglas, the governor of Vancouver Island.

No goldfield lasts forever, and by late 1859 the sandbars of the Fraser were pretty thoroughly picked over all the way to Lillooet more than 200 miles upriver. Prospectors drifted on and merchants selling prospecting supplies in Victoria had little to do but 'stand by their doors and project idle spittle into the streets'. Then in the autumn of 1860, electrifying news hit: gold was found by the ton in the Cariboo. By the time the ice broke up on the Fraser in the spring of 1861, all the prospectors who left were surging back again: from New York, Australia and Liverpool. This time there seemed to be enough gold to go around and Victoria began to boom again. By the autumn of 1861, it was estimated that more than $5 million in gold had been taken out.

By the time the Fathers of Confederation sat down to create a country, they realised they wanted the gold- and resource-rich territory on the Pacific Ocean to be a part of it. Since BC was toying with the idea of either joining the US or declaring independence, the British were panicked that the crucial last link in their much-desired safe land route to India might slip from their hands. To lure British Columbia into the family of Canada, it was promised a transcontinental railroad to link it to the East. In a country as diverse as Canada, the railroad proved to be one of the few real national bonds: it not only created a dependable physical link in a territory usually cut off by snow, rampaging rivers, mountains and landslides, but an emotional link as well. The story of the building of the transcontinental railway is one of Canada's great legends, well told in Pierre Berton's book *The Last Spike*. It not only created 'a dominion from sea to sea' but shaped the ethnic diversity of the province as well.

The people

Until the 20th century, Canada received most of its immigrants from either Britain or France, but the opening of the prairies required a different kind of settler. One official, Clifford Sifton, Minister of the Interior in 1896, laid out the specifications: 'I think we require a stalwart peasant in a sheepskin coat, born on the soil, whose forefathers have been farmers for ten generations, with a stout wife and a half-dozen children of good quality.'

To meet this demand, thousands who fitted this description flooded into the plains from the Ukraine, Scandinavia, Germany, The Netherlands and Poland, lured by the offer of 160 acres (64.8ha) of 'virgin farmland' for free. Most were bitterly disappointed to find a brutal landscape filled with trees and bogs. Western Canada became the promised land for all sorts of religious dissidents as well, looking for peace, freedom and hope. Mennonites and Doukhobors came from the Netherlands and Russia respectively, as well as Jewish survivors of tsarist pogroms; Mormons and Hutterites came from the US. Later, refugees from other countries fighting oppressive governments came in waves: in 1956 Hungarians after their revolution, Czechs after the Prague Spring and thousands of Hong Kong Chinese fearful of the China takeover. Unlike in the US where immigrants found themselves dropped into a 'melting pot', the new Canadians held onto their languages and customs, forming instead a 'mosaic' of people.

The Chinese were here even before this, drawn to the frontier as labourers to pound in the spikes on the great transcontinental railroad. Today parts of Vancouver are densely Asian (in Richmond 40 per cent of the residents are Chinese), but the history of Chinese immigration and the treatment of the Japanese have left a sorry historical blot. Until the mid-20th century, the Chinese were subject to a 'Head Tax' and the families of Chinese male immigrants were not allowed to join them. During World War II Japanese who were born in Canada were sent to concentration camps in the Interior as 'undesirable aliens', their possessions confiscated.

Like any place with a frontier history, BC and Alberta have had more than their fair share of colourful characters. During the gold rush days, a Cornish sailor named Billy Barker jumped ship in Victoria and headed into the Cariboo to seek his fortune. Billy made the biggest strike ever in 1862, led a lusty life and died in poverty. 'Hanging Judge' Begby brought law and order to the restless frontier, and one of BC's most colourful bank robbers was an ageing grey-haired desperado called 'The Grey Fox'. Vancouver's unofficial 'father' was a drunken publican named 'Gassy Jack' Deighton who arrived on the wooded shores, set up a sawhorse and a barrel of whiskey and thereby opened Vancouver for business. Politics has been a magnet for colourful characters in BC, especially premiers. When he was elected as premier, John Smith decided his name was too plain for such a lofty position so he legally changed it instead to Amor de Cosmos (Lover of the Universe). In more recent history, one of the longest reigning premiers was known as 'Wacky' Bennett, and three premiers in a row following him were thrown out of office because of scandals. Cabinet ministers have been equally colourful, such as 'Flying Phil' Gaglardi, Minister of Transportation, who clocked up an astounding number of speeding tickets while he was in office. We don't even want to get onto the subject of hucksters and charlatans: suffice to mention Brother XII, a charismatic character who started a cult near Nanaimo and left just hours ahead of the law with a fortune in gold stuffed in jam jars conned from his devoted followers.

First Nations

As in the United States, Central and South America and Australia, the historical relationship of aboriginal people and the newcomers is a blemished one full of shame and tragedy. It is only within the last few decades that some of the historical wrongs have been addressed and the many aboriginal communities, formerly called 'Indians', have assumed their rightful place as Canada's First Nations. All through BC and Alberta, treaty negotiations have taken place to restore lands and establish self-government to the people, reclaiming their languages and identities as Gitxsan or Dakelh or Quw'utsun'.

Canadians in recent years have become more aware of aboriginal landscape, issues and history, and to build on this First Nations communities have been opening their doors and inviting guests to learn from them. More and more First Nations cultural centres are opening up along with interpretative tours, art galleries and special events. At Duncan's Cowichan Native Village, for example, visitors hear traditional stories around a smoking fire, listen to the songs, watch the dance performances and get to dine on a traditional feast of pit-barbecued salmon, venison and clams. At Xa:ytem National Historic Site outside Mission, Sto:lo guides share lessons taught by the Transformer, Xexa:ls. *A Traveler's Guide to Aboriginal BC* (*see Reading, page 20*) provides an excellent guide to places where visitors can share in the stories and cultural events.

The wildlife

Of all the reasons people are drawn to the Rockies and BC, a chance to experience wilderness and its animals – and to test oneself in a multitude of wilderness activities – probably places first. There are more resident wild animal species here than anywhere else in Canada. It's said that more than three-quarters of Canada's wildlife species actually breed here. On the coast, there are resident pods of whales and among the regular visiting species, nearly all of the world's 24,000 Pacific grey whales swim past the length of BC's coast in the spring and autumn. Sea lions, dolphins, seals and porpoises are full-time residents; in fact BC's coastal waters are so alluring to sea mammals and fish that they are considered by scuba divers as some of the best in the world. Visibility is phenomenal and many species come in 'industrial size': the world's largest octopus and sea urchins are here, as well as mussels so huge, one alone would make a chowder.

The Rockies are home to grizzly and black bears, cougars, wolves, coyotes, mountain goat, bighorn sheep, caribou, elk and moose just to name a few. Banff National Park has 53 species of mammals alone, ranging from the pygmy shrew, weighing a fraction of an ounce, to huge bison. Many of the larger animals will be spotted just grazing by the side of the road. There are in fact more big-game species here than in any other place on earth.

Birdlife is even more abundant, from tiny chickadees to regal bald eagles. More than a million birds migrate on the Pacific flyway and hundreds of thousands stop to rest. For birdwatchers, the western wetlands are filled with an endless procession of waterfowl: trumpeter and whistling swans, pelicans, loons, Canada geese and snow geese. To make things easier for visitors, provincial wildlife viewing programmes have been set up so that people may observe wildlife in their natural habitats. For details, check the **BC Wildlife Watch website:** *www3.telus.net/driftwood/bcwwhome*

The sporting life

Next to wilderness and wildlife, the biggest lure in the West is sport, the more active the better. The Rockies and BC have become world-famous not only for the quantity but also the quality of skiing terrain available to all levels and types of skiers. Whether downhill, snowboard, cross-country, helicopter or powder-cat skiing, the resorts are fully equipped, the snow is plentiful, the scenery grand and the air as fresh as it can be. Banff, Jasper and Lake Louise are long-time favourites in the Rockies, but Kananaskis is coming up hard as a family favourite and Kicking Horse Pass nearby plans to be 'the new Whistler'. In BC, Whistler/Blackcombe is world-famous for its extraordinary runs and scenery but many of the Okanagan ski resorts are equally good, cheaper and less crowded.

'Watching' has become one of the West's hottest sports. Bird watchers have been around for aeons but the latest favourites are whale watching, bear watching and now storm watching. Just driving through wilderness areas can be a non-packaged watching event as moose, herds of deer, bighorn sheep and elk nibble beside the road.

Guest ranches have sprung up all over, with visitors encouraged to take an active part in rounding up cattle, sheep shearing and day-to-day ranch chores. In the Cariboo, guest ranches or outfitters provide horse riding trips on a daily basis or on lengthy forays into the wilderness. A new twist on this is llama-trekking where hiking becomes a novel experience when you have a llama as a companion.

Provincial parks have hundreds of miles of trails for the fit and experienced or the casual stroller, some easy walks for a few minutes, others for hours and days. Among the most challenging and popular are the West Coast Trail that takes 5–7 days along Vancouver Island's west coast and the 25-day Nuxalk–Carrier Heritage Trail in the Cariboo to trace aboriginal footsteps. A number of outfitters also take people heli-hiking where a helicopter lifts you from a plateau near a wilderness lodge up to the highest peaks and alpine meadows for unparalleled walking experiences.

Fishing also draws passionate anglers to cast for giant halibut, lingcod and BC's five salmon species found along thousands of kilometres of shoreline or in remote rivers and streams. Trout fishing is also huge in the myriad freshwater lakes all through the West.

There's more: caving in some of the thousands of charted and explored caves, particularly on Vancouver Island; mountain biking through the Rockies; scuba diving along the entire BC coast and its islands; gold panning in the Cariboo, mountaineering and rock climbing that is among the best in the world; and for something a little different, soaking in a remote cove on the edge of the world in hot water bubbling up from the core of the earth.

Highlights and touring itineraries

Top ten sights

These are not the most frequently visited places but are certainly some of the best:

- **Barkerville Historic Town** (*page 140*)
  Where the Cariboo Gold Rush began.
- **Fort Steele Heritage Town** (*page 107*)
  A frontier town that has brought the 1890s vividly back to life.
- **Fraser Valley Canyon and Hell's Gate** (*page 144*)
  Raging rivers and spectacularly rugged landscapes.
- **Head-Smashed-In Buffalo Jump, Fort Macleod** (*page 96*)
  A UNESCO World Heritage Site that tells the story of how Plains Indians ingeniously harvested buffalo.
- **Heritage Park, Calgary** (*page 42*)
  The largest historical village in Canada recreates pre-1915 life in western Canada.
- **Kettle Valley Railway** (*page 210*)
  The KVR runs all through the Okanagan and is a masterpiece example of 'recycling'.
- **Nelson** (*page 118*)
  The entire town is quaint, friendly and a favourite with film makers from Hollywood.
- **The Royal BC Museum, Victoria** (*page 254*)
  Rated one of the 10-best museums in the world for its permanent holdings and its highly imaginative special shows.
- **The Royal Tyrrell Museum of Palaeontology, Drumheller** (*page 67*)
  Some of the most stunning reconstructed dinosaur skeletons in the world stalk the museum.
- **Stanley Park, Vancouver** (*page 274*)
  This is just about the perfect city park and a monument to foresight by the original city planners.

The best of Alberta and BC

Two of these three circular tours start and end in Calgary, the other in Vancouver. Suggested overnight stops are shown in **bold**.

Two weeks

This is the Best of the West, a journey with coastal activities as its theme.

Day 1   Arrive in **Vancouver** (*see page 268*).
Day 2   **Vancouver**.
Day 3   BC Ferries to **Mayne Island** (*see page 261*).
Day 4   BC Ferries to **Salt Spring Island** (*see page 263*).
Day 5   BC Ferries to **Victoria** (*see page 248*).
Day 6   **Victoria**.
Day 7   Hwy 1 to the **Cowichan Valley** (*see page 234*).
Day 8   Take Hwys 1 and 19 to **Campbell River** (*see page 227*).
Day 9   **Strathcona Park** (*see page 230*) and drive via Hwys 9 and 4 to **Ucluelet** (*see page 245*).
Day 10   **Ucluelet** and **Tofino** (*see page 242*).
Day 11   **Tofino**.
Day 12   BC Ferries to **Vancouver** via **Nanaimo**, then drive via Hwy 1 to **Fort Langley** and **Harrison Hot Springs** (*see page 221*).
Day 13   Return to **Vancouver**.
Day 14   **Home**.

Three weeks

See most of Alberta, from the Rockies to the prairies.

Day 1   Arrive in **Calgary** (*see page 38*).
Day 2   **Calgary**.
Day 3   Trans-Canada Highway (Hwy 1) to Brooks, then Hwys 550/544/876 to

Dinosaur Provincial Park. Follow Hwy 876 to Trans-Canada Highway and continue on to **Medicine Hat** (*see page 98*).

Day 4   Crowsnest Highway (Hwy 3) to **Lethbridge/Fort Macleod/Head-Smashed-In Buffalo Jump** (*see pages 96–7*).

Day 5   Hwy 2 to Cardston, then Hwy 5 to **Waterton Lakes National Park** (*see page 99*).

Day 6   **Waterton Lakes National Park.**

Day 7   Cowboy Trail (Hwy 6) to Pincher Creek, then Hwy 22 to **Rocky Mountain House** (*see page 78*).

Day 8   Hwy 11 to Red Deer/Innisfail/Olds then Hwys 27/21/837 to **Drumheller** (*see page 67*).

Day 9   Hwys 56/26/2A to Stettler/Wetaskiwin/Leduc/Devon, then Hwys 60/16 to **Edmonton** (*see page 50*).

Day 10   **Edmonton.**

Day 11   Yellowhead Highway (Hwy 16) to **Jasper** (*see page 87*).

Day 12   **Jasper.**

Day 13   Icefields Parkway (Hwy 93) to **Columbia Icefield/Lake Louise** (*see pages 86, 88*).

Day 14   **Lake Louise.**

Day 15   Bow Valley Parkway (Hwy 1A) to **Banff** (*see page 84*).

Day 16   **Banff.**

Day 17   Trans-Canada Highway (Hwy 1) and Hwy 40 to **Kananaskis** (*see page 76*).

Day 18   **Kananaskis.**

Day 19   Continue on Hwys 40/541/22 to **Bragg Creek** (*see page 74*).

Day 20   Return to **Calgary.**

Day 21   **Home.**

Four weeks
From mountains to ocean, this covers a lot of territory.

Day 1   Arrive in **Calgary** (*see page 38*).

Day 2   **Calgary.**

Day 3   Hwy 9 to **Drumheller** (*see page 67*) and then Hwy 2 to **Head-Smashed-In Buffalo Jump** (*see page 96*).

Day 4   Return to **Calgary** and Hwy 1 for **Kananaskis** (*see page 76*).

Day 5   Take Hwy 1 to **Banff** (*see page 84*).

Day 6   Continue up Hwy 1 for **Lake Louise** (*see page 86*).

Day 7   Follow Hwy 1 to **Revelstoke** (*see page 126*).

Day 8   **Shuswap Lakes** (*see page 160*).

Day 9   Take Hwy 97B to **Vernon** and **Kelowna** (*see pages 204, 208*).

Day 10   The **Okanagan Valley** tourings (*see page 198*).

Day 11   Follow Hwys 97C to **Merritt**, then 5A to the **Nicola Valley** (*see page 194*).

Day 12   The **Nicola Valley.**

Day 13   Follow Hwys 5A north via **Kamloops** and then 97 to **Williams Lake** (*see page 137*).

Day 14   Take Hwy 97 south for the **Gold Rush Trail** (*see page 140*) to join Hwy 1 south to **Hope** (*see page 223*).

Day 15   Continue on Hwy 1 through the **Fraser Valley** (*see page 218*) and Fort Langley.

Day 16   Hwy 1 to **Vancouver** (*see page 268*).

Day 17   **Vancouver.**

Day 18   BC Ferries to the **Gulf Islands** (*see page 260*).

Day 19   BC Ferries to **Victoria** (*see page 248*).

Day 20   Take Hwy 1 north to the **Malahat and the Cowichan Valley** (*see page 234*).

Day 21   Follow Hwys 1 then 19 to **Parksville**, then 4 to **Ucluelet** (*see page 245*).

Day 22   **Tofino** (*see page 242*) for eco-adventures.

Day 23   Take Hwys 4 west and 19 north to **Campbell River** (*see page 227*).

Day 24   Continue on to **Port Hardy** for BC Ferries to **Prince Rupert** (*see page 184*).

Day 25   Follow Hwy 16 east to **Jasper** (*see page 87*).

Day 26   **Jasper.**

Day 27   Drive to **Calgary.**

Day 28   **Home.**

Calgary

Bounded by the Rocky Mountains on the west and the vast wheat fields and rangeland on the east, Calgary sprawls over the largest landscape of any Canadian city. The oil and gas financial centre of Western Canada, downtown Calgary is a Lego-size Manhattan with towering skyscrapers housing banks, insurance firms and oil companies. Despite its size, openness and party atmosphere, 'Cowtown' is a clean, safe and friendly city. The fastest-growing city in North America is regarded as one of the world's finest: UNESCO has rated Calgary one of the best in the world to live in. There are numerous parks, a world-class zoo and the famous Stampede held every July. The 1988 Winter Olympics not only helped Calgary emerge from relative obscurity but also changed Calgarians. Visitor numbers increased, especially international travellers who introduced new expectations of fine galleries, haute cuisine and comfortable accommodation, without changing the loveable cowboy image.

ⓘ Calgary Tourism Info has two offices: *Calgary Tower, 101 9th Ave; tel: (403) 263-8510, tollfree (800) 661-1678; www.tourismcalgary.com. Open daily 0800–2000 in summer, 0900–1700 in winter (subject to change). Calgary Airport; open daily 0600–2300.*

🗘 Calgary International Airport *Open 24 hrs, 7 days a week.*

Arriving and departing

Canada's fourth busiest airport, **Calgary International Airport** *tel: (403) 735-1200; e-mail: calgaryairport@yyc.com; www.calgaryairport.com,* is no more than one stop from any major airport in the world as well as many points in Canada and the US. A $10 domestic, $20 international airport-improvement fee is added to tickets for domestic and international flights. Roving volunteer 'White Hatters' greet arrivals, answer questions and solve problems. A 20-minute drive to the city centre, **Airport Shuttle Express** $ *tel: (403) 509-4799; tollfree (888) 438-2992; e-mail: airportshuttle@canada.com; www.airportshuttle.ca,* operates door-to-door 24 hours a day; **Banff Airporter** $$ *tel: (403) 762-3330; tollfree (888) 449-2901; e-mail: reservations@banffairporter.com; www.banffairporter.com,* provides door-to-door service to Banff; taxi $$ to downtown. Many hotels have courtesy shuttles.

Calgary

0 500 metres
0 500 yards

Bow River

Calgary Zoo

Fort Calgary Historic Park

MEMORIAL DRIVE NE

MACDOUGALL ROAD NE

EDMONTON TRAIL NE

4 AVENUE NE

MEMORIAL DRIVE NW

Rotary Park

Prince's Island Park

Chinese Cultural Centre

Glenbow Museum

Calgary Tower

Bankers Hall

Alta Sports Hall of Fame

Eau Claire Park

Heliport

LOUISE BRIDGE

KENSINGTON ROAD NW

GLADSTONE ROAD NW

to STREET NW

MEMORIAL DRIVE NW

Canada Olympic Park

TELUS World of Science

Calaway Park

14TH STREET NW

Stampede Park

OLYMPIC WAY

STAMPEDE TRAIL

MACLEOD TRAIL SE

Elbow River

Burnsilsland Cemetery

Union Cemetery

St Mary's Cemetery

MACLEOD TRAIL SE

Glenmore Reservoir & Bow Valley Ranch

PORTLAND STREET SE

BLACKFOOT TRAIL

DARTMOOR ROAD SE

HIGHFIELD ROAD SE

SHULER ROAD

Attraction
Important building
Park
Main Road
Other Road
Railway

N

CALGARY

Bow River

Fish Creek Provincial Park

Bow Valley Ranch

Weaselhead Natural Area

Glenmore Reservoir

Heritage Park Historic Village

Fish Creek Provincial Park

Canada Olympic Park

Calaway Park

CROWCHILD TRAIL

MACLEOD TRAIL

CANYON MEADOWS DR

14 STREET SW

Fish Creek

Getting around

Breeze through the city on the C-Train light-rail transit (LRT) or hop aboard a Calgary Transit bus (*www.calgarytransit.com*), with free transfers from bus drivers with an all-day pass ($6.75). Easy access is provided for all passengers with priority seating for wheelchairs and scooters. Calgary has an extensive bike path system of some 300km of well-groomed paths. Afternoon bike rentals are available at cycle shops.

Brewster Banff
Tel: (403) 762-6700, tollfree (800) 661-1152; www.brewster.ca.
The Graylines Sightseeing division provides airport service between Calgary and Banff as well as specialised tours. With over 80 motorcoaches, Brewster has been in business for over a century.

Greyhound Canada
Tel: tollfree (800) 661-8747; www.greyhound.ca.
Provides service to numerous points in Alberta and BC. Canada's largest intercity bus company. Greyhound also operates motorcoach charters.

Sights

Calaway Park

Western Canada's largest outdoor family amusement park, Calaway Park (*www.calawaypark.com*) is a 20-minute drive from Canada Olympic Park. Among the more than 30 rides are the Vortex Rollercoaster, Bumper Boat Splash Challenge, the Rocky Mountain Rail and the new Free Fallin' and Balloon Ascension. Spectacular musical productions are performed at the Showtime Theatre and Celebration Stage.

Calgary Chinese Cultural Centre

Modelled on the 1420 Temple of Heaven in Beijing, the Chinese Cultural Centre was built by artisans from China using traditional tools. Centrepiece is the Hall of Prayers of the Temple of Heaven, a 21m-high dome ceiling decorated with 40 phoenixes and 561 dragons. Situated in the heart of Chinatown, the ornate Centre contains a craft shop, cultural museum, herbal medicine store and restaurant.

Red Arrow Motorcoach *205
9 Ave southeast, tel: (403)
531-0350, tollfree (800)
232-1958; www.redarrow.ca.*
Provides a de luxe, daily
express service between
Calgary, Red Deer,
Edmonton and Fort
McMurray, offering
complimentary snacks and
refreshments, fold-down
work tables and laptop
plug-ins.

Calaway Park $$
*245033 Range Rd 33;
tel: (403) 240-3822. Open
May, Jun & Sept weekends
only; e-mail:
calaway@calawaypark.com;
www.calawaypark.com*

**Calgary Chinese
Cultural Centre $**
*197 First St southwest;
tel: (403) 262-5071;
www.culturalcentre.ca.
Open year round.*

Below
Canada Olympic Park

Calgary Tower

It may not be the tallest structure in the city, but the Calgary Tower is the most recognisable outline on the horizon. The 190.8m sceptre-shaped edifice provides stunning views of the city, the vast plains and the rugged Rocky Mountains from the Observation Terrace. Two 18-passenger elevators (lifts) whisk visitors to the top in 62 seconds, or if you feel energetic, try the 802-step staircase. After the Olympian workout, dine at the revolving Panorama Dining Room.

Calgary Zoo, Botanical Garden and Prehistoric Park

Home to more than 1,000 animals and 275 species of animals in their natural habitats, the zoo is a world-renowned institution containing many rare and endangered species. Situated on St George's Island in the middle of the Bow River in downtown Calgary, the Prehistoric Park teems with 22 life-size dinosaur models, giving visitors an opportunity to step back in time to a world when T Rex shook the earth. The Canadian Wilds, the Aspen Woodlands and the Canadian Rockies exhibits each represent a slice of Canada's wilderness.

Canada Olympic Park

As the premier site of the XV Olympic Winter Games in Calgary, Canada Olympic Park is perhaps the most visible legacy of the 1988 Games to visitors and Calgary alike – truly a one-of-a-kind attraction. Situated 15 minutes from downtown Calgary, at the gateway to the magnificent Rocky Mountains, Calgary's premier recreational and sport learning centre is unique from most Olympic venues in that it continues to function as a multi-purpose competition, training and recreation area designed for year-round use by both athletes and the general public. A two-hour guided Olympic Odyssey Tour of the Park includes visitor access to the Olympic Hall of Fame and Museum; the Ice House – CODA's national sliding centre and the world's only

🅘 Calgary Tower $
101 9th Ave; tel: (403)
266-7171. Call for hours.
www.calgarytower.com

Calgary Zoo $$
1300 Zoo Road northeast;
tel: (403) 232-9300 or
tollfree (800) 588-9993.
Open daily 0900–1700;
www.calgaryzoo.org

Canada Olympic Park $
88 Canada Olympic Rd
southwest; tel: (403) 247-
5452; e-mail: info@coda.ca;
www.canadaolympicpark.ca

Fort Calgary Historic
Park $
750 9 Ave southeast; tel:
(403) 290-1875. Open every
day year-round 0900–1700;
www.fortcalgary.com

Glenbow Museum $
130 9 Ave southeast; tel:
(403) 268-4100; e-mail:
glenbow@glenbow.org;
www.glenbow.org.
Open daily 0900–1700;
Thur and Fri 0900–2100.

Heritage Park Historic
Village $
1900 Heritage Dr.
southwest; tel: (403) 268-
8500; e-mail: reception@
heritagepark.ab.ca;
www.heritagepark.ca. Open
mid-May–Labour Day
weekend daily 0900–1700;
weekends Labour
Day–Thanksgiving.

TELUS World of
Science Calgary $$ *701*
11 St southwest; tel: (403)
268-8300; e-mail:
discover@calgaryscience.ca;
www.calgaryscience.ca.
Open Tue–Thur
1000–1600; Fri–Sun
1000–1700.

indoor refrigerator track where the world's leading sliding athletes practise the ever-important push start; the Olympic Track; and the 90-metre ski jump tower – the highest point in Calgary. Self-guided tours are also permitted.

Fort Calgary Historic Park

Amid a sea of scarlet jackets and thundering hooves, 'F' Troop of the North West Mounted Police crossed the Bow River in 1875 to build Fort Calgary. Now, the reconstructed Fort Calgary brings history to life on the 40-acre (16.2ha) park on the banks of the Elbow River. Across the river, enjoy lunch, dinner or a murder mystery evening at the elegant Deane House. Behind the building is the Hunt House, the oldest structure in Calgary, built by the Hudson's Bay Company in 1876.

Glenbow Museum

Visitors to the vast Glenbow Museum journey into the heritage of the Canadian West and the richness of First Nations cultures. There are exhibits of a Blackfoot tepee, elegant quillwork of the Plains Cree, and the hard-won comforts of a settler's cabin. Permanent displays are laid out over four floors, with the top floor provided for military history. The Museum Shop offers a variety of unique souvenir items, while the Lazy Loaf and Kettle café offers snacks and quick, fresh meals.

Heritage Park Historic Village

Recreating all the sights and sounds of pre-1914 life in Western Canada, Heritage Park is the largest living historical village in Canada. The park contains dozens of structures collected from across the West, including outhouses and a two-storey hotel. The SS *Moyie* sternwheeler takes visitors on a 30-minute cruise around the Glenmore Reservoir, while electric streetcars provide rides to and from the front gates. Thundering steam trains and horse-drawn buses add to the atmosphere. During summer, there is a free breakfast 0900–1000 with regular paid admission.

TELUS World of Science Calgary

Holograms, frozen shadows and laser beams delight visitors at the 35-plus hands-on exhibits. The latest in computer graphics are featured in the Discovery Dome, all brought to life on the huge domed screen. The stars are observed Friday evenings through the observatory's high-powered telescope.

Opposite
Prehistoric Park

Accommodation and food

Calgary has a wide selection of accommodation that ranges from budget to de luxe. Vacancies are tight June–September and prices are higher. As Calgary is a convention city, reservations well in advance are recommended year round.

Calgarians and visitors enjoy a variety of fine cuisine, cooked over an open fire or served on the finest linens. Flapjacks, buffalo burgers and Alberta beef are renowned but locals also enjoy dim sum, grilled tuna and New Zealand lamb.

Calgary Tower $$$ *101 9 Ave southwest; tel: (403) 266-7171; www.calgarytower.com.* Has the best views of Calgary and the Rockies from atop the revolving Panorama Dining Room.

Calgary Westways B&B $$ *216 25 Ave southwest; tel: (403) 229-1758, tollfree (866) 846-7038; e-mail: calgary@westways.ab.ca; www.westways. ab.ca.* A delightful downtown B&B located in a 1912 heritage home.

Carriage House Inn $$ *9030 Macleod Trail South; tel: (403) 253-1101, tollfree (800) 661-9566; e-mail: reserv@carriagehouse.net; www. carriagehouse.net.* Located close to Heritage Park, about a 10-minute drive from downtown.

Eau Claire Market *200 Barclay Parade; tel: (403) 264-6450; www.eauclairemarket.com. Open Mon–Wed 1000–1800, Thur and Fri 1000–2000, Sat 1000–1800, Sun and holidays 1100–1700.*

Elements Bistro $$ *Delta Bow Valley, 209 4 Ave southeast; tel: (403) 266-1980.* Has an outstanding chef's menu – try the Buffalo Rib Eye.

Essence $$$ *Westin Hotel, 320 4 Ave southwest; tel: (403) 266-1611.* Excellent menu featuring flavours of Alberta.

Fairmont Palliser $$$ *133 9 Ave southwest; tel: (403) 262-1234; e-mail: palliserhotel@fairmont.com; www.fairmont.com/palliser.* The former Canadian Pacific Railway hotel is the *grande dame* of Calgary hotels situated in the heart of downtown.

Hampton Inn and Suites $$ *2231 Banff Trail Northwest; tel: (403) 289-9800, tollfree (888) 432-6777; e-mail: info@hamptoncalgary.com; www.hamptoncalgary.com.* Conveniently located on the Trans-Canada Highway, has a superb recreation area with a rainforest theme.

Inn on Lake Bonavista $$$ *747 Lake Bonavista Dr. southeast; tel: (403) 271-6711.* Overlooks a man-made lake where guests enjoy New Zealand lamb or grass-fed Alberta beef.

Joey Tomato's $$ *Eau Claire Market; tel: (403) 263-6336.* Is packed with good humour, from the Auntie Pasta sign over the kitchen to the Italian flag-wrapped pillars.

La Chaumière $$$ *139 17 Ave southwest; tel: (403) 228-5690.* One of Calgary's finest restaurants; choose a fine wine from the 11,000-bottle cellar to go with the caviar, seafood and Alberta beef.

Lazy Loaf and Kettle $ *8 Parkdale Crescent; tel: (403) 270-7810.* Has healthy food, wonderful sandwiches and takeaway picnic lunches.

Right
Old City Hall clocktower

River Café $$ *Prince's Island Park; tel: (403) 261-7670; www.river-cafe.com.* Prepares organic and locally-grown ingredients such as Saskatchewan venison chops, Saskatoon berries and crispy risotto cakes.

Teatro $$ *200 8 Ave southeast; tel: (403) 290-1012; www.teatro.ca.* Located downtown in a former bank building, the Italian cuisine prepared in a traditional wood-burning oven.

The *Eye Opener*

The hard-drinking, cigar-smoking editor of the *Eye Opener*, Robert Chambers Edwards, was one of Canada's most colourful newspaper men. With an unmatched reputation for his wit and scathing editorials, Bob Edwards's itinerant newspaper was published 'semi-occasionally' from 1902 until his death in 1922. Born in Edinburgh, the lampooning journalist waged war on big business, self-righteous individuals, and hard-line social institutions. The targets of his strong social conscience – politicians, politics and organised religion – were lambasted for their pomposity and pretension. He faced legal action when he called the three biggest liars in Alberta: 'Robert Edwards, Gentleman; Hon. A L Sifton (Premier); and Bob Edwards, Editor of the *Eye Opener*'. The suit was dropped when similar suits were filed on behalf of Robert Edwards and Bob Edwards. His favourite inspiration was the Alberta Hotel and its Long Bar, reputed to be the longest drinking beam between Winnipeg and Hong Kong.

Right
City Hall, Calgary

Shopping

Competition and variety provide shoppers with good value. An overhead pedestrian walkway, Plus-15, connects over 600 stores through 16km of downtown. Bankers Hall has three levels of speciality stores and one-of-a-kind boutiques. Canadian Wilderness features Albertan- and Canadian-made souvenirs, clothing and native art. Alberta Boot Co. has the best selection of men's and women's cowboy boots, all made in Calgary. The Bay has the famous Hudson's Bay point blankets as well as international gift foods, cheeses and fashions. The Wine Cottage has an inviting atmosphere with an extensive selection of wine, scotch and speciality beer.

Suggested tour

Total distance: 55km.

Time: Allow $1^1/_2$ hours for driving, longer during rush hour, to drive the circuit, which cannot be reversed because of one-way streets.

Links: The Trans-Canada Highway (Hwy 1) runs from the Saskatchewan boundary to the east, and Banff to the west. The C&E Trail (Hwy 2) links with Calgary from the north and Macleod Trail (Hwy 2) from the south. Hwy 1A runs in a northeasterly direction towards Cochrane, then angles southwesterly to Canmore.

Route: Exit Tower Centre parkade near the **CALGARY TOWER ❶** onto 10 Ave southwest and go right. Turn right on 1 St southwest for one block and right again past Calgary Tower on 9 Ave southwest for three blocks. Go left onto Macleod Trail southeast, staying in the left lane. Turn left on 6 Ave southeast and go west 13 blocks. Go left on 11 St southwest one block to 7 Ave southwest and the right-hand entrance to the **TELUS WORLD OF SCIENCE CALGARY ❷**.

Continue south on 11 St southwest. Go left on 9 Ave southwest, then turn right on 5 St southwest and go under an overpass. Turn right

Calgary Stampede

Billed as 'The Greatest Outdoor Show on Earth', the world-famous Calgary Exhibition and Stampede in July was born in 1912, instigated by an American trick roper, Guy Weadick, who envisioned a big rodeo in the heart of cattle country. Interrupted by World War I, chuckwagon races were introduced a decade later, which now see 4-horse teams and four mounted outriders racing for more than $350,000 in prize money. But the biggest draws are the rugged saddlebronc and bull riding events, the cowboys competing for a purse of over $500,000. **Stampede Park** *tollfree (800) 661-1767; www.calgarystampede.com*

Opposite
Calgary Stampede, chuckwagon racing

onto 17 Ave southwest, nine blocks of trendy eateries, coffee houses, galleries, bookstores and boutiques. Turn left on 24 St southwest. Two blocks beyond, 24 St southwest joins Crowchild Trail. Continue south and take the Flanders Ave turn. Go right on Arras Dr. following signs to the Museum of the Regiments.

Return to Crowchild Trail and continue south. Follow signs to go left on Glenmore Trail, crossing a short causeway over Glenmore Park Reservoir. Go right on 14 St southwest and look for the Canadian Pacific locomotive on the right at the entrance to **HERITAGE PARK HISTORIC VILLAGE ❸** .

Leave Heritage Park at Heritage Dr. turning right to go 4km south on 14 St southwest. Turn left on Canyon Meadows Dr., which winds 5km around the northern side of Fish Creek Provincial Park, Canada's largest urban park. Turn right 2.5km on Bow Bottom Trail to Bow Valley Ranch. Return north 4km on Bow Bottom Trail, left and then right on Acadia Drive to Anderson Road southeast. Turn left there, then right onto Macleod Trail and go 7.5km north to the main entrance of Stampede Park.

Continue three blocks north on Macleod Trail, then turn right onto 9 Ave southeast. **FORT CALGARY HISTORIC PARK ❹** and its Interpretive Centre are east on 9 Ave southeast. Continue east, crossing the Elbow River via the 9 Avenue Bridge, otherwise known as the 'Duck' Inglewood Bridge. Go right onto 8 St southeast across the railway crossing, then turn right to go up 17 Ave southeast to Scotman's Hill. Turn left onto Salisbury St for a panoramic view of downtown highrise buildings, with the Elbow River below. Stampede Park and the saddle-shaped Saddledome are below to the left.

Go around the block and return to 17 Ave southeast. Go right, then turn left on 8 St southeast. Go right on 9 Ave southeast to the shops and pleasant restaurants of the Inglewood District. Turn left on 12 St southeast, crossing over two Bow River bridges to the **CALGARY ZOO, BOTANICAL GARDEN and PREHISTORIC PARK ❺** .

Leave the zoo on Memorial Dr. northeast, continuing 3.5km towards downtown. Take the exit for 4 Ave southeast into Chinatown, and go right on Centre St. Before reaching the imposing stone lions flanking the Centre Street Bridge, turn left onto 2 Ave southwest. Go right on 1 St southwest for one block, then left onto 1 Ave southwest, and left one block on 2 St southwest to Eau Claire Market.

Turn right onto 2 Ave southwest for one block. Barclay Parkade is on the right. Go left on 3 St southwest, south along the Barclay Mall. Turn left on 9 Ave southwest, passing a regal Canadian Pacific locomotive engine and the Fairmont Palliser Hotel on the right, to return to Calgary Tower.

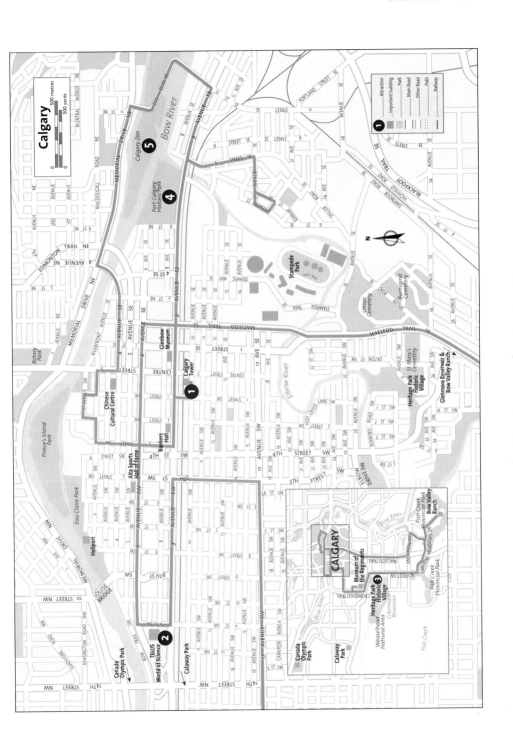

Calgary

0 500 metres
0 500 yards

	Attraction
	Important building
	Park
	Main Road
	Other Road
	Path
	Railway

1

Bow River

Calgary Zoo **5**

Fort Calgary Historic Park **4**

MEMORIAL DRIVE NE

PORTLAND STREET SE

BLACKFOOT TRAIL

DARTMOOR ROAD SE

BENTAL AVENUE NE

MACDOUGALL ROAD NE

CENTRAL AVENUE NE

2ND AVENUE NE

3RD AVENUE NE

4TH AVENUE NE

EDMONTON TRAIL NE

AVENUE NE

MEMORIAL DRIVE NE

Rotary Park

RIVERFRONT AVENUE SE

AVENUE SE

Glenbow Museum

CENTRE STREET

Calgary Tower **1**

MACLEOD TRAIL SE

MACLEOD TRAIL SE

Stampede Park

OLYMPIC WAY

STAMPEDE TRAIL

Union Cemetery

Burnsland Cemetery

SPILLER ROAD

Heritage Park Historic Village

Glenmore Reservoir & Bow Valley Ranch

St Mary's Cemetery

ELBOW DRIVE SW

Prince's Island Park

Chinese Cultural Centre

Bankers Hall

Alta Sports Hall of Fame

4TH ST SW

Eau Claire Park

Heliport

MEMORIAL DRIVE NW

LOUISE BRIDGE

to 10 STREET NW

KENSINGTON ROAD NW

GLADSTONE ROAD NW

Canada Olympic Park

TELUS World of Science **2**

Calaway Park

9TH ST SW

14TH STREET NW

Elbow River

HOLY CROSS LANE SW

4TH STREET SW

5TH STREET SW

CALGARY

Bow River

Fish Creek Provincial Park

Bow Valley Ranch

Museum of the Regiments **3**

Heritage Park Historic Village

CROWCHILD TRAIL

MACLEOD TRAIL

Weaselhead Natural Area

Glenmore Reservoir

Fish Creek

Canada Olympic Park

Calaway Park

ANDERSON ROAD

BOW BOTTOM TRAIL

CANYON MEADOWS DR

Fish Creek Provincial Park

N

Edmonton

Ratings

Children	●●●●●
Entertainment	●●●●●
Food and drink	●●●●●
Historical sights	●●●●●
Museums	●●●●●
Outdoor activities	●●●●●
Scenery	●●●●●
Shopping	●●●●●

Edmonton comes as a big surprise – not only is it huge, but it's lovely as well, fanning out from a deep valley along the meandering North Saskatchewan River. This greenbelt includes ravines and beautifully landscaped parks, golf courses, woodland trains and neat residential areas highlighted by the majestic Alberta Legislature, the striking glass pyramids of the Muttart Conservatory and historic Fort Edmonton Park. The capital of Alberta and thriving oil capital of Canada, Edmonton is best known to visitors as the home of the gargantuan West Edmonton Mall, one of the bigger tourist draws in Canada, but there's so much more to the city. During the summer months, the streets explode with fun and colour as one festival – streets fairs, summer and ethnic festivals – blends into another. In the winter, the city proves that cold temperatures are a spur to culture as opera, ballet and theatre provide an endless choice of things to do.

ℹ Edmonton Tourism Gateway Park Visitor Information Centre, *2404 Gateway Blvd southwest, tel: (780) 496-8400 or (800) 463-4667; e-mail: gateway@edmonton.com; www.edmonton.com/tourism. Open daily 0800–2000 (summer); Mon–Fri 0830–1630; weekends (winter) 0900–1700.*

Opposite
Edmonton skyline

Arriving and departing

By air: Edmonton International Airport, located 29km from downtown, is Canada's fifth busiest airport, providing non-stop service in summer from London and many points in Canada and the US. A $15 airport-improvement fee is added to tickets for domestic and international flights originating in Edmonton. **Airport Shuttle Bus $$** has service to downtown, west end and University of Alberta; taxi $$ to downtown is about a 30-minute drive, depending on traffic. Independently operated **Sky Shuttle $$** (from door #7 arrivals level; *tel: (780) 465-8515 or tollfree: (888) 438-2342*) has three routes to Edmonton: downtown (*every 20 min weekdays and 30 min weekends and holidays*); westend (*every 45 min weekdays, every hour weekends and holidays*); university (*every 45 min Sun–Fri, every hour Sat and holidays*). Courtesy shuttles are also available to many hotels. Conveniently located in the heart of Edmonton, **City Centre Airport,**

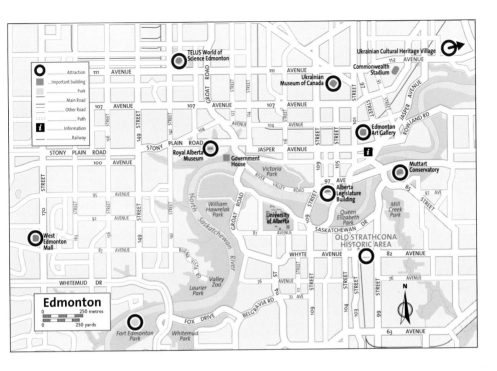

Edmonton map legend:
- Attraction
- ...Important building
- Park
- Main Road
- Other Road
- Path
- Information
- Railway

TELUS World of Science Edmonton

Ukrainian Cultural Heritage Village

Commonwealth Stadium

Ukrainian Museum of Canada

Edmonton Art Gallery

Royal Alberta Museum

Government House

Muttart Conservatory

Alberta Legislature Building

Victoria Park

William Hawrelak Park

University of Alberta

Queen Elizabeth Park

Mill Creek Park

OLD STRATHCONA HISTORIC AREA

West Edmonton Mall

North Saskatchewan River

Valley Zoo

Laurier Park

Fort Edmonton Park

Whitemud Park

STONY PLAIN ROAD

JASPER AVENUE

WHYTE AVENUE

WHITEMUD DR

FOX DRIVE

BELGRAVIA RD

Edmonton

0   250 metres
0   250 yards

ⓘ Edmonton Tourism Visitor Information Centre
9990 Jasper Ave; tel: (780) 401-7696, tollfree (800) 463-4667. Open Mon–Fri 0600–2000, weekends 0900–1700.

⤵ Edmonton International Airport Information Booths *Arrivals Level, North and South Terminals; tel: (780) 890-8900; e-mail: info@edmontonairports.com; www.edmontonairports.com*

VIA Rail *12360 121 St; tollfree (888) 842-7245; www.viarail.ca.*
Provides national rail service. The transcontinental *Canadian* provides service three times a week to Toronto, Jasper and Vancouver.

Greyhound Canada
10324 103 St; tel: (780) 420-2400, tollfree (800) 661-8747; www.greyhound.ca.
Has service to numerous points in Alberta and British Columbia. Canada's largest intercity bus company, Greyhound also operates motorcoach charters.

Red Arrow Motorcoach
Several locations; tel: (780) 425-0825, tollfree (800) 232-1958; www.redarrow.ca.
Offers a de luxe, daily express service between Calgary, Red Deer, Edmonton and Fort McMurray, offering complimentary snacks, fold-down work tables and computer plug-ins.

www.edmontonairports.com, is a hub for a few regional carriers providing service to smaller centres in Alberta, Saskatchewan and the Northwest Territories. Most passenger services use the Esso Avitat Passenger Lounge.

Downtown Info Centre *Churchill LRT Station, 99th St & 102A Ave; tel: (780) 496-1600. Open Mon–Fri 0830–1730 for tickets, passes and route maps.*

ETS route information
tel: (780) 496-1611, is available Mon–Fri 0630–2200, Sat and Sun 0800–1730.

Edmonton Art Gallery *$ 2 Sir Winston Churchill Square; tel: (780) 422-6223; www.artgalleryalberta.com. Open Tue–Fri 1030–1700, Thur until 2000; Sat and Sun 1100–1700; closed Mon and public holidays.*

Fort Edmonton Park $
Fox Dr. and Whitemud Dr.; tel: (780) 496-8787; fax: (780) 496-8797; www.edmonton.ca/fort. Open May and Jun Mon–Fri 1000–1600, Sat and Sun 1000–1800; Jul–Sept, daily 1000–1800.

Legislature Building $
10800 97 Ave; tel: (780) 427-7362; fax: (780) 427-0980; e-mail: visitorinfo@ assembly.ab.ca; www.assembly.ab.ca. Open May–mid-Oct Mon–Fri 0830–1700, Sat, Sun & public holidays 0900–1700, tours on the hour 0900–1200, every half hour 1230–1600; mid-Oct–Apr, Mon–Fri 0900–1630, Sat, Sun & public holidays 1200–1700; tours on the hour 0900–1500, every half hour 1200–1600.

Opposite
Hudson's Bay Company fort

By car: Highway access is Hwy 16 (Yellowhead Highway) from the east and west, and Hwy 2 (Calgary Trail and Gateway Blvd in Edmonton) from the north and south. This corridor was renamed Queen Elizabeth II Highway in 2005.

Getting around

Public transport

A quick, easy and inexpensive option throughout the city is Edmonton Transit Service (ETS; *etransit@edmonton.ca; www.takeets.com*). LRT (light rail transit), trolleys and buses cover Edmonton but not the airport. Billed as a trip across the world's highest streetcar bridge, **High Level Streetcar**, *tel: (780) 437-7721*, follows a 2.5km route across the old CPR rail line from Old Strathcona across the High Level Bridge to the Grandin LRT Station, adjacent to the Legislature Building.

Sights

Edmonton Art Gallery

The gallery with an open central stairway contains an extensive, high-quality collection of more than 5,000 works of art by regional, national and international artists. The Children's Gallery contains interactive exhibits. There is also a delightful coffee bar and gallery shop.

Fort Edmonton Park

A reconstruction of the fur trading fort, Fort Edmonton Park is set in a ravine of the North Saskatchewan River. The vast living history museum is an adventure through four time periods. Guides in period costume recreate the atmosphere and perform the daily duties of the early days. Nostalgic steam train and street car rides are included in the price of admission.

Legislature Building

Alberta's foremost historic structure, the stately, domed Legislature Building has a prominent setting on the verdant banks of the North Saskatchewan River. The yellow sandstone building is graced with beautifully landscaped grounds in summer, and a huge skating rink in winter. Opened in 1912 on the site of the original Fort Edmonton, the building contains a portrait of Princess Louise Caroline Alberta, daughter of Queen Victoria and wife of the Governor-General of Canada 1878–83, after whom the province is named.

Muttart Conservatory

Four spectacular glass pyramids contain some 700 species of plants and flowers collected from around the world. Explore a steaming jungle, trek across a sun-baked desert, and stroll through the scents of

a floral paradise. One-hour guided tours for groups should be booked two weeks in advance. Refreshments, light lunches and after-hour visits are available.

Old Strathcona Historic Area

Restored houses and shops line Whyte Ave (82nd) and 104th St on the south side of the river, the early town of Strathcona before it was amalgamated with Edmonton in 1912. Wide streets and low buildings give it an Old West atmosphere, a good place to walk around and browse through the museums, theatres, restaurants and Saturday farmers' market.

Old Strathcona Historic Area $
104th St and Whyte (82nd) Ave; tel: (780) 433-4657 for information; www.oldstrathcona.ca. Open daily.

Royal Alberta Museum $
12845 102 Ave; tel: (780) 453-9100; www.royalalbertamuseum.ca. Open daily 0900–1700, closed Christmas Day and Boxing Day.

TELUS World of Science Edmonton $
11211 142 St; tel: (780) 451-3344; fax: (780) 455-5882; www.telusworldofscience.com. Open mid-Jun–Aug daily 1000–2100; winter Sun–Thur and holidays 1000–1700, Fri and Sat 1000–2100; closed Christmas Day.

Ukrainian Cultural Heritage Village $
c/o 9920–112 St; tel: (780) 662-3640; e-mail: uchv@gov.ab.ca; www.cd.gov.ab.ca/uchv. Open Victoria Day weekend–Labour Day daily 1000–1800; Labour Day–Thanksgiving weekends only.

Ukrainian Museum of Canada $
10611 110 Ave; tel: (780) 483-5932. Open May–Aug Mon–Fri 1000–1600; weekends and Sept–Apr by appointment only.

Right
TELUS World of Science Edmonton

Opposite
Old Strathcona

Royal Alberta Museum
Highlight of the museum is the stunning Syncrude Gallery of Aboriginal Culture which showcases native artefacts in North America. Other galleries include Habitat and Natural History, and the live Bug Room. Tour menus are available for breaks, lunch and dinner in the restaurant.

TELUS World of Science Edmonton
The largest planetarium in Canada, the complex contains an IMAX theatre, interactive exhibits, an observatory, the Dow Computer lab, a ham radio station, and Environment, Forensics and Health galleries.

Ukrainian Cultural Heritage Village
Over 30 historic buildings including churches, blacksmith and sod huts built by the Ukrainian population. Try traditional food and meet local interpreters.

Ukrainian Museum of Canada
Edmonton's rich Ukrainian heritage is celebrated with displays of colourful costumes, dolls, tapestries, paintings and Easter eggs.

Right
Grain elevator,
Ukrainian village

**West Edmonton
Mall** *8882 170 St; tel:
(780) 444-5300, tollfree
(800) 661-8890;
e-mail: tourism@
westedmontonmall.com;
www.westedmontonmall.com.
Open daily.* Individual
attraction's hours vary; call
for information.

West Edmonton Mall

Once billed by the *Guinness Book of Records* as the world's largest indoor playground and shopping complex, the West Edmonton Mall is still the 'greatest indoor show on earth' and a destination in itself. Alberta's No 1 destination has over 800 retail stores, 100 eating establishments, and such varied attractions as *World Waterpark* and a replica of Christopher Columbus's *Santa Maria*.

Accommodation and food

Edmonton has a variety of accommodation, from budget to deluxe. Most hotels can be booked through Alberta Express Reservations: *tel: (780) 621-2855, tollfree (800) 884-8803.*

Edmonton is a multicultural city and its culinary expertise shines at the 1,700 restaurants, offering traditional fare to Ukrainian and Russian delicacies.

Bourbon Street $$ *West Edmonton Mall.* Has a collection of restaurants in a New Orleans atmosphere such as Albert's (Montreal-smoked meat), Hooters (scantily-clad waitresses) and Sherlock Holmes (great selection of imported beer).

Century Grill $$ *3975 Calgary Trail; tel: (780) 431-0303; www.centurygrill.com.* Features Canadian dishes such as rack of lamb, herb roasted chicken and fine Alberta beef.

The Crêperie $$$ *10220 103 St; tel: (780) 420-6656.* Has a cosy, romantic ambience. Located in downtown Edmonton, The Crêperie is widely regarded as the best French restaurant in the city.

Fairmont Hotel Macdonald $$$ *10065 100 St; tel: (780) 424-2450, tollfree (800) 441-1414; fax: (780) 429-6481; www.fairmont.com.* Edmonton's foremost hotel with sweeping views of the North Saskatchewan River valley.

Fantasyland Hotel $$$ *17700 87th Ave; tel: (780) 444-3000; fax: (780) 444-3294; e-mail: info@fantasylandhotel.com; www.fantasylandhotel.com.* Part of the West Edmonton Mall and has regular and theme rooms such as Polynesian, Victorian and Roman.

Glenora B&B Inn $$ *12327 102 Ave; tel: (780) 488-6766, tollfree (877) 453-6672; fax: (780) 488-5168; www.glenorabnb.com.* Has full breakfast, and is located in a historic building near the Provincial Museum of Alberta.

Unheardof Restaurant $$ *9602 82nd Ave; tel: (780) 432-0480.* Located in an old house in Old Strathcona. This popular eatery (the owner's name is 'Heard') is noted for its 5-course *prix-fixe* (fixed price) dinners.

Union Bank Inn $$$ *10053 Jasper Ave; tel: (780) 423-3600, tollfree (888) 423-3601; fax: (780) 423-4623; www.unionbankinn.com.* Has an art deco look, located in the heart of downtown Edmonton in a restored bank building.

ℹ **Vue Weekly**
10303 108 St; tel:
(780) 426-1996;
www.vueweekly.com, and
See Magazine e-mail:
info@see.greatwest.ca;
www.seemagazine.com,
are free distribution
publications which provide
information on local
events, cultural attractions,
performances, cinemas and
other happenings.

📖 **The Front Page**
10356 Jasper Ave; tel:
(780) 426-1206, for books,
magazines and newspapers:
carries an extensive
selection at its downtown
location.

**Wine and Spirits
Warehouse – Cost Plus**
11452 Jasper Ave; tel: (780)
488-7973, for wine and
spirits.

Shopping

Edmonton has a huge variety of shopping centres such as the downtown Edmonton City Centre and ManuLife Place, all connected by tunnels above and below, and street-level pedways. Over 800 stores and services are tucked into the huge West Edmonton Mall. Boutiques, restaurants and the Saturday farmers' market line Old Strathcona.

Suggested tour

Total distance: 53km.

Time: Allow $1^1/2$ hours to drive the circuit, longer during rush hour, which limits the route to the direction indicated because of the one-way streets.

Links: The Yellowhead Highway (Hwy 16) links with Edmonton from the Saskatchewan boundary to the east and Jasper to the west. The Queen Elizabeth II Hwy (Hwy 2) connects from the north and south. The Poundmaker Trail (Hwy 14) runs in a southeasterly direction to Wainwright and the Saskatchewan boundary.

Note: The scale of the map on page 61 is quite small, and not all roads will be marked on it. The directions will make sense, though, when you are in the car.

Route: Begin at the Edmonton Tourism Visitor Information Centre, 9990 Jasper Ave northwest. Turn left onto 97 St and continue to 102A Ave and turn left again, heading west. **EDMONTON ART GALLERY** ❶ is on the right. To the right on 99 St, also called Rue Hull, is City Hall's fountain/winter ice rink, pyramid and carillon. Turn left at 100 St down to Jasper Ave; the landmark Fairmont Hotel Macdonald is on the left.

Turn right on McDougall Hill and over the Low Level Bridge, following signs for the **MUTTART CONSERVATORY** ❷ east via 98 Ave through a circular spaghetti maze of roads, then turn right on 96A St. Go east on 97 Ave, turn right onto Cloverdale Rd, and at the top turn left onto Connors Rd. Go right on 85 St to Whyte (82nd Ave) to **OLD STRATHCONA HISTORIC AREA** ❸, a delightful place to get out and wander.

Continue along Whyte (82nd Ave) and turn left at the 114 St exit, then turn right at 71st Ave/Belgravia Rd and veer right onto Fox Dr. Turn right onto Fort Edmonton Park Rd to the reconstructed **FORT EDMONTON PARK** ❹. Leave Fort Edmonton Park and retrace the route to 71st Ave/Belgravia Rd. Half-way around the traffic circle, continue east on 72 Ave. Turn left on 111 St, go right one-half block

Opposite
Alberta's Legislature Building

on University Ave, then left on 110 St. Turn left onto Saskatchewan Dr. Rutherford House Provincial House is on the left, with the handsome University of Alberta campus ahead.

Go left onto 111 St then to 87 Ave, left on 109 St. Take a sharp right onto Saskatchewan Dr. East. Just beyond the Strathcona Information Caboose turn left onto Queen Elizabeth Dr. and cross Walterdale Hill and the 105 Street Bridge, then veer right onto 103 St. Go left on 97 Ave, left again on 106 St, then right on 96 Ave and right on Fort Way Dr. to the lovely and picturesque **LEGISLATURE BUILDING** ❺.

Take Fort Way Dr. around the legislature grounds through the gracious park. Fort Way Dr. becomes 107 St as it turns north. The striking pillars and modern architecture of Grant MacEwan College are straight ahead. Drive left on Jasper Ave to 124 Street, turning right to browse nine blocks of art galleries. Go left on 111 Ave to 142 St and the **TELUS WORLD OF SCIENCE EDMONTON** ❻.

Continue west of 111 Ave as it becomes Mayfield Rd. Go south at 170 St to the **WEST EDMONTON MALL** (WEM) ❼. Exit WEM and go left to 87 Ave, then left on 149 St and right to Stony Plain Rd which turns into 104 Ave. The **ROYAL ALBERTA MUSEUM** ❽ is on the right. Continue on 104 Ave, crossing over Groat Rd, then right on 124 St to follow Jasper Ave left to Downtown Edmonton and the Visitor Information Centre.

Also worth exploring

Drive 45km east of Edmonton on the Yellowhead Highway (Hwy 16) to Elk Island National Park. A popular day trip from Edmonton, the Elk Island was established as Canada's first animal sanctuary in 1906, home to prairie elk, plains bison and the larger yet rarer wood bison. The **South Gate Visitor Centre**, *tel: (780) 922-5833*, is open daily May–October. Three kilometres farther east on Hwy 16 is the **Ukrainian Cultural Heritage Village**, *tel: (780) 662-3640. Open Victoria Day weekend–Labour Day daily 1000–1800; Labour Day–Thanksgiving weekends only.*

Gateway to the North

Edmonton is frequently called the 'Gateway to the North' because of its northerly location. Occupying the same latitude as Liverpool, Edmonton was first settled by the Hudson's Bay Company and North West Co. in 1795 as Fort Edmonton, yet it was more than a century before Edmonton was incorporated as a city in 1904.

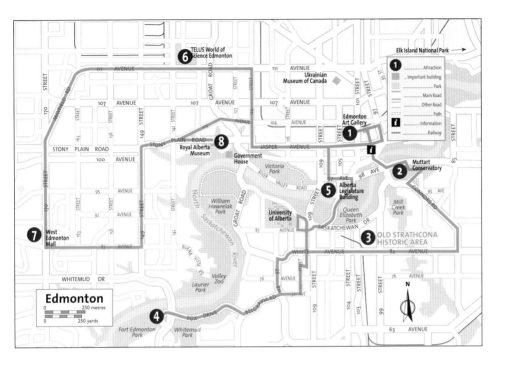

Edmonton takes flight

Edmonton has had a long association with aviation. Dating from 1910 when Hugh Robinson flew a Curtis Flyer to the Edmonton Exhibition, the legendary Wilfred 'Wop' May gets credit for ushering in the era when he introduced mail delivery service and flying passengers in 1919. Wop and his brother Court formed May Airplanes Ltd, which led to Canadian Pacific Airlines. Edmonton became a vibrant centre of aviation and earned its nickname 'Gateway to the North' when bush pilots such as C H 'Punch' Dickins, Grant McConachie and 'Wop' May flew prospectors, mail and supplies into the far north. As traffic increased, a larger airfield was needed so the municipal airport site (now City Centre Airport) was established in 1926. During World War II, the 'Muni' was a crucial link in the war effort, chosen for the No 2 Air Observer School (British Commonwealth Air Training Plan). As Edmonton grew, there was considerable controversy about whether to save the airport or move all flights to the Edmonton International Airport south of the city. With the creation of the privatised Edmonton Airports Authority, the City Centre Airport became the hub for general aviation, aircraft smaller than ten seats.

Calgary–Edmonton Trail

Ratings

Children	●●●●●
History	●●●●●
Museums	●●●●●
Towns	●●●●●
Food and drink	●●●●○
Outdoor activities	●●●●○
Parks	●●●●○
Historical sights	●●●○○

Linking Alberta's major cities, the Calgary–Edmonton Trail is an easy morning drive across broad plains, over rolling hills and through the verdant city of Red Deer. A vital transportation route since the 19th century, the Calgary–Edmonton Trail was surveyed after the Canadian Pacific Railway reached Calgary. At first little more than a worn pathway used by wagons and Red River carts which connected the North West Mounted Police post in Calgary and the fur trading centre of Edmonton, many motorists now refer to the busy highway as Alberta's autobahn. A stopover point for Scottish settlers, Red Deer is the midway point and beginning of the David Thompson Highway, a less travelled yet no less picturesque route to the Rocky Mountains at the southern end of Jasper National Park. A side trip to Devon describes Leduc No 1, which ushered in Alberta's oil industry and age of prosperity.

ALBERTA HERITAGE EXPOSITION PARK

Alberta Heritage Exposition Park $
5km west of Leduc on Hwy 39; tel: (780) 986-5912; www.leducwestantique.com. Open year round, summer 1000–1700. Appointments recommended off-season.

The 32ha site contains restored historic buildings which house artefacts and private collections. The 400-member Leduc West Antique Society began as an antique tractor club, and has expanded to include collectables and antiques associated with Western Canada.

CANADIAN PETROLEUM INTERPRETIVE CENTRE

Situated on the site of the well which ushered in Alberta's oil era, the Canadian Petroleum Interpretive Centre salutes the spirit, resolve and success of the Alberta oil patch. Owned and operated by the

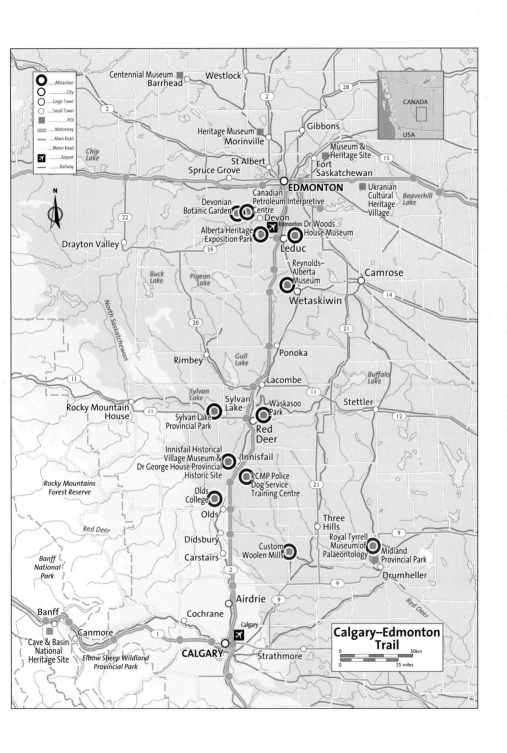

Calgary–Edmonton
Trail

Canadian Petroleum Interpretive Centre $
12km west of Hwy 2 on Hwy 19, 2km north of Devon; tel: (780) 987-4323, (866) 987-4323; www.c-pic. org. Open year round daily 0900–1700.

Leduc/Devon Oil Field Historical Society, the towering 53m conventional oil derrick adjacent to the Interpretive Centre is a replica of the original that tapped into the huge Leduc oilfield (*see page 69*). Other outside displays include oilfield equipment, a field battery and four types of full-scale drilling rigs. Videos, guides and drilling rig equipment tell the story of the oil industry.

Right
Canadian Petroleum Interpretive Centre

Opposite
Horseshoe Canyon

CUSTOM WOOLEN MILLS LTD

Custom Woolen Mills Ltd
30km east of Carstairs on Hwy 791; tel: (403) 337-2221; e-mail: info@ customwoolenmills.com; www.customwoolenmills.com. Open Mon–Fri 0900–1700.

Demonstrations give visitors an opportunity to see early wool processing. The Wool Shoppe sells finished yarns, knitting and wool craft supplies. Carding machinery in use was made between 1860 and 1910, the spinning mule dates from 1910 and the knotting machine is circa 1917.

DEVONIAN BOTANIC GARDEN

Devonian Botanic Garden $ *12km west of Hwy 2 on Hwy 19, 5km north of Devon on Hwy 60; tel: (780) 987-3054; www.devonian.ualberta.ca. Open daily Apr and May 1000–1600; Jun 1000–1800; Jul and Aug 1000–2100; Sept–mid-Oct 1000–1800.*

A tropical garden in the prairies, Devonian Botanic Garden is home to a collection of exotic orchids, free-flying butterflies and a succulent greenhouse. The Kurimoto Japanese garden is set in a picturesque landscape and peaceful atmosphere. Operated by the University of Alberta, the Garden is home to their microfungus collection, second largest in Canada. Spread over a 77ha site, the Garden is a delightful setting for picnics and birdwatching. There is a berry patch where visitors may pick and taste the fruit, and a gift shop and restaurant.

DR GEORGE HOUSE PROVINCIAL HISTORIC SITE

Dr George House Provincial Historic Site $ *5713 51 Ave, Innisfail; tel: (403) 227-7744. Open late May–Aug, Mon–Fri 0830–1630.*

Built in 1893 by Innisfail's original physician, the red brick house combines a natural history museum and offices. Though Dr Henry George and his wife, an artist who designed the Alberta provincial crest, later moved to Red Deer, the doctor was a collector and had established the first museum in the then Northwest Territories.

DR WOODS HOUSE MUSEUM

Dr Woods House Museum $ *4801 49 Ave, Leduc; tel: (780) 986-1517. Open year round: Jun–Aug 1100–1700; winter Tue and Fri 1000–1700.*

The home of pioneer physician Dr Robert Woods and his family, the Craftsman bungalow contains his medical wing and attached garage as it was in the 1920s. There is a collection of photographs, textiles and archival material. A registered historic site, the attached garage contains a tea room.

INNISFAIL HISTORICAL VILLAGE MUSEUM

 **Innisfail Historical Village Museum $** 52 Ave and 42 St, Innisfail; tel: (403) 227-2906. Open mid-May–Labour Day Mon–Sat 1600–1700, Sun and hols 1200–1700.

Hudson's Bay Company scout, Anthony Henday, with Cree guides, spotted the Rockies from nearby Mud Creek in 1754. The 1886 Spruces log building, the only extant Stopping House between Calgary and Edmonton, is one of the 13 historic buildings encompassed by the Innisfail Historical Village Museum.

OLDS COLLEGE

Olds College Hwy 2A and Hwy 27, Olds; tel: (403) 556-8371, tollfree (800) 661-6537; www.oldscollege.ab.ca. Open year round, best viewing months May–Oct. Farm buildings off-limits without permission.

Known for innovative agricultural development, Olds College has beautiful flower beds and botanical gardens along with fruit trees and specimens of trees grown in Alberta. The 700ha campus and farm also has greenhouses, a natural fibre centre and an alpaca farm, offering a limited number of sweaters and blankets for sale.

RCMP POLICE DOG SERVICE TRAINING CENTRE

RCMP Police Dog Service Training Centre 4km south of Innisfail on Hwy 2; tel: (403) 227-3346; www.rcmp.ca/pds. Open year round, phone ahead for tours; demonstrations late May–Labour Day Wed 1400. Free.

The national dog training centre for the Royal Canadian Mounted Police, the centre conducts tours and demonstrations, though should be booked in advance. At the centre visitors can pick up tips in dog handling; it also buys, breeds and sells dogs.

REYNOLDS–ALBERTA MUSEUM

Reynolds–Alberta Museum $ 2km west of Wetaskiwin on Hwy 13; tel: (780) 361-1351, tollfree (800) 661-4726; e-mail: ram@gov.ab.ca; www.machinemuseum.net. Open year round: mid-May–Jun 1000–1700; Jul–early Sept 1000–1800. Off season 6 days a week (closed Monday).

The Reynolds–Alberta Museum contains some 60 vintage aircraft, 300 restored vehicles, and 1,000 pieces of ageing agricultural and industrial equipment. Cruise the grounds in a pristine 1935 Chevrolet or soar in a glorious open cockpit biplane. The Exhibition Hall contains artefacts, audio-visual presentations and guided tours. Self-guided and interpreter-led tours.

ROYAL TYRRELL MUSEUM OF PALAEONTOLOGY

🚩 **Royal Tyrrell Museum of Palaeontology** *6km northwest of downtown Drumheller; tel: (403) 823-7707, tollfree Alberta 310-0000 then (403) 823-7707; e-mail: tyrrell.info@gov.ab.ca; www.tyrrellmuseum.com. Open daily, Victoria Day–Labour Day 0900–2100, Labour Day–Thanksgiving 1000–1700; mid-Oct–mid-May Tue–Sun 1000–1700.*

A world-class exhibition, museum and research facility, the Royal Tyrrell Museum of Palaeontology is the only museum in Canada dedicated to the study and display of prehistoric life. Some 800 fossil specimens and over 50 dramatically exhibited dinosaur skeletons take visitors through 4.5 billion years of the earth's history. At least three hours are recommended for a visit. If you are a die-hard Lost World explorer, spend a week working in the field with palaeontologists during the summer in the richest dinosaur burial grounds in the world. Situated in the barren badlands of Midland Provincial Park, the lunar-like region was a marshland with a semi-tropical climate similar to the Florida Everglades when dinosaurs roamed the valley of the Red Deer River.

Below
Royal Tyrrell Museum of Palaeontology dinosaur

SYLVAN LAKE PROVINCIAL PARK

🚩 **Sylvan Lake Provincial Park $** *11km west of Red Deer; tel: (403) 340-7657; www.cd.gov.ab.ca. Townsite open year round, park activities May–Oct.*

One of Alberta's favourite summer resorts, Sylvan Lake Provincial Park is busy on weekends when the sun shines, the throngs of visitors attracted to the golf course, golden beaches and the enormous Wild Rapids Water Slide. Home of the only functioning lighthouse between Winnipeg and the West Coast, water activities include fishing, boating and windsurfing.

WASKASOO PARK

ⓟ Waskasoo Park
entrance at Heritage Ranch, Red Deer; tel: (403) 342-8259; www.city.red-deer.ab.ca. Open year round.

Kerry Wood Nature Centre
6300 45th Ave, Red Deer; tel: (403) 346-2010; e-mail: general@waskasoopark.ca. Open year round.

Fort Normandeau Historic Site and Interpretive Centre $
west of Hwy 2 on 32nd St, Red Deer. Open May–Sept. www.waskasoopark.ca

Spanning 11km along the Red Deer River through the centre of the city of Red Deer, the expansive park was made to preserve and enhance the natural open space while incorporating developed facilities. Among the attractions are Heritage Ranch, the **Kerry Wood Nature Centre**, Gaetz Lakes Sanctuary, the Victorian-style Cronquist House and **Fort Normandeau Historic Site and Interpretive Centre**, a reconstruction of a North West Mounted Police fort. The park provides some 80km of bicycle, pedestrian and equestrian trails.

Accommodation and food

Most of the motels, hotels and B&Bs are moderately priced, reflecting their modest furnishings. Prices are generally higher in summer and on weekdays. Book in advance for accommodation in Red Deer, a convention and conference centre.

Aladdin Motor Inn $ *7444 50 Ave, Red Deer; tel: (403) 343-2711; fax: (403) 343-2711; e-mail: aladdinmotorinn@hotmail.ca; www.aladdinmotorinn.com.* On North Hill; has a lounge and the China Bens Restaurant in the plaza.

Apples & Angels B&B $$ *304 Waterstone Place, Airdrie; tel: (403) 912-4441, tollfree (877) 346-9399; www.lanierbb.com.* Lovely rooms with many amenities such as soaker tub, fireplace and music room.

Café Noble & Bakery $ *5005–50 Ave, Red Deer; tel: (403) 358-6058.* A downtown, family-run quaint café that features fresh baking and home cooking. Also vegetarian, vegan, wheat-free and dairy-free selections.

Country Pleasures B&B $$ *5712–45 Ave, Wetaskiwin; tel: (780) 352-4335; e-mail: relax@country-pleasures-bb.com.* Spacious rooms with fireplaces and en suite baths. Lovely decor and dining.

Graham's Beachfront Resort $ *4505 Lakeshore Dr., Sylvan Lake; tel: (403) 887-2407; www.grahamsbeachfront.com.* Has an outdoor hot tub.

Joey's Only and Tennessee Jack's $ *4 5220 Lakeshore Dr., Sylvan Lake; tel: (403) 887-2788.* Has great ribs and a patio with a view of the lake.

La Casa Pergola $$ *4909 48 St, Red Deer; tel: (403) 342-2404.* A comfortable dining room that features fine Italian food.

MacEachern Tea House $ *4719 50 Ave, Wetaskiwin; tel: (780) 352-0606; open Tue–Fri 1100–1700, Sat 1100–1600.* Amid 1930s period furniture, the tea house serves 180 loose teas and a menu with everything freshly made.

Red Deer Lodge $$ *4311 49 Ave, Red Deer; tel: (403) 346-8841, tollfree (reservations) (800) 661-1657; www.reddeerlodge.ca.* Largest motel in the city; on the edge of downtown.

Rosebud Country Inn $$ *320 north Railway Ave east, Rosebud; tel: (403) 677-2211; www.experiencerosebud.com.* A cosy inn near Rosebud Theatre, about a 20-minute drive southwest of Drumheller.

Voyageur Inn $ *Hwy 11, Rocky Mountain House; tel: (403) 845-3381.* Kitchenettes with microwaves and coffee makers.

Dr Joseph Burr Tyrrell

A geologist with the Geological Survey of Canada 1881–98, Joseph Burr Tyrrell is widely recognised as the dean of Canadian mining. After exploring the Northwest Territories, Tyrrell discovered the extensive coal beds at Fernie in BC and at Drumheller. But it was a 70 million-year-old fossilised dinosaur skull, christened Albertosaurus, that attracted world-wide interest. Found in 1884 in the rich dinosaur beds of the Drumheller Valley, the cousin of the fierce, meat-eating T Rex was the first of hundreds of complete dinosaur skeletons removed from the Badlands. A cartographer, explorer, geologist and mining consultant, Tyrrell later took over a faltering gold mine at Kirkland Lake, Ontario, which kept producing well after his death in 1957. Namesake of the Tyrrell Museum of Palaeontology which opened in 1985; Queen Elizabeth II granted the 'Royal' appellation in 1990.

Leduc No 1

After drilling 133 dry holes in Alberta and Saskatchewan, Imperial Oil was about to give up but decided to drill another line of wildcat wells across Alberta. The first of the wells was on a farm 15km west of Leduc and 50km south of Edmonton. Three months after drilling 1,544m, the company was confident that the hole would be a gusher. On a cold winter day on 13 February 1947, Imperial Oil invited businessmen, dignitaries and government officials to the site. As luck would have it, equipment failures the night before delayed the ceremony for hours. Sure enough, drillers hit paydirt at 1600 hours as the drilling mud blew out of the hole, the guests treated to a spectacular sight of towering columns of smoke and fire flaring across the darkening sky. While the oil industry had long been established in the Turner Valley south of Calgary, Leduc No 1 was the big one that ushered in Alberta's booming oil industry.

Suggested tour

Total distance: 300km.

Time: 3 hours to drive, 2–3 days to explore.

Links: The Yellowhead Highway (Hwy 16) links with Edmonton (*see page 50*), the Trans-Canada Highway (Hwy 1) with Calgary (*see page 38*), the David Thompson Highway (Hwy 11) connects with Red Deer, and Hwys 72 and 9 continue east to Drumheller.

Route: From Calgary, take the Deerfoot Trail (Hwy 2) north. The divided highway bypasses Calgary International Airport on the right and continues through barren rangeland to Airdrie, a one-time railway depot and now a booming dormitory community for Calgary. Continue north and take the Hwy 581 exit to the right, then left on Hwy 791 to **CUSTOM WOOLEN MILLS** ❶ where workers demonstrate wool processing with ancient machines and sell finished yarns, knitting and wool craft supplies.

Return to Hwy 2 and head north to Olds on the west side on Hwy 2A, predecessor to the original Calgary–Edmonton Trail. **OLDS COLLEGE** ❷ trains some 1,300 students in innovative agricultural development, and provides a delightful setting for a leisurely stroll through the flower beds, gardens and greenhouse. Return to Hwy 2 and continue north to the **RCMP POLICE DOG SERVICE TRAINING CENTRE** ❸, 4km south of Innisfail, where dogs imported from Europe are trained with their masters for active duty across Canada.

Back on Hwy 2, the highway angles right towards **RED DEER** ❹ and the midway point. Founded in 1882 by Scottish settlers as a stopover point for travellers, Red Deer is the commercial hub for the rolling parkland district of central Alberta. It is also the junction of the David Thompson Highway, a less travelled though no less scenic route to the Rocky Mountains. Hwy 11A is an access road to one of Alberta's most popular summer resorts, **SYLVAN LAKE** ❺, which also connects with Hwy 11 to Rocky Mountain House and Saskatchewan River Crossing.

Hwy 2 continues in a northerly direction through rolling parkland, the divided highway bypassing several small communities such as Lacombe, named after the famous priest and diplomat Father Albert Lacombe, and Ponoka, which means 'elk' in the Blackfoot language. Turn right at the junction of Hwy 13 to Wetaskiwin, home of the **REYNOLDS–ALBERTA MUSEUM** ❻, a provincial heritage collection of machinery, aircraft and transportation-related gadgets from the 1890–1950 era. Continue north on Hwy 2A to the city of Leduc, home of the **DR WOODS HOUSE MUSEUM** ❼, the pioneer living quarters and doctor's office in a Craftsman bungalow.

Opposite
Fort Normandeau Historic Site

Above
A 1927 International Model
54-C at Alberta Heritage
Exposition Park

Return to Hwy 2 and continue north past Edmonton International Airport on the left, then exit onto the Hwy 19 turnoff and head west to the town of Devon, home of the **DEVONIAN BOTANIC GARDEN** ❽, **CANADIAN PETROLEUM INTERPRETIVE CENTRE** ❾ and **ALBERTA HERITAGE EXPOSITION PARK** ❿. Return to Hwy 2, and continue on into the city of Edmonton (*see pages 50–61*).

Also worth exploring

Some 800 fossil specimens and over 50 dramatically exhibited dinosaur skeletons take a visitor through 4.5 billion years of the earth's history at the **Royal Tyrrell Museum of Palaeontology** in Drumheller (*see pages 67 and 69*). The research centre studies all forms of ancient life, including the Burgess Shale exhibit which provides a 3-D look at the unusual creatures that swam in prehistoric waters. The museum's theme, 'A Celebration of Life', explores the origin of life in the 11,200sq m facility which also contains an auditorium, cafeteria, gift shop and bookstore.

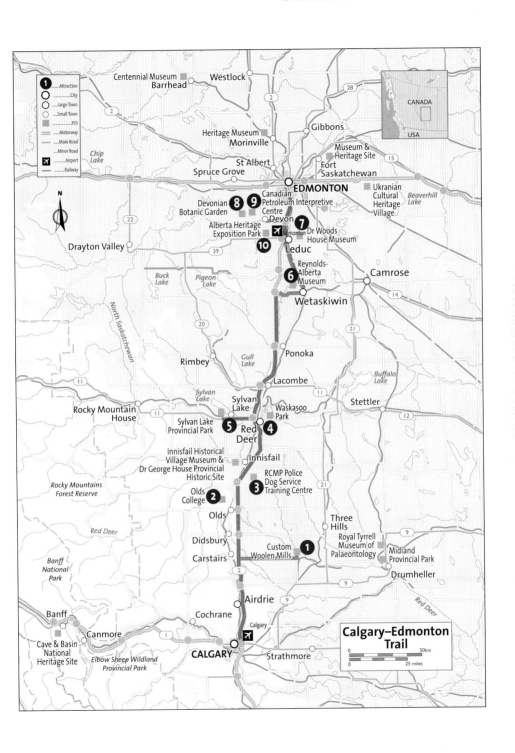

Calgary–Edmonton Trail

- **1** Attraction
- ○ City
- ○ Large Town
- ○ Small Town
- ▪ POI
- Motorway
- Main Road
- Minor Road
- ✈ Airport
- Railway

CANADA

USA

N

Centennial Museum
Barrhead
Westlock

28

2

Heritage Museum
Morinville
Gibbons

Museum &
Heritage Site

15

St Albert
Spruce Grove
Fort
Saskatchewan

Chip
Lake

2

EDMONTON

Ukrainian
Cultural
Heritage
Village

Beaverhill
Lake

Devonian
Botanic Garden
8 **9** Canadian
Petroleum Interpretive
Centre

22

Devon

7 Dr Woods
House Museum

Alberta Heritage
Exposition Park
✈ Edmonton
10 Leduc

Drayton Valley

39

Reynolds-
Alberta
Museum
6

Camrose

Buck
Lake
Pigeon
Lake
Wetaskiwin

14

North Saskatchewan

20

21

Rimbey
Gull
Lake
Ponoka

Lacombe
11
Buffalo
Lake

11
Sylvan
Lake
Sylvan
Lake
Waskasoo
Park
Stettler

Rocky Mountain
House
11
Sylvan Lake
Provincial Park
5 Red
Deer
4

12

Innisfail Historical
Village Museum &
Dr George House Provincial
Historic Site
Innisfail

Rocky Mountains
Forest Reserve

Olds
College
2
RCMP Police
Dog Service
Training Centre
3

21

Olds

Three
Hills

Royal Tyrrell
Museum of
Palaeontology

9

Red Deer

Didsbury
Custom
Woolen Mills
1

Midland
Provincial Park

Banff
National
Park
Carstairs

2
Drumheller

Airdrie
9

Red Deer

Banff
Cochrane

Cave & Basin
National
Heritage Site
Canmore

Calgary
✈

1

CALGARY
Strathmore

Elbow Sheep Wildland
Provincial Park

Calgary–Edmonton
Trail

0   50km
0   25 miles

Cowboy Trail

Ratings

Foothills	●●●●●
History	●●●●●
Scenery	●●●●●
Walking	●●●●●
Wildlife	●●●●●
Children	●●●●○
Towns	●●●●○
Food and drink	●●○○○

Alberta's historic Cowboy Trail links the fur-trading post of Rocky Mountain House, the rolling prairie of the foothills and the icy peaks of the Waterton Lakes National Park. This north–south highway is home to sprawling ranches, spectacular vistas and friendly towns where cowboys resplendent in high heels and magnificent silver belt buckles tip their ten-gallon hats and greet strangers with a smile. Along the way you will see the gentlemen of the range herding cattle, graceful quarter horses running free and native dancers performing at a colourful powwow. Wildlife is abundant and it is not uncommon to see bears, wolves, cougars, elk, moose and deer roaming freely in their natural habitat. The Cowboy Trail crosses cold mountain rivers and streams where fly fishermen test their skills, and leads to country inns, rustic lodges and stunning scenery: a favourite setting for many Hollywood films.

BAR U RANCH NATIONAL HISTORIC SITE

Bar U Ranch National Historic Site $ 13km south of Longview on Hwy 22; tel: (403) 395-3044, tollfree (888) 773-8888; www.thecowboytrail.com or www.pc.gc.ca. Open Jun–Oct daily 0900–1700.

Once one of the leading ranches in Canada, the Bar U Ranch was named after its brand by the North West Cattle Co. syndicate. Dating from 1882, the ranch earned international repute as a centre of breeding excellence for cattle and purebred Percheron draught horses. The Bar U remained one of the largest ranches in the country until 1950, when land was sold to other ranchers from the estate of the millionaire meatpacker Patrick Burns, one of the 'Big Four' who helped launch the Calgary Stampede. The Bar U's buildings sprawl over rangeland near Pekisco Creek, a riparian area favoured by wapiti (elk), moose and beavers. The Rocky Mountains provide a dramatic backdrop due west. Costumed interpreters lead guided tours through the 35 ranch buildings. The Visitor Centre has ranching exhibits and a video of Bar U history. The Roadhouse Restaurant serves ranch-style food, while the General Store sells local arts and crafts.

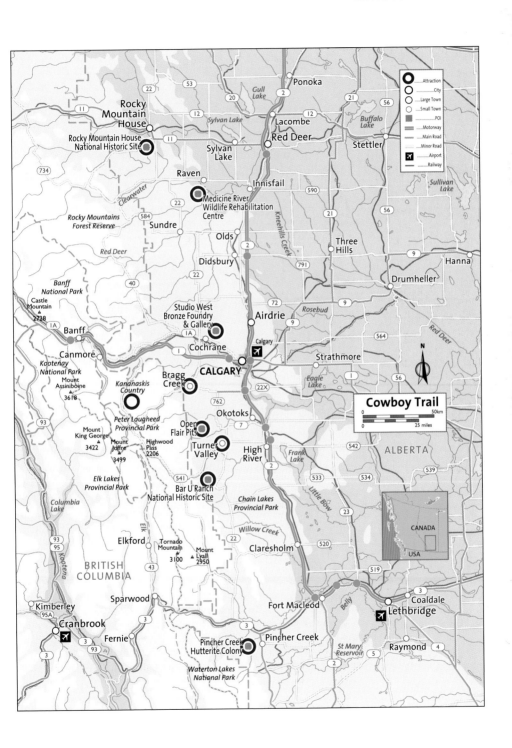

Bragg Creek

A funky village full of artisans, Bragg Creek is a pleasant community for a picnic, hiking and horse riding as well as shopping for Western arts and crafts, sampling cowboy cuisine and taking in a native dinner theatre. A dormitory community with many young residents, Bragg Creek dates from 1914 when the first post office opened, the mail carried on horseback along the Stoney Trail. When the first settlers arrived in 1885, Bragg Creek was an open meadow, a contrast to the heavy forests of aspen, fir, poplar and spruce. Several ranches are tended by descendants of the early settlers yet most who live on the acreages now are young, recent arrivals who work in Calgary but prefer to live in these picturesque foothills.

Kananaskis Country

Barrier Lake Information Centre *26km southeast of Canmore on Kananaskis Trail (Hwy 40); tel: (403) 673-3985; www. canmore.canmorealberta.ca. Open year-round with varying hours.*

Kananaskis Country Course $$ *Highway 40 south, 1 Lorette Dr.; in season, tel: (403) 591-7272; www.kananaskisgolf.com. Has two 18-hole golf courses.*

Named by explorer John Palliser after a legendary Indian who survived a stunning axe blow to the head, Kananaskis, a Blackfoot word for 'Meeting of the Waters', is a year-round recreational area containing superb golf courses and magnificent areas for hiking, biking, fishing, skiing and camping. Some 500km of equestrian riding trails provide unique camping facilities in the valleys of the Elbow, Highwood and Sheep. A full-service dining, lodging and golf resort, Kananaskis Village was purpose-built for the 1988 Winter Olympics. Adjoining Peter Lougheed Provincial Park comprises some 500sq km of beautiful lakes and valleys.

Accommodation and food in Kananaskis Country

Delta Lodge at Kananaskis $$$ *1 Centennial Dr., Kananaskis Village; tel: (403) 591-7711, tollfree (866) 432-4322; www.deltalodgeatkananaskis.ca.* The best address in the foothills.

The Executive Resort at Kananaskis $$ *2 Terrace Dr., Kananaskis Village (Hwy 40, 28km south of Hwy 1); tel: (403) 591-7229, tollfree (888) 388-3932; www.executivehotels.net; e-mail: resortinfo@royalinn.com.* Great mountain views, creative cuisine and a variety of outdoor activities.

Seasons $$$ *Delta Lodge at Kananaskis; tel: (403) 591-7711.* Creative Canadian dishes, served to the sounds of an easy-going dance band.

William Watson Lodge $ *30km south of Kananaskis Village; tel: (403) 591-7227; www.tprc.alberta.ca/parks/kananaskis/facilities_wwlodge.asp.* A resort for visitors with a disability. Non-Alberta residents should reserve 60 days in advance.

Opposite
Bar U Ranch sculpture

MEDICINE RIVER WILDLIFE REHABILITATION CENTRE

Medicine River Wildlife Rehabilitation Centre $
5.5km south of Raven; tel: (403) 728-3467; www. medicineriverwildlifecentre.ca. Open daily May–Oct 1000–1700.

Injured and orphaned wildlife, which can range from hummingbirds to grizzly bears, are provided for at the Medicine River Wildlife Rehabilitation Centre before returning them to the wild. The animals can be viewed in the reception area and education wing, while birds can be viewed at an outdoor observation tower. The centre also has educational and interactive displays.

OPEN FLAIR PITS

Open Flair Pits
Turner Valley Info Centre, 223 Main St, Turner Valley; tel: (403) 933-4944; www.turnervalley.ca. Open mid-May–Aug Mon–Fri 1000–1600; pits open daily year round.

Natural gas burns around the clock at the Open Flair Pits in the broad Turner Valley. The unusual sight of ground burning is caused by raw gas which seeps through the hillside soil. Site of the first major oil and gas find in Alberta in 1914, the oil was depleted by the time Leduc No 1 blew in in 1947.

PINCHER CREEK HUTTERITE COLONY

Pincher Creek Hutterite Colony $
3km west of Pincher Creek; tel: (403) 627-4021; phone ahead for tour. Open year round daily 0900–1500.

Retaining the dress, customs and simple lifestyle of their 16th-century ancestors, the Pincher Creek Hutterite Colony welcomes visitors year round at their extensive mixed farming operation. Some 90 men, women and children live communally on the self-contained farm that covers some 2,000ha. Visitors are shown a variety of animals, including sheep, poultry and dairy cattle, though the enclosed hog operation is off-limits to prevent the possibility of infection. The colony contains a kitchen, church and school.

ROCKY MOUNTAIN HOUSE NATIONAL HISTORIC SITE

Rocky Mountain House National Historic Site $
82km west of Red Deer on Hwy 11 and 5km south of Rocky Mountain House on Hwy 52A; tel: (403) 845-2412; fax: (403) 845-5320; e-mail: rockinfo@pc.gc.ca. Open May–Sept 1000–1700.

The site commemorates a series of fur trade posts built 1799–1864 by the Hudson's Bay Company and its rival, the North West Co., near the junction of the Clearwater and Saskatchewan rivers. An interpretation centre describes the posts and Rocky Mountain House, the centre for sporadic trade with the Blackfoot, who kept the post in operation until 1875. Canada's greatest geographer, David Thompson, used Rocky Mountain House as a base while he explored, surveyed and established trading posts in present-day British Columbia, Washington, Oregon, Idaho and Montana.

STUDIO WEST BRONZE FOUNDRY AND GALLERY

Studio West Bronze Foundry and Gallery $$ *205 2nd Ave southeast, Cochrane; tel: (403) 932-2611. Open year round Mon–Fri 0800–1700, Sat and Sun 0900–1700.*

Skilled artisans perform the age-old art of bronze casting at Studio West Bronze Foundry and Gallery. Owned and operated by Don and Shirley Beggs, Studio West specialises in lifesize bronze casts of bison and horses. See artisans at work in the studio and foundry as they work with clay and wax, making miniature to monumental sculptures at the largest sculpture foundry in Western Canada.

Above
Medicine River Wildlife
Rehabilitation Centre

TURNER VALLEY

Named after the first settlers in the area, James and Robert Turner, the town was the first cornerstone of the Alberta petroleum industry. Oil was apparent for years through seepage but it was not until 1914 that Dingman No 1 came in, heralding the first major oil and gas discovery in Alberta. The oil ran out by the time Leduc No 1 blew in in 1947.

Accommodation and food

Accommodation is moderate to budget along the Cowboy Trail. Best bet are the B&Bs, many on working cattle ranches.

Bloomin' Inn Guest Ranch $$ *5km east of Pincher Creek on Tower Rd; tel: (403) 627-5829; www.bloomin-inn.com.* A working cattle ranch that provides a full breakfast.

Burger Baron $ *Hwy 11, Rocky Mountain House; tel: (403) 845-6009.* Known for its fine pizza.

Georgetown Inn $$ *1101 Bow Valley Trail, Canmore; tel: (403) 678-3439, reservations (800) 657-5955; www.georgetowninn.net.* A family owned lodge with an English country inn atmosphere.

Highwood River Inn and Nature Bound Tours $$ *23km west of Longview on Hwy 541; tel: (403) 558-2456; e-mail: info@highwoodriverinn.com; www.highwoodriverinn.com.* On the Highwood River in the gorgeous rolling foothills, has a video theatre and licensed dining room.

Lazy M Ranch $$ *Off Hwy 761, Caroline; tel: (403) 722-3053; e-mail: thelazym@telusplanet.net; www.lazymcanada.com; open year round.* Overnight accommodation or a week-long package of riding, fly fishing and horse training.

Silver Willow Lodge $$$ *3km west of Bragg Creek on Hwy 66; tel: (403) 949-3108.* A B&B offering a full breakfast, situated on acreage along the Elbow River.

Turner Valley Lodge $ *112 Kennedy Dr. Turner Valley; tel: (403) 933-7878; e-mail: desk@turnervalleylodge.com; www.turnervalleylodge.com.* Has live entertainment Friday–Saturday nights and jam sessions Saturday afternoon.

Voyageur Motel $ *Hwy 11, Rocky Mountain House; tel: (403) 845-3381, tollfree (888) 845-3569; e-mail: voymote@telusplanet.net.* Has kitchenettes with microwaves and coffee makers.

Above
Red barn post box

Suggested tour

Total distance: 450km. Detour to Kananaskis Country: 70km southwest of Cochrane.

Time: 6–7 hours to drive, 3–5 days to explore.

Links: The Cowboy Trail (Hwy 22) begins at Rocky Mountain House, which links on the west with Hwy 11 from the northern end of Banff National Park, and Red Deer to the east. Hwy 22 connects with numerous secondary roads along its north–south route and crosses over the Trans-Canada Highway (Hwy 1) west of Calgary.

Route: From **ROCKY MOUNTAIN HOUSE** ❶, take Hwy 22 south 25km, turn left and pass through the ranching town of Caroline. Continue east on Hwy 54 to Raven and turn right to the **MEDICINE RIVER WILDLIFE REHABILITATION CENTRE** ❷. Return to Raven, turn left and just before Caroline turn left on Hwy 22 and go through the town of Sundre. Turn right just after Sundre and pass by the villages of Elkton, Cremona and Bottrel before the junction of Hwy 1A, which leads through Cochrane, named after Sen M H Cochrane who founded the historic Cochrane Ranch in 1881; Cochrane became a shipping point for cattle and a dormitory town for Calgary. Hwy 1A continues east to Calgary, or west to Canmore and Banff.

Continue south over the Trans-Canada Highway (Hwy 1) past the trendy estate village of Redwood Meadows, then follow the highway in a southwesterly direction towards **BRAGG CREEK** ❸, a Calgary dormitory community and home to interesting gift shops. Travel east on Hwy 22 for 20km and turn right through the village of Millarville,

Right
Cowboy weather vane

home to a great farmers' market on Sundays during summer. Continue south to **TURNER VALLEY ❹**, centre of the first major oil strike in Alberta, and the neighbouring community of Black Diamond. Travel south to Longview, film location for Clint Eastwood's *Unforgiven*, and 13km south on the west (right) side of the road, pass by the historic **BAR U RANCH ❺**, once the largest ranch in Canada.

The scenery may start to look familiar as many Hollywood films have been made in this area. Drive through Chain Lakes Provincial Park, a favourite summer home for ducks, pelicans and Canada geese. The scenic countryside is dotted with lodges, country inns and B&Bs. Hwy 22 continues through the rolling foothills to the junction of Crowsnest Pass Highway (Hwy 3). Turn left, and pass through the villages of Lundbreck and Cowley before the junction with Hwy 6; turn right to the town of **Pincher Creek ❻**.

Detour: to **KANANASKIS COUNTRY**. From Cochrane travel south on Hwy 22, then right onto the Trans-Canada Highway (Hwy 1). Follow the signs, turn onto Hwy 40 and travel through rolling foothills to Kananaskis Village, 50km from the highway. Return to Cochrane or continue south to Highwood Pass and Highwood House, which is closed December–mid-June to protect and manage animal species along the 44.5km-long Highwood Road Corridor Wildlife Sanctuary. The road meets Hwy 22 just above Longview.

Bar U Ranch

After gold rushes in BC and the arrival of the railway, ranching reached into the sheltered, well-watered foothills of southern Alberta. Nurtured by Englishmen wooed by the glamour of cattle ranching, the newly minted cowboys made time for polo and afternoon tea breaks. One of the great cattle companies developed over the years was the Bar U Ranch, owned over time by Fred Stinson, George Lane and Patrick Burns, who helped underwrite the first Calgary Stampede. From 1882 to 1950, the Bar U (the brand of the North West Cattle Co.) earned an international reputation as a centre of breeding excellence. One of the largest ranches in Canada, there were 10 million cattle grazing in the early 1900s, and later some 9,000 Percheron draught horses. The ranch was so large that Pat Burns boasted he could drive from Calgary to the US border (244km) without stepping off his property. The Bar U is now a thumbnail of its original size but the cattle, horses and chickens, along with the guides in period dress, give a good image of the rugged life of the cowboy on the range.

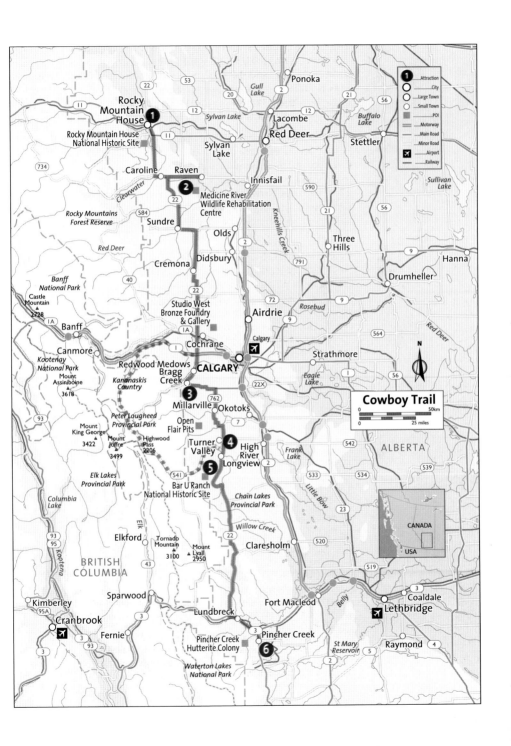

UNESCO Trail North

Ratings

Children	●●●●●
Mountains	●●●●●
National parks	●●●●●
Nature	●●●●●
Outdoor activities	●●●●●
Scenery	●●●●●
Walking	●●●●●
Wildlife	●●●●●

Full of extravagant natural wonders, UNESCO Trail North is one of the most spectacular drives imaginable. Covering the largest body of mountain parkland in the world, the adjoining national parks of Banff, Jasper, Kootenay and Yoho, together with the provincial parks of Mount Assiniboine, Mount Robson and Hamber, make up the Rocky Mountain National Parks World Heritage Site, a 20,238sq km wilderness area straddling the Continental Divide. The Rockies of painting, postcard and song are an endless procession of ragged peaks, sweeping valleys and spectacular mountain passes. Most visitors stop just long enough to shop in Banff, stroll around Banff Springs Hotel and Chateau Lake Louise, and drive along the Icefields Parkway, a rugged alpine wonderland that tests the vocabulary. Watch elk wander through the town of Banff and bighorn sheep graze along the roadway, while other wildlife keep their distance in the forests and alpine meadows.

BANFF NATIONAL PARK

Rocky Mountain National Parks Canada provides a free tabloid-size newspaper with a page of highlights from each of the six parks: Banff, Glacier, Jasper, Kootenay, Mount Revelstoke and Yoho. The same summaries can be found online: *www.pc.gc.ca*

Canada's oldest national park, the Banff Hot Springs Reserve, was created on 4ha of land in 1885 to preserve the sulphur hot springs for public use. It became the Rocky Mountain Parks Reserve shortly after, and was then renamed Banff National Park. Stretching 240km along the eastern slope of the Continental Divide, Banff National Park is a blend of towering peaks, flowery meadows and cold, aquamarine lakes and rivers. The hub of most activities in the Rocky Mountains, the town of Banff, founded in 1883 as 'Siding 29', was renamed by Lord Strathcona (financier and fur trader Donald Alexander Smith) after his home town in Scotland. There is a fee to enter the park – currently $9 per adult, per day.

Banff Park Museum. A taxidermy collection of park wildlife dating back to 1860 is housed in this Victorian-style railway museum. A National Historic Site, the 'museum of a museum' contains a library on natural history; the interior is lined with Douglas fir and balconies

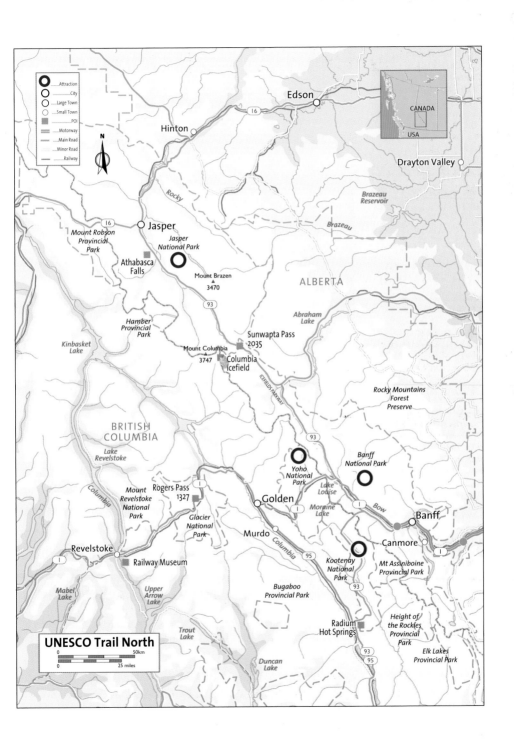

ⓘ Banff National Park Visitor Centre *224 Banff Ave; tel: (403) 762-1550; fax: (403) 762-1551; e-mail: banff.vrc@pc.gc.ca; www.pc.gc.ca. Open late May, Jun & Sept 0900–1900; mid-Jun–early Sept 0800–2000; late Sept–mid-May 0900–1700.*

Lake Louise Visitor Centre *Samson Mall; tel: (403) 522-3833. Open May–late Jun 0800–1800; late Jun–mid-Sept 0800–2000; mid-Sept–1 Apr 0900–1700; e-mail: ll.info@gc.ca; www.pc.gc.ca*

⬤ Banff Book and Art Den *94 Banff Ave; tel: (403) 762-3919, tollfree (866) 418-6613; e-mail: info@banffbooks.com; www.banffbooks.com. Has a good selection of books on the Canadian Rockies.*

ⓕ Banff Park Museum National Historic Site *$ Banff Ave by Bow River Bridge; tel: (403) 762-1588; e-mail: banff.vrc@pc.gc.ca; www.pc.gc.ca. Open mid-May–Sept 1000–1800; Oct–mid-May 1300–1700.*

Cave and Basin National Historic Site *$ 311 Cave Ave; tel: (403) 762-1566; e-mail: banff.vrc@pc.gc.ca. Open mid-May–Sept daily 0900–1800 (site tours 1100 daily); Oct–mid-May Mon–Fri 1100–1600 (inc statutory holidays), Sat and Sun 0930–1700 (guided tour 1100). Closed 25–26 Dec, 1 Jan.*

Right
Lake Louise, 'the Mona Lisa of the Mountains'

set around an atrium. **Banff Springs Hotel**. Dating from 1888 and rebuilt after a fire, this landmark hotel was designed to resemble a Scottish baronial castle. The hotel caters to large groups and can be a circus during busy periods, but the luxurious spa can wipe away the stress, for a price. **Cave and Basin National Historic Site**. Site of the sulphuric hot springs found by railway workers in 1883 that led to the creation of Banff. Hands-on displays describe the wildlife and history of the park, while interpretive trails provide an insight into the geology and plant life.

Lake Louise. Known as the 'Mona Lisa of the Mountains' for its calm, aquamarine waters, and 'Lake of the Little Fishes' by local aboriginal people. Chateau Lake Louise overlooks the lake and stunning Mount Victoria and the Victoria Glacier. Hikers take the **Lake Agnes Trail** in summer to a tea house or follow the 1.5km return **Lakeshore Trail/Plain of the Six Glaciers Trail**. Beloved by canoeists and photographers, **Moraine Lake** rivals Lake Louise in beauty and fame. Set below the 'Valley of Ten Peaks', Moraine Lake was named after the moraine boulders (rock pushed along by a glacier) which dammed the valley and created the lake.

Accommodation and food in Banff National Park

Banff Rocky Mountain Resort $$$ *1029 Banff Ave and Tunnel Mountain Rd; tel: (403) 762-5531, tollfree (800) 661-9563; e-mail: info@rockymountainresort.com; www.rockymountainresort.com.* A chalet-style building with fireplaces and kitchens.

Banff Springs Hotel $$$ *405 Spray Ave; tel: (403) 762-2211, tollfree (800) 257-7544; e-mail: banffsprings@fairmont.com; www.fairmont.com/banffsprings.* An enormous castle-like hotel that caters to tour groups; a big draw is its world-class spa.

First sighting

The first European known to have seen the Rocky Mountains was the explorer Anthony Henday. Viewed near present-day Innisfail, Alberta on 17 October 1754, he called them the 'Shining Mountains', a description Aborigines gave the rugged vista. Yet it was not until 1793 that Alexander Mackenzie made the first crossing of the Rockies, and 1885 before the CPR (Canadian Pacific Railway) completed 'The National Dream'.

🄸 **Snocoach Tours on Athabasca Glacier**
$ Brewster Transport; tel: tollfree (877) 766-7433; e-mail: icefield@brewster.ca; www.brewster.ca. Weather-dependent Snocoach tours run mid-Apr–mid-Oct.

Bumper's The Beef House $$ *603 Banff Ave, Banff; tel: (403) 762-2622. Open from 1630.* Features Alberta beef and all-you-can-eat salad bar.

Caboose $$ *Railway Depot, Elk and Lynx Sts, Banff; tel: (403) 762-3622.* Has railway mementoes and serves basic yet good Continental dishes.

Chateau Lake Louise $$$ *111 Lake Louise Dr.; tel: (403) 522-3511, tollfree (800) 257-7544; fax: (403) 522-3834; e-mail: chateaulakelouise@fairmont.com; www.fairmont.com/lakelouise.* Caters to tour groups so individuals may get neglected, though all can enjoy the stunning view of the glacier and aquamarine lake.

Edelweiss Dining Room $$$ *Chateau Lake Louise; tel: (403) 522-3511.* Has a dress code for the elegant eatery.

Joe Btfsplk's Diner $ *221 Banff Ave, Banff; tel: (403) 762-5529.* Named after an Al Capp cartoon character, an informal 1950s-style diner that has tasty burgers, cookies and muffins.

Le Beaujolais $$$ *212 Buffalo St at Banff Ave; tel: (403) 762-2712; www.lebeaujolais.com.* A French gourmet restaurant with an extensive wine selection, frequently rated one of the best in Canada.

Post Hotel $$$ *200 Pipestone Rd, Lake Louise; tel: (403) 522-3989, tollfree (800) 661-1586; e-mail: info@posthotel.com; www.posthotel.com.* An elegant pine and stone lodge alongside a river, best known for its outstanding dining room.

Rimrock Resort Hotel $$$ *Mountain Ave, Banff; tel: (403) 762-3356, tollfree (888) 372-9270; e-mail: info@rimrockresort.com; www.rimrockresort. com.* Perched on the side of a mountain with stunning views of the Bow Valley.

The Station $$ *200 Sentinel Rd, Lake Louise; tel: (403) 522-2600.* In the restored CPR station along with early rail cars and period furnishings.

Storm Mountain Lodge $$$ *5km west of Trans-Canada Highway (Hwy 1) on Hwy 93; tel: (403) 762-4155; fax: (403) 762-4155; e-mail: info@stormmountainlodge.com; www.stormmountainlodge.com. Open Jun–Sept.* A log cabin-style lodge built by the CPR.

JASPER NATIONAL PARK

The largest and most northerly of the adjoining national parks, Jasper Park Reserve was created in 1907. You will need to pay to enter the park – tickets currently cost $9 per adult, per day. Originally called Fitzhugh, the town was named after Jasper House, a nearby North West Co. post which was established a century earlier. Yet nomadic

Above
Columbia Icefield, Jasper
National Park

**ⓘ Jasper National
Park Info Centre**
*409 Patricia St; tel: (780)
852-3858; e-mail:
jasper@incentre.net;
www.pc.gc.ca. Open daily.*

people have lived in the valleys of the park for some 10,000 years, about the time the big glaciers receded. When the park was established, Aborigines and Métis were called squatters on Crown land, and were paid off and ordered to leave the park. Tourists began arriving in 1915, and the first hotel, the Athabasca, opened in 1921, followed by the landmark Jasper Park Lodge.

Columbia Icefield. A mass of ice on the boundary of Banff and Jasper national parks, Columbia Icefield lies at the hydrographic apex of North America. Astride the Continental Divide, the 325sq km of ice is called the 'mother of rivers', feeding the Athabasca, Columbia, Fraser and Saskatchewan river systems. Meltwater flows into three oceans: west to the Pacific, east to the Atlantic via Hudson Bay, and north to the Arctic. **Icefields Parkway**. The 230km drive along Hwy 93 between Jasper and Lake Louise offers glaciers, waterfalls, wildlife and awesome vistas for several hours' drive by car or narrated by Brewster Coach Tours.

ⓘ Jasper Tourism and Commerce
409 Patricia St; tel: (780) 852-3858; e-mail: jaspercc@infocentre.net; www.jaspercanadianrockies. com. Open daily.

Icefield Info Centre
Icefields Parkway; tel: (780) 852-6288. Open daily May–mid-Oct.

Right
Patricia Lake, Jasper National Park

Accommodation and food in Jasper National Park

Alpine Village $$ *2km south of Jasper on Hwy 93A; tel: (780) 852-3285; fax: (780) 852-1955.* Has sun decks that overlook Athabasca River and Mount Edith Cavell.

Becker's Gourmet Restaurant (L'Auberge) $$$ *8km south of Jasper on Hwy 93; tel: (780) 852-3535.* A French restaurant with panoramic views of the Athabasca River.

Below
Downtown Jasper

Columbia Icefield Chalet $$$ *100km south of Jasper and 130km north of Lake Louise on Icefields Parkway (Hwy 93); tel: (403) 762-0260, tollfree (877) 226-3348; fax: (403) 762-0266; e-mail: icefield@brewster.ca. Open May–Oct.* Has spectacular views of the glaciers.

Jasper Park Lodge $$$ *4km northeast of Jasper off Hwy 16; tel: (780) 852-3301 or (780) 852-5107, tollfree (800) 441-1414; e-mail: jasperparklodge@fairmont.com.* Caters to large groups, though the heated year-round outdoor pool is a hit with everyone.

Le Beauvallon $$$ *96 Giekie St, Chateau Jasper, Jasper; tel: (780) 852-5644.* An elegant restaurant best known for its lamb and venison, served to the strains of a harpist.

KOOTENAY NATIONAL PARK

ⓘ Vermilion Crossing Visitor Centre *68km northeast of Radium; no phone. Open daily late May–Jun and Sept 1000–1700; Jul and Aug 0900–1900. Closed winter.*

ⓗ Kootenay National Park $ *7556 Main St E. Radium Hot Springs; tel: (250) 347-9505 or (403) 522-3833; e-mail: kootenay.info@pc.gc.ca; www.pc.gc.ca. Open late May–late Jun 0900–1700; late Jun–early Sept 0900–1900; early–mid-Sept 0900–1700; mid-Sept–mid-Oct 0900–1600.*

Radium Hot Springs Pools $ *3km east of Radium; tel: (250) 347-9485, tollfree (800) 767-1611; www.rhs.bc.ca. Open mid-May–mid-Oct 0900–2300; mid-Oct–mid-May 1200–2100.*

On the west slope of the Continental Divide, Kootenay was a travel route during the golden age of exploration. Ancient pictographs at Radium Hot Springs indicate it was a meeting point for plains and mountain Indians, who enjoyed the soothing waters for centuries. The Kootenay (pronounced 'coo-teh-knee': 'people from beyond the hills'), settled in the area, and made trips across the mountains to hunt for bison on the prairies. The Banff–Windermere Parkway, built over nearly a decade starting in 1912, is one of the most stunning drives in the Rocky Mountains. Most of the park's 1.2 million annual visitors make a pilgrimage to soak, swim or absorb the atmosphere in the hot mineral waters of **Radium Hot Springs Pools** in the village of Radium, which has more hotel rooms, coffee shops and flower-filled pots than residents.

Accommodation and food in Kootenay National Park

Alpen Motel $$ *5022 Hwy 93, Radium Hot Springs; tel: (250) 347-9823, tollfree (888) 788-3891; e-mail: info@alpenmotel.com; www.alpenmotel. com.* Cheerful with flower boxes and 14 spotless, non-smoking rooms a block from the park portal.

Kootenay Park Lodge $$$ *Hwy 93 at Vermilion Crossing; tel: (403) 762-9196 or (403) 283-7482; e-mail: info@kootenayparklodge.com; www.kootenayparklodge.com. Open mid-May–Sept.* CPR built the lodge in 1923. The home-made sandwiches in the gift shop are outstanding.

Old Salzburg Restaurant $$ *4943 Hwy 93; tel: (250) 347-6553.* Matches the style of many nearby alpine-chalet-style motels with Austrian specialities such as schnitzel.

Radium Hot Springs Resort $$$ *8100 Golf Course Rd, Hwy 93/95; tel: (250) 347-9311, tollfree (800) 667-6444; fax: (250) 347-6299; www.radiumresort.com.* All rooms face one of the two golf courses at this pricey, three-storey boutique hotel.

Above
Radium Hot Springs town sign

YOHO NATIONAL PARK

❶ Yoho National Visitor Info Centre
$ Trans-Canada Hwy 1, Field; tel: (250) 343-6783; e-mail: yoho.info@pc.gc.ca; www.pc.gc.ca. Open early May–late Jun 0900–1700; late Jun–early Sept 0900–1900; early–mid-Sept 0900–1700; mid-Sept–Mar 0900–1600. A big attraction is the Burgess Shale Fossil exhibit; the bookshop has a good selection of titles.

With 28 towering peaks, Yoho National Park is appropriately named after the Cree words expressing 'awe and wonder'. Bordered by Banff and Kootenay national parks on the western side of the Rockies in BC, the park contains some of the most outstanding scenery in the Rocky Mountains. Waterfalls, emerald lakes, crashing rivers, hanging glaciers, distinctive rock escarpments, and sheer ranges of mountains are divided by the Trans-Canada Highway (Hwy 1). **Emerald Lake.** Greener than green, the glassy, glacier-formed, 28m-deep lake is perfect for canoeing. Walk clockwise from the wooden car bridge near the parking area for the best views of the President Range northwards.

Accommodation and food in Yoho National Park

Cathedral Mountain Lodge and Chalets $$$ *Yoho Valley Rd; tel: (250) 343-6442, tollfree (866) 619-6442; fax: (250) 343-6424; e-mail: info@cathedralmountain.com; www.cathedralmountain.com. Open mid-May–mid-Sept.* Log cabins with fireplaces along the pale blue Kicking Horse River and stunning views of the mountains. A grocery store is good for provisioning before Takakkaw Falls.

Emerald Lake Lodge $$$ *9km north of Field at Emerald Lake; tel: (250) 343-6321, tollfree (800) 663-6336.* Chalets surround the lodge-cum-resort, often booked out by executive conferences. **Cilantro's $$** restaurant serves meals and drinks on an umbrella-decked terrace.

Below
Canadian flag

Kicking Horse Lodge and Café $$ *Hwy 1, across from Info Centre at Field; tel: (250) 343-6303, tollfree (800) 659-4944.* Sells sandwiches, Aboriginal-style souvenirs and books, and is the meeting place for the Yoho-Burgess Shale Foundation tours.

Picnic lunches

Evelyn's Coffee Bar $ *201 Banff Ave, Banff; tel: (403) 762-0352.* Has great sandwiches, quiches and home-made soups.

Laggan's Mountain Bakery and Deli $ *Samson Mall, Lake Louise; tel: (403) 522-2017.* Makes great sandwiches from sweet poppy-seed breads.

Truffles and Trout $ *Jasper Marketplace, corner of Patricia St and Hazel Ave, Jasper; tel: (780) 852-3152.* Specialises in light gourmet meals and boxed lunches.

Suggested tour

Mount Eisenhower

Dwight D Eisenhower, Supreme Allied Commander in World War II, was honoured in 1946 when Canadian Premier Mackenzie King named a mountain in Banff National Park after the man who was later to become US President. The decision to name a Canadian treasure after an American was unpopular and Premier Joe Clark reversed the decision in 1979, returning to the name Castle Mountain, which the 2,766m mountain had borne for 99 years. Situated midway between Banff and Lake Louise, its red-brown peak of layered rock is weathered into turrets and towers: the first tower called Eisenhower Peak.

Total distance: 540km.

Time: One long day to drive; 2–5 days to explore.

Links: The BC Rockies at Castle Junction for Kootenay National Park, at the Hwy 1 fork to Yoho National Park and Hwy 16 west from Jasper to Mount Robson National Park.

Route: Trans-Canada Highway (Hwy 1) runs from **BANFF NATIONAL PARK ❶** east gate by Banff townsite to just north of the Lake Louise exit. Veer left at Castle Mountain junction to take the Banff–Windermere Highway (Hwy 93) through **KOOTENAY NATIONAL PARK ❷** for 105km to **Radium Hot Springs ❸**.

Detour along Bow Valley Parkway: Hwy 1A between Banff and Lake Louise parallels the Trans-Canada Highway for 55km but is considered the more scenic, if slower (60kph) route. Pick up the Bow Valley Parkway 5.5km west of Banff townsite.

Leaving Radium Hot Springs, turn right onto Hwy 95 and travel 120km through a superb wildlife habitat. Continue on to the scenic mountain setting of Golden *(see page 125)*. Turn right onto the Trans-Canada Highway (Hwy 1) and 25km away is the western boundary of **YOHO NATIONAL PARK ❹**. A Cree word expressing 'awe', Yoho is just 45km from west to east yet has some 400km of hiking trails, from short walks to day hikes.

Continue on the Trans-Canada to Lake Louise Village. Another 4.5km up a winding road is **Lake Louise ❺**, the 'Mona Lisa of the Mountain', the most famous landmark of the Rockies. Chateau Lake Louise overlooks the calm waters, which change from aquamarine to emerald green. Rivalling Lake Louise in fame and beauty is Moraine Lake, 3km up an access road then 12km on Moraine Lake Road.

Return to the Trans-Canada and follow signs to the **Icefields Parkway ❻** (Hwy 93), a spectacular drive following a natural corridor through an unspoiled wilderness, 230km to Jasper. The route could be driven in about 3 hours; however, in the peak summer tourist season, the parkway is busy with vehicles, cyclists and pedestrians criss-crossing the roadway to view the scenery and wildlife.

Sunwapta Pass at 2,035m marks the southern end of **JASPER NATIONAL PARK ❼** and the **Columbia Icefield**. Wapiti (elk) wander everywhere around Jasper, a relaxed, tourist-catering town strung along the CN Rail line. Drive out to Jasper Park Lodge for a lovely series of water sports recreation lakes, epitomised by the lodge's own Lac Beauvert.

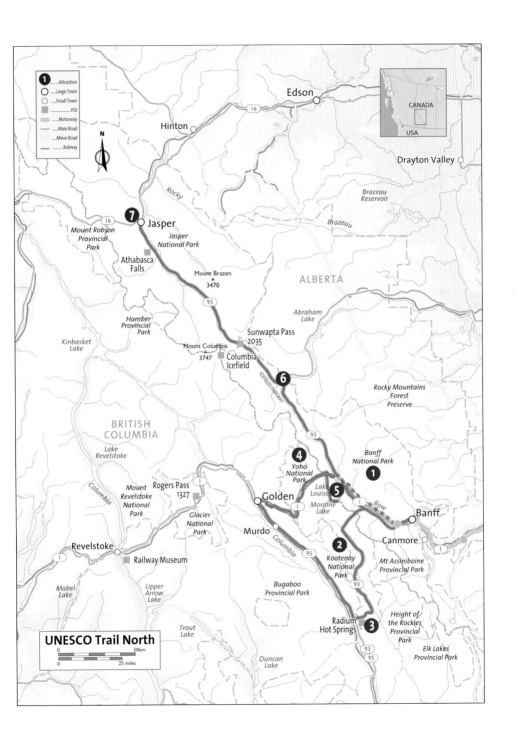

UNESCO Trail North

Legend
- 1 Attraction
- Large Town
- Small Town
- POI
- Motorway
- Main Road
- Minor Road
- Railway

Edson

Hinton

CANADA

USA

Drayton Valley

Rocky

Brazeau Reservoir

Brazeau

7 Jasper

Mount Robson Provincial Park

Jasper National Park

ALBERTA

Athabasca Falls

Mount Brazen 3470

93

Hamber Provincial Park

Abraham Lake

Kinbasket Lake

Sunwapta Pass 2035

Mount Columbia 3747

Columbia Icefield

ICEFIELD PARKWAY

6

Rocky Mountains Forest Preserve

BRITISH COLUMBIA

Lake Revelstoke

93

Columbia

Mount Revelstoke National Park

Rogers Pass 1327

4

Yoho National Park

Banff National Park

1

Glacier National Park

Lake Louise

5

Golden

Moraine Lake

Bow

Banff

Revelstoke

Murdo

Columbia

Railway Museum

95

2

Kootenay National Park

Canmore

Mt Assiniboine Provincial Park

Mabel Lake

Upper Arrow Lake

Bugaboo Provincial Park

93

Height of the Rockies Provincial Park

Trout Lake

Radium Hot Springs

3

Elk Lakes Provincial Park

UNESCO Trail North

0   50km

0   25 miles

Duncan Lake

93

95

UNESCO Trail South

Ratings

Children	•••••
Geology	•••••
History	•••••
Nature	•••••
Walking	•••••
Scenery	••••○
Towns and villages	••••○
Food and Drink	••○○○

Spanning the earliest syllable of time, the World Heritage Sites in UNESCO Trail South preserve a spectacular registry of adventure, heritage and nature. One of the oldest inhabited parts of North America, early aboriginal people settled here up to 28,000 years ago, setting up camp in what is now Waterton Lakes National Park. For some 10,000 years until as recently as the 19th century, Plains Indians used an ingenious system to harvest bison at Head-Smashed-In Buffalo Jump. The grandaddy of all treasures is Dinosaur Provincial Park, for 79 million years a favourite haunt of the huge reptiles when this barren lunar landscape resembled the lush Florida Everglades. As you drive through the tapestry of southern Alberta, the rolling foothills expand into semi-arid grassland, short-grass prairie and the eerie Badlands, once the domain of the dinosaur and now one of the richest fossil beds in the world.

BROOKS AQUEDUCT

Brooks Aqueduct
$ *3km south of Hwy 1, east of Brooks; tel: (403) 362-4451 (summer); tel: (403) 653-5139 (winter); e-mail: aqueduct@eid.awinc. com; www.eidnet.org/ local/aqueduct. Open mid-May–Labour Day 1000–1800.*

Spanning a 3.2km-wide valley, the elevated Brooks Aqueduct is a National/Provincial Historic Site: a monument to pioneers who developed this bone-dry region. Built by the CPR between 1912 and 1914, the 3,186m-long concrete aqueduct was part of a scheme to irrigate the region so the railway could sell land to prospective farmers. Connected to the Bow River 50km away, the aqueduct was discontinued because of costly repairs. A new clay-lined earthen canal now provides farmers with the much-needed moisture to irrigate their crops.

CARDSTON

Cardston Visitor Information
Centre *67 3rd Ave W;*
tel: (403) 653-3366,
tollfree (888) 434-3366;
www.town.cardston.ab.ca.
Open summer 0830–1630.

Mormon Temple
348 3rd St west; tel:
(403) 653-1696. Open
May–Sept daily 0900–2100.

Remington–Alberta Carriage Centre $
623 Main St, Cardston;
tel: (403) 653-5139; www.
remingtoncarriagemuseum.
com. Open daily year round.

Nestled in the rolling foothills, Cardston was established in 1887 by Mormons to escape anti-polygamy laws in the US. Named after Charles Card, a son-in-law of Brigham Young, work began in 1913 on the towering **Mormon Temple**. Completed ten years later, the Visitor Centre depicts the history of the marble temple and the pioneers who arrived in one of the last great covered wagon migrations. Visitors are welcome, though only church members may enter the temple. The **Remington–Alberta Carriage Centre** contains one of the largest collections of horse-drawn vehicles in North America. Over 200 carriages, sleighs and wagons whisk visitors back in time to the days of horses and buggies.

DINOSAUR PROVINCIAL PARK

Dinosaur Provincial Park $
49km northeast of Brooks; tel: (403) 378-4342 (administration), (403) 378-4344 (tour reservations), tollfree (Alberta) 310-0000; www.dinosaurpark.ca. Park is open year round though many services are available seasonally.

Established in 1955 to protect one of the world's richest fossil beds, Dinosaur Provincial Park contains 35 dinosaur species, plus thousands of fossil finds. Chiselled by years of wind, water and ice, the 73sq km World Heritage Site has numerous trails to explore, though much of the park is a nature preserve and has limited public access. The best way to visit the World Heritage Site is by bus tour. The Field Station contains several dinosaur skeletons and a workshop. The park recommends two full days for an in-depth experience.

FORT MACLEOD

Fort Macleod Museum $
219 25th St, Fort Macleod; tel: (403) 553-4703 or 553-4425; www.fortmacleod.com. Open Mar–Jun daily 0900–1700; Jul–mid-Sept 0900–1800; mid-Sept–Dec 0900–1700; closed 24 Dec–28 Feb.

The oldest town in southern Alberta, Fort Macleod was founded in 1874 when the North West Mounted Police established a police post on an island on the Oldman River. Named after an assistant commissioner, James F Macleod, the fort became a police headquarters that wiped out the illegal whiskey trade. The original site was moved because of constant flooding, and now the reconstructed Fort Museum tells the story of the colourful past. Downtown Fort Macleod contains some 30 buildings of historical significance. Walking tour brochures are available at several locations. A guided walking tour is conducted at the Information Centre next to the Fort Museum and musical rides are performed four times a day 1 July–Labour Day.

HEAD-SMASHED-IN BUFFALO JUMP

Head-Smashed-In Buffalo Jump $
18km west of Fort Macleod on Hwy 785; tel: (403) 553-2731; e-mail: info@head-smashed-in.com; www.head-smashed-in.com. Open mid-Sept–mid-May 1000–1700; mid-May–mid-Sept 0900–1800.

Bison provided Aboriginal people with many of life's needs, including food, hides for clothing and shelter, sinew, bone and horns for tools, and dung for fires – and Head-Smashed-In Buffalo Jump provided the clever setting to harvest the bison. As the herds stampeded across the Porcupine Hills, up to 500 Plains Indians at a time guided the huge animals over the edge, falling 10m to their death. A World Heritage Site, Head-Smashed-In Buffalo Jump is the biggest, oldest and best preserved buffalo jump in North America, believed to have been first used 10,000 years ago and continuing until the mid-19th century. Built into the side of a cliff, the seven-level Interpretive Centre contains a theatre, cafeteria and audio-visual exhibits. Blackfoot guides describe the site and the hunting techniques of the Northwest Plains people, and provide guided tours along 2km of outdoor trails. The site is named after an absent-minded brave whose head was smashed in as he watched a stampede from the base of the cliff.

Right
Head-Smashed-In Buffalo Jump
Heritage Site display

LETHBRIDGE

① Chinook Country Tourist Association
2805 Scenic Dr., Lethbridge; tel: (403) 320-1222, tollfree (800) 661-1222; e-mail: info@chinookcountry.com; www.chinookcountry.com

⑪ Fort Whoop-up Interpretive Centre $ Indian Battle Park; tel: (403) 329-0444; fax: (403) 329-0645; e-mail: whoopup@telus.net; www.fortwhoopup.com. Open Tue–Sun 1000–1700; closed Mon.

Nikka Yuko Japanese Gardens $ Henderson Park; tel: (403) 328-3511; fax: (403) 328-0511; e-mail: info@nikkayuko.com; www. japanesegarden.ab.ca. Open May, Jun & Sept 0900–1700; Jul and Aug 0900–2000.

While modern Lethbridge was founded in 1885 with the start of large-scale coal mining, some 500 generations of Blackfoot Indians have inhabited the area since prehistoric times. Located on the steep banks of the coulee-scarred Oldman River, the city was named after William Lethbridge, president of the North Western Coal and Navigation Co. Set into the side of a coulee are the impressive buildings of the University of Lethbridge, facing the spindle leg High Level Railway Bridge, 1.5km long and 96m high. **Nikka Yuko Japanese Gardens** is a symbol of Japanese–Canadian friendship, a memorial to the forced and humiliating evacuation of Japanese Canadians during World War II. Situated along the man-made Henderson Lake, the lovely 1.6ha oasis features elements of five traditional Japanese gardens, joined by a meandering path which combines ponds, shrubs, pebbled beaches, moon-shaped bridges, pagoda, bell tower and a Cultural Centre representing a Tea Room and Japanese house styles. Built in Japan and reassembled as a Canadian Centennial project in 1967, the Nikka Yuko Japanese Gardens is an elegant setting of peace and tranquillity. **Fort Whoop-up** is a replica of a notorious 19th-century fort built by American whiskey traders on Canadian territory to further their illicit and often deadly business. Guided and self-guided trails lead through the coulees and river flood plain.

MEDICINE HAT

ⓘ **Tourism Medicine Hat**
413 6th Ave southeast, Medicine Hat; tel: (403) 527-6422, (800) 481-2822; fax: (403) 528-2682; e-mail: info@tourismmedicinehat.com; www.tourismmedicinehat.com. Open mid-May–Labour Day Mon–Fri 0800–1900, Sat and Sun 0800–1700; Labour Day–Victoria Day, Mon–Fri 0900–1700, Sat 1000–1500.

Straddling the winding South Saskatchewan River Valley, the city of Medicine Hat is the natural gas capital of Canada. Standing guard over the city and adjacent to the Trans-Canada Highway is the Saamis Tepee, a 20-storey structure which towered above the 1988 Winter Olympics in Calgary. Below the tepee is Seven Persons Coulee, one of the most important archaeological sites of the northern plains, a native camp and buffalo jump spanning over 6,000 years. The Blackfoot word for eagle tail feather headdress, *saamis* was a hat worn by the Medicine Man, or simply, medicine hat, after which the city was named. Founded in 1883 with the arrival of the CPR, the abundant supply of natural gas and clay led to the manufacturing of bricks, pottery and tiles. The **Historic Clay District** describes the industry, and takes visitors through the kilns and products. Self-

⊕ Historic Clay District $
713 Medalta Ave SE, Medicine Hat; tel: (403) 529-1070. Self-guided tours winter months Tue–Sat 0900–1700; summer (May–Aug) guided tours on the hour daily 0900–1700.

guided downtown walking tours feature the early 20th-century houses, churches and businesses. Charming copper gaslights imported from Shugg, England add a touch of class and a reminder of Medicine Hat's source of prosperity. Another memorial is the glass-sided City Hall on the banks of the river, which received a Canadian Architectural Award after it opened in 1985.

WATERTON LAKES NATIONAL PARK

⊕ Waterton Lakes National Park $
Open year round; tel: (403) 859-2224. Reservations (406) 892-2525; e-mail: waterton.info@pch.gc.ca; www.watertoninfo.ab.ca.

Officially known as Waterton–Glacier International Peace Park, Waterton Lakes National Park graces the Canada–US border. The world's first international peace park, Waterton was established in 1932, uniting Alberta's Waterton Lakes National Park and Montana's Glacier National Park. Embracing prairie and mountain, the World Heritage Site contains a variety of plants and animals such as coyotes roaming the grasslands, and bighorn sheep and grizzly bears on the Trail of the Grizzly Bear, the Yellowstone–Yukon corridor where bears are active day and night. Discovered by European fur traders in the mid-19th century, the area was once a Blackfoot stronghold. Horse riding, lake cruises, sightseeing and shopping are favourite activities, though the **Prince of Wales Hotel** (*open mid-May–mid-October*) is the centre of attention. Perched high on a windy bluff overlooking Lake Waterton, the pricey 87-room hotel, named after the popular Prince Edward when the Great Northern Railway opened the chalet-style lodge in 1927, provides a dramatic backdrop to the lake and mountains.

Opposite
Nikka Yuko Japanese Gardens, Lethbridge

Right
Prince of Wales Hotel, Waterton Lakes National Park

Prince of Wales Hotel

The first recorded white man to visit the area, Thomas Blakiston of the Palliser Expedition, named the region of rolling prairie, icy peaks and deep lakes after English naturalist Charles Waterton. Designated a World Heritage Site, the centre of attraction is the Prince of Wales Hotel, named after Prince Edward, son of Queen Mary and King George V. Opened in 1927 as a chain of chalets and hotels by the Great Northern Railway, the chalet-style lodge with steep, gabled roofs over a butter-yellow façade is a romantic landmark that dominates the story-book setting. Now owned by Parks Canada and managed by Glacier Park Inc., the baronial, dark-panelled interior projects the air of a Scottish hunting lodge. Enjoy afternoon tea in Valerie's Tea Room or sample traditional English entrées in the Royal Stewart Dining Room.

Accommodation and food

Aspen Village Inn $ *111 Wildflower Ave, Waterton; tel: (403) 859-2255; fax: (403) 859-8669; www.aspenvillageinn.com.* Has a variety of accommodation from de luxe to family cottages.

Bayshore Inn $$ *111 Waterton Ave, Waterton; tel: (403) 859-2211; tollfree (888) 527-9555; www.bayshoreinn.com. Open Apr–mid-Oct.* A two-storey, motel-style inn with rooms that have balconies with views of the lake and mountains.

Bloomin' Inn Guest Ranch $$ *5km east of Pincher Creek on Tower Rd; tel: (403) 627-5829; e-mail: bloomin-inn@telusplanet.net; www.bloomin-inn.com. Open year round.* The working ranch serves home-cooked meals.

Four Winds Café $$ *526 Mayor Magrath Dr., Lethbridge; tel: (403) 327-5701.* The Travelodge Hotel is noted for its tender Alberta steaks.

Kilmorey Lodge $$ *117 Evergreen Ave, Waterton Park; tel: (403) 859-2334; e-mail: kilmorey@telusplanet.net; www.kilmoreylodge.com.* Has a log-cabin façade with antique furnishings, situated on the edge of Waterton National Park.

Medicine Hat Lodge $$$ *1051 Ross Glen Dr. southeast, Medicine Hat; tel: (403) 529-2222, tollfree (800) 661-8095; www.medhatlodge.com.* Has rooms that face an indoor pool, steam room and a huge waterslide.

M Grill $$ *Medicine Hat Lodge, 1051 Ross Glen Dr. southeast, Medicine Hat; tel: (403) 529-2222, tollfree (800) 661-8095.* A popular spot for fine Continental dining.

Pepper Tree Inn $$ *1142 Mayor Magrath Dr. south, Lethbridge; tel: (403) 328-4436; fax: (403) 328-4436; www.peppertreeinn.ca.* Located near Henderson Park and Nikka Yuko Japanese Gardens.

Plains Motel $$ *1004 2nd St West, Brooks; tel: (403) 362-3367.* Has an indoor pool and sauna.

Prince of Wales Hotel $$$ *Waterton Park; year round reservations (406) 892-2525, (403) 236-3400; www.princeofwaleswaterton.com. Open 4 Jun –18 Sept.* Has creaky floors and rattles in the wind, yet this historic hotel is a Canadian favourite.

Sven Eriksen's Family Restaurant $$ *1715 Mayor Magrath Dr., Lethbridge; tel: (403) 328-7756.* A colonial-style restaurant that specialises in chicken and prime rib.

Valerie's Tea Room $$$ *Prince of Wales Hotel, Waterton; tel: (403) 859-2231. Open mid-May–mid-Oct.* Serves breakfast buffet, English and Continental cuisine, and afternoon tea.

Suggested tour

Total distance: 265km. Detour: 165km from Lethbridge to Medicine Hat; 145km Medicine Hat–Dinosaur Provincial Park.

Time: 3 hours to drive; 2–3 days to explore; 2 hours to drive Lethbridge–Medicine Hat; 2 hours to drive Medicine Hat–Dinosaur Provincial Park.

Links: Hwy 2 connects Calgary and Fort Macleod, then Hwy 3 (Crowsnest Pass Highway) to Lethbridge and continues on to Medicine Hat. Hwy 3 connects with Hwy 36 to Brooks and the Trans-Canada Highway (Hwy 1), and Hwy 36 north of Brooks.

Route: From **LETHBRIDGE ❶**, travel south on Hwy 5, which angles in a southwesterly direction towards the town of **CARDSTON ❷**, founded by Mormons who travelled by covered wagon in the late 1800s from Utah. Main attractions are the grandiose Mormon Temple and the Remington-Alberta Carriage Centre Museum, which houses a handsome collection of buggies and sleighs. Hwy 5 continues in a westerly direction to **WATERTON LAKES NATIONAL PARK ❸**, a UNESCO World Heritage Site on the Alberta–Montana border. Dry rolling hills of the prairies soar to icy peaks nearly 3,000m high. Hwy 6, which originates a few kilometres south at the US border, skirts the eastern side of the park, continues north to the town of **Pincher Creek ❹**. North of the town, the highway meets the Crowsnest Pass Highway (Hwy 3), which runs in an east–west direction. Turn right on Hwy 3, then left onto Hwy 2, then left again onto Hwy 785, a secondary road which leads to **HEAD-SMASHED-IN BUFFALO JUMP ❺**, a World Heritage Site. Return to Hwy 3 to the town of **FORT MACLEOD ❻**, the oldest community in southern Alberta, established to crack the illicit and frequently poisonous whiskey trading. Continue on Hwy 3 back to the city of Lethbridge, the largest centre in southern Alberta.

Detour: to Medicine Hat and Dinosaur Provincial Park. From Lethbridge, take the Crowsnest Pass Highway (Hwy 3) east to Taber, passing through several small communities and the lush irrigated farmlands of sweetcorn and sugar beets and on to the natural gas city of **MEDICINE HAT ❼** on the Trans-Canada Highway (Hwy 1). Continue on the Trans-Canada Highway and watch for signs, turning right onto Hwy 876, a good gravel road which then becomes paved,

Below
Dinosaur Provincial Park

and on to **DINOSAUR PROVINCIAL PARK** ❽. Return to the Trans-Canada Highway and watch for signs for the **BROOKS AQUEDUCT** ❾ south of the highway on the east side of Brooks.

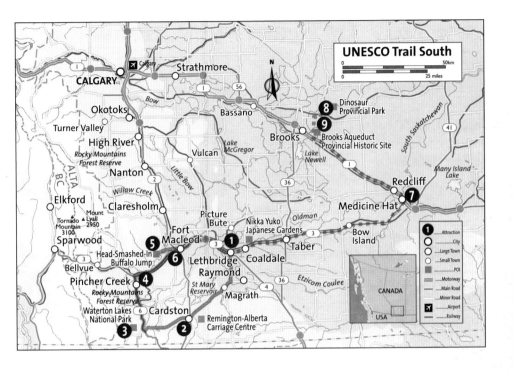

Dinosaurs

Dinosaur life ended abruptly and for a much-debated reason 66.4 million years ago. The huge reptiles were especially common in southern Alberta, their domain a tropical swamp similar to what is now the Everglades in Florida. With changing weather patterns, the region became a barren outback of sandstone and mudstone after rain, drought and wind-driven sand eroded the region, burying the dinosaur remains and preserving them for all time. The desert-like badlands of the Red Deer River valley, which include Dinosaur Provincial Park, contain one of the most diverse collections of dinosaur specimens in the world. Reconstructed dinosaur skeletons are exhibited some 170km northwest at the highly acclaimed Royal Tyrrell Museum of Palaeontology (see page 67) at Drumheller.

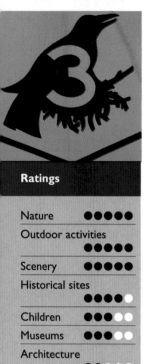

Crowsnest Highway

Ratings

Nature	●●●●○
Outdoor activities	●●●●●
Scenery	●●●●○
Historical sites	●●●●○
Children	●●●○○
Museums	●●●○○
Architecture	●●○○○
Food and Drink	●●○○○

Skirting the US border, the Crowsnest Highway is the most southerly of the highway passes crossing the Continental Divide. Originating in Medicine Hat and ending just east of Vancouver at Hope, the highway probably takes its name from Crow Indians who 'nested' after a fight with nomadic Cree; for centuries the 1,357m Crowsnest Pass was an access to hunt bison in the Alberta foothills. Zigzagging west and south for several hundred kilometres, the 'Crow Highway' links Aboriginal, gold mining, lumbering and railway history, and the tragic coal-mining past with scenic recreation lakes, a magnificent waterfall and an alpine village, famous for accordions and alpenhorns. Some call Fernie the Aspen of BC, and few dispute the world's largest operating cuckoo clock in Kimberley, though its homespun Bavarian alpine theme is somewhat of a curiosity. The scenic alps in winter transform into a wonderland, with major ski resorts at Kimberley and Fernie.

BLAIRMORE

 Frank Slide Interpretive Centre $
1.5km north of Hwy 3, Blairmore; tel: (403) 562-7388; e-mail: info@frankslide.com; www.frankslide.com. Open daily mid-May–mid-Sept 0900–1800; mid-Sept–mid-May 1000–1700; closed Christmas Eve, Christmas Day, New Year's Day, Easter Sunday.

The bustling coal mining town of Frank was devastated in 1903 when unstable limestone crashed from the east slope of Turtle Mountain and buried a section of the sleeping town. Called 'The Mountain that Walks' by aboriginals, it is monitored daily for movement, though the only activity now is wandering sheep.

Accommodation and food in Blairmore

Cosmopolitan Hotel $ *13001 20th Ave; tel: (403) 562-7321.* A moderate hotel, providing a base for exploring the mining areas.

Inn on the Border $ *Hwy 3, Crowsnest Pass; tel: (403) 563-3101; e-mail: innontheborder@yahoo.com.* A moderate B&B in a scenic spot.

CRANBROOK

ℹ Cranbrook and District Chamber of Commerce Info Centre *2279 Cranbrook St north; tel: (250) 426-5914, tollfree (800) 222-6174; www.city.cranbrook.bc.ca. Open year round Mon–Fri 0830–1700, weekends 0900–1700.*

ℹ Canadian Museum of Rail Travel $$ 57 *Van Horne St north at Baker St (Hwy 3/95); tel: (250) 489-3918; e-mail: mail@trainsdeluxe.com; www.crowsnest.bc.ca/cmrt; www.trainsdeluxe.com. Open mid-Apr–mid-Oct daily 1000–1800; winter Tue–Sat 1000–1700.*

A major city in the Rocky Mountains, Cranbrook was a Ktunaxa camp and pasture before the 1870s known as Joseph's Prairie. Despite local protest, Col James Baker, member of the Legislature 1886–1900, bought the land and named it Cranbrook Farm after his birthplace in England. Located at the apex of three valleys, the city became a divisional point on the CPR and new capital of the region, serving the forestry and coal mining industries. **Canadian Museum of Rail Travel**. Train buffs are in their glory touring through the nine original cars from the Trans-Canada Limited, a CPR luxury service between Vancouver and Montreal. Built in 1929 and designed as a nine-car travelling hotel, the cars are the last of their type made in Canada. The *Argyle* dining car serves tea and light snacks in a stunning restored carriage.

Elizabeth Lake Sanctuary Wildlife Area. A 113ha section of the Rocky Mountain Trench on the south side of Cranbrook is preserved for birds on their annual migration. Watch mallards, songbirds and Canada geese from a viewing hide as they share the marsh with moose, painted turtles and white-tailed deer. **Jimsmith Lake Provincial Park**. Join the locals swimming, canoeing, picnicking and camping. You can cross-country ski to the lake in winter and lace up the skates to enjoy the ice.

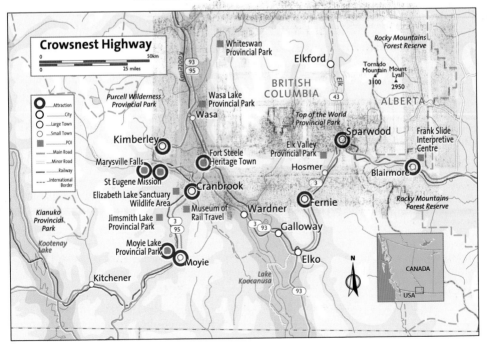

Elizabeth Lake Sanctuary Wildlife Area and Info Centre *1101 1st Ave south. Open Jun–Labour Day 0900–1700.*

Jimsmith Lake Provincial Park $ *2km west of Cranbrook on Jim Smith Lake Rd; wlapwww.gov.bc.ca. Open May–Oct.*

Accommodation and food in Cranbrook

Bavarian Chalet $$ *1617 Cranbrook St north; tel: (250) 489-3305.* On Thursday–Sunday have the prime rib, otherwise it's a mixture of German specialities and all-Canadian.

Casa Della Pasta & Deli $–$$ *202 Van Horne St south; tel: (250) 426-5331.* Home-made Italian pastas and sauces.

Heritage Inn $$ *803 Cranbrook St north; tel: (250) 489-4301, tollfree (888) 888-4374; fax: (250) 489-5758; e-mail: info.cranbrook@ heritageinn.net; www.heritageinn.net.* This motor inn has 101 rooms and a central location.

Prestige Rocky Mountain Resort $$$ *209 Van Horne St south; tel: (250) 417-0444, tollfree (877) 737-8443; www.prestigeinn.com.* A modern, de luxe railway-theme hotel has 108 rooms adjacent to the railway museum.

Super 8 $ *2370 Cranbrook St north; tel: (250) 489-8028, tollfree (800) 800-8000.* Clean and comfortable at the north end of town, the hotel is across from the Info Centre.

FERNIE

Fernie Chamber of Commerce Info Centre *102 Commerce Rd; tel: (250) 423-6868, tollfree (877) 433-7643; e-mail: info@ferniechamber.com; www.ferniechamber.com. Open summer 0900–1800; winter Mon–Fri 0900–1700.*

Fernie Alpine Resort $$ *Ski Area Rd; tel: (250) 423-4655; www.skifernie.com. For snow information tel: (250) 423-4655 or tollfree (866)-6FERNIE; e-mail: info@skifernie.com. Ski season: open late Nov–mid-Apr daily 0900–1600.*

With its mountain setting and fine heritage buildings, Fernie could be called the Aspen of BC. Skiing in winter and fly-fishing in summer are the big draws to this former coal mining town, once a base for the Ktunaxa. **Fernie Alpine Resort.** Lizard Range forms an impressive drop, and with 9m annual snowfall the resort is a paradise for alpine and Nordic skiers. Mountain bike, ride a horse, kayak, raft, hike, fly fish or take a chairlift ride to scenic views in summer.

Accommodation and food in Fernie

Fernie Log Inn $$ *141 Commerce Rd; tel: (250) 423-6222, tollfree (877) 733-7643.* Radiant floor heating completes the cosy feeling of this log cabin, chalet-style lodge.

Lizard Creek Lodge $$ *5346 Highline Dr; tel: (250) 423-2057, tollfree (877) 228-1948; fax: (250) 423-2058.* A hit with skiers but also an excellent summer base with easy access to summer activities. Spa and other amenities.

Mug Shots Bistro $ *592 3rd Ave; tel: (250) 423-8081.* Have a relaxed coffee on comfy couches or dine on home-made soups, pastries and wraps.

Wolf's Den Mountain Lodge **$$** *5339 Ski Hill Rd, Fernie Alpine Ski Resort; tel: (250) 423-9202, tollfree (800) 258-7669.* Open all year, the 42-room lodge offers ski-in, ski-out slope access.

FORT STEELE HERITAGE TOWN

Fort Steele Heritage Town $$
Hwy 93, 8km north of Hwys 3/93 junction; tel: (250) 417-6000; e-mail: info@FortSteele.bc.ca; www.fortsteele.bc.ca. Open daily sunrise–dusk. Actors and artisans in period costume in summer.

Named after North West Mounted Police Supt Sam Steele who brought law and order during the 1864 Kootenay Gold Rush, Fort Steele boomed until the CPR bypassed the town for Cranbrook. At the confluence of the Kootenay and St Mary rivers, the *de facto* capital of the East Kootenay's rich mining economy declined when BC legislator Col James Baker persuaded the CPR to build its divisional point on his Cranbrook holdings. The restoration of Fort Steele contains some 50 buildings, including several from the original NWMP post. Guides and artisans in period costume bring history to life, providing a well-rounded introduction to Fort Steele's golden years, as a steam train and a Clydesdale-drawn wagon offer rides through the complex.

Right
Fort Steele Heritage Town tanner at work

KIMBERLEY

ⓘ Kimberley Visitor Info Centre
270 Kimberley Ave; tel: (250) 427-3666; e-mail: info@kimberleychamber.ca; www.kimberleychamber.ca

Ⓗ Kimberley Underground Mining Railway and Cominco Powerhouse Mining Tours $
Open late Jun–Labour Day, in conjunction with the Railway ride, tel: (250) 427-0022; www.kumr.ca. The Power House tour is a stop en route on the railway.

Cominco Gardens $
306 3rd Ave. Open May–Sept dawn–dusk. Tea room open daily in summer 1000–1800.

Happy Hans
Located at the Kimberley Visitor Info Centre.

Platzl
T-shaped pedestrian street encircled by Wallinger Ave, Howard St, Kimberley Ave and Ross St.

Named after her South African namesake, BC's highest city (1,113m) was dedicated to silver, zinc and lead mining production at the Cominco (Sullivan Mine). Happy Hans, the world's largest operating cuckoo clock, Bavarian kitsch and a ski resort at North Star Mountain have replaced the mining industry. Salvaged railway cars at the **Kimberley Underground Mining Railway** show off the countryside on a 12km, one-hour ride through the scenic countryside. The mining company wanted to promote fertiliser in 1927. The resultant **Cominco Gardens** boast 48,000 blooms annually, with dedicated rose, prairie and Victorian gazebo areas. In the **Platzl** Bavarian architecture, restaurants, shops, wandering accordion players and depictions of the Happy Hans town mascot reflect the transition the town economy has made from mining lead to mining tourists. The beer-stein-waving **Happy Hans** statue in *lederhosen* is hard to miss.

Accommodation and food in Kimberley

Chef Bernard's $$ *170 Spokane St, on the Platzl; tel: (250) 427-4820. Open daily 0800–2200.* The chef is well known and locally beloved in this Bavarian schnitzelhaus which serves excellent pasta dishes.

Old Bauernhaus $$$ *280 Norton St, up the ski hill; tel: (250) 427-5133 Open Thur–Mon 1700–2300.* Bavarian cuisine was never so authentic as in this 350 plus year-old building, dismantled and reassembled here.

Right
Platzl, downtown Kimberley

Above
Happy Hans, town mascot, Kimberley

Snowdrift Café $ *110 Spokane St on the Platzl; tel: (250) 427-5272. Open Mon–Sat 1000–2200, Sun 1200–1800.* Big, rich cups of *latte* and home-grown spinach salad with gorgonzola cheese, walnuts, mushrooms, carrots and wholewheat bread reflect the quality of the menu at this superb vegetarian restaurant.

Wild Rose Ranch and Resort $$$ *east of Wasa Lake, north 8km on Wolf Creek Rd; tel: (250) 422-3403, tollfree (800) 324-6188; www.wildrose-ranch.com.* A family-owned tourist ranch purpose-built for horse riders and fly fishers in a stunning mountain-view setting. A variety of adventures organised by the family.

MARYSVILLE FALLS

Marysville Falls $
7km south of Kimberley.

An easy 10-minute afternoon walk along rocky Mark Creek to a spectacularly crashing 30m cascade is worth a brief stop.

MOYIE AND MOYIE LAKE PROVINCIAL PARK

Moyie and Moyie Lake Provincial Park $
31km south of Cranbrook, Hwy 3; www.env.gov.bc.ca/bcparks. Open Apr–Oct.

Nestled within the Purcell Mountains, bears roam around the popular windsurfing and swimming lake. Explorer David Thompson's party was almost swept away by Moyie River spring floods in 1808. Today's 200 Moyie residents point with pride to lovely buildings and a well-preserved fire hall which served when the St Eugene Mine flourished in the late-19th century, one of the richest lead–silver mines in the province.

SPARWOOD

Sparwood and District Visitor Info Centre *141 Aspen Dr., Sparwood; tel: (250) 425-2423, tollfree (877) 485-8185; www.sparwood.bc.ca. Information on accommodation, dining, Titan truck and coal mine tours.*

The town that replaced the blackened, bulldozed coal-mining towns of Natal and Michel, Sparwood lays claim to the world's largest dump truck, a 9m-high green Terex Titan with 3m-high wheels, at the Info Centre.

Accommodation in Sparwood

Blue Collar B&B $ *124 Pine Ave, Sparwood; tel: (250) 425-2952 or (250) 425-4223; e-mail: bobbyhut@telus.net; www.bobbyhutchinson.com.* For something different, stay with a romance writer who likes to cook.

ST EUGENE MISSION

St Eugene Mission
$ 7731 Mission Rd,
Cranbrook; tel: (250) 420-
2000 or (866) 292-2020;
www.steugene.ca. Stop by
nearby Ktunaxa Tribal
Office for information and
to go inside the church.

A restored 1897 Gothic-style mission church has hand-painted Italian stained and leaded glass and interior supports resembling a barn. Across Old Airport Road is the former Kootenay Indian Residential School, now a destination resort.

Suggested tour

Total distance: 270km Blairmore to Cranbrook, including the circular route to Kimberley and Fort Steele and back to Cranbrook. Detour: 90km south to Moyie.

Time: An easy day to drive. 2–3 days to explore, including detour.

Links: The Columbia River (*see page 122*) lies north of Wasa. Continue south on Hwy 3, the Crowsnest Highway, to Creston and the Kootenays (*see page 114*). North of Fernie, Hwy 3 runs east to the Crowsnest Pass and enters Alberta, and continues on to Blairmore.

Route: The Crowsnest Highway (Hwy 3) goes through **BLAIRMORE** ❶, where a tragic slide on Turtle Mountain killed 70 people in their sleep in 1903. The Frank Slide Interpretive Centre explains the avalanche, mining and living conditions in the mine's heyday.

Hwy 3 continues west over the Crowsnest Pass (1,357m) on the BC–Alberta boundary to the town of **SPARWOOD** ❷, home of the world's largest dump truck. The route follows a southerly direction to the town of **FERNIE** ❸. Coal mining boomed around 1900 from the valley into Alberta, and Fernie and area became rich, though plagued by a legendary curse on the mines, claiming many lives. Fernie Alpine Resort buzzes with winter activity in a stunning range of mountains.

The Elk Valley traverses the Elk River, named after the numerous wapiti (elk) spotted by settlers. Hwy 3 continues through Elko, then joins up with Hwy 93, turning in a northwesterly direction to a T-junction. Turn right and follow the signs to **FORT STEELE HERITAGE TOWN** ❹ for time travel through one of BC's best and most authentic historic site restorations. Continue along Hwy 93/95 to Wasa Lake Provincial Park for swimming in the Kootenay's warmest lake (May–Oct). Turn left onto Hwy 95A past Ta Ta Creek to **KIMBERLEY** ❺.

British Columbia Provincial Parks–Kootenay District Wasa Lake Dr., Wasa; tel: (250) 422-4200; www.pc.gc.ca/pn-np/bc/kootenay. Information on all Crowsnest area provincial parks.

Kimberley's heart is the Platzl, the Bavarian chalet-style pedestrian plaza, with a cuckoo clock that claims to be the world's largest. It chimes on the hour, revealing the ubiquitous Happy Hans yodelling. Catch the Bavarian City Mining Railway excursion train at the Platzl. A short drive up the hill provides vistas over the Kootenay River Valley. Before leaving town, take in the thousands of blooms at Cominco Gardens.

Take Hwy 95A south in the direction of Marysville, stop at the bridge and hike down Mark Creek for a view of the magnificent **MARYSVILLE FALLS** ❻. Continue towards Cranbrook, then left on to Old Airport Road to **ST EUGENE MISSION** ❼ in the bucolic midst of the tribal headquarters for the Ktunaxa/Kinbasket First Nation St Mary's Reserve. The restored historic church is lovely. Ask at the tribal centre to have the church unlocked. Continue on to Hwy 95A and **CRANBROOK** ❽.

The main city in the area, Cranbrook's big attraction is the Canadian Museum of Rail Travel and the red wooden railway Water Tower nearby, situated along the CPR line where rolling stock provides a realistic background for the historic railway carriages. A graceful reconstructed red-brick Rotary Clock Tower (Baker and Cranbrook Sts) is the focal point for a Chamber of Commerce Heritage Tour brochure at Cranbrook's downtown and Baker Hill residential area buildings. Elizabeth Lake Sanctuary Wildlife Area is a peaceful spot for picnicking and walking the lakeside trail accompanied by birdsong. Follow signs when crossing Hwy 3 to Jimsmith Lake Provincial Park for swimming, fishing and canoeing.

Detour: to Moyie. Take Hwy 3/95 south of Cranbrook to **MOYIE** ❾, a village set on a scenic hillside. **MOYIE LAKE PROVINCIAL PARK** has watersports and sailing.

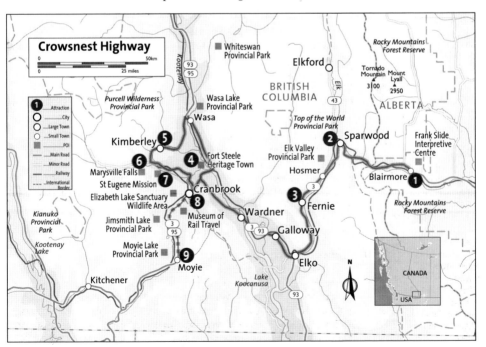

The Kootenays

Ratings

History	●●●●●
Mountains	●●●●●
Nature	●●●●●
Scenery	●●●●●
Children	●●●●○
Outdoor activities	●●●●○
Parks	●●●●○
Food and drink	●●○○○

Dominated by the sinuous and raucous waterways of the Kootenay River and Kootenay Lake, and the soaring peaks of the Purcell and Selkirk mountains, the region is heaven for lovers of rugged mountains and lakes. Following a dirt track carved open from Hope to Fort Steele, the one highway linking southern BC is more vertical than horizontal. What little flat space exists between mountain ranges is more often filled with water. Ghost towns abound in the Upper and Lower Kootenay (named after a small Aboriginal band), no surprise in a region best known for rushes in search of gold, copper, silver and lead, as do smelter ruins, decaying mine shafts and abandoned cemeteries. The future is as bright as the past. Urban professionals from across Canada have transformed one-time backwaters into modern enclaves surrounding golden opportunities for boating, hiking, fishing and skiing.

AINSWORTH HOT SPRINGS

Ainsworth Hot Springs $$
Hwy 31, 13km north of Balfour; tel: (250) 229-4212, tollfree (800) 668-1171; www.hotnaturally.com. Pool open daily 1000–2130.

The hot springs flow from a steam bath with stalactites, an abandoned horseshoe-shaped mine shaft. Spa aficionados swear by the water which has the highest mineral content of any natural springs in Canada. Everyone else swears by the stunning views across Kootenay Lake from the 45°C (113°F) outdoor baths.

BOUNDARY CREEK PROVINCIAL PARK

Boundary Creek Provincial Park $
Hwy 3, west of Greenwood. Open May–Oct.

A slag heap and crumbling chimney are all that remain of the largest copper processor in North America before World War I, serving up to 20 mines in the surrounding hills. The park also has pleasant camping and picnicking spots along Boundary Creek.

CASTLEGAR

**ⓘ Castlegar Info
Centre** *1995 6th Ave;
tel: (250) 365-6313;
www.castlegar.com*

**ⓘ Brilliant
Suspension Bridge**
*$ Base of Airport Hill. Park
at the south end of the
Kootenay River Bridge and
walk 500m down the old
highway.*

Castlegar Museum $
*400 13th Ave; tel: (250)
365-6440. Open Jul and Aug
Mon–Sat 0900–1700.*

**Doukhobor Historical
Village $** *112 Heritage
Way, across from Castlegar
Airport; tel: (250) 365-6622.
Open daily May–Sept.*

Perched dramatically on benchlands west of the Columbia River and opposite the junction of the Kootenay River, Castlegar began as a railway and timber town. Odorous fumes still blow from a pulp mill just below **Hugh Keenleyside Dam**, which backs the Columbia into Arrow Lakes, stretching 230km north of Revelstoke (*see page 126*). Doukhobor farms added an important agricultural element to the economy. When local authorities ignored requests for a bridge across the Kootenay River, the Doukhobors (*see page 120*) designed and built their own span in 1913, which carried Hwy 3 traffic for decades. It forms part of the **Brilliant Suspension Bridge**, a National Heritage Site.

    Castlegar Museum, an old CPR station, concentrates on area history from the early stages of the 20th century. **Doukhobor Historical Village** is a reproduction of a typical village and includes the communal main house, cottages and workrooms. The furnishings, photographs and artworks are authentic, as are the costumed guides who explain traditional Doukhobor life and beliefs. The small river island which forms **Zuckerberg Island Heritage Park** was named after a local Russian teacher who built an onion-dome home in the forest. Reached by the 91m pedestrian-only suspension bridge, Zuckerberg's home has been restored as a museum and tea room.

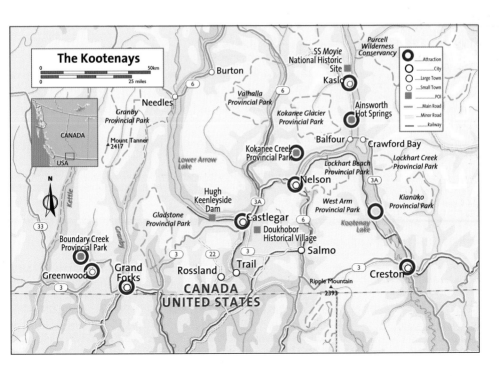

Hugh Keenleyside Dam $ *8km west of town; tel: (250) 365-3115. Open daily.*

Zuckerberg Island Bridge $ *8th St and 7th Ave; tel: (250) 365-6440. Open May–Aug.*

Accommodation and food in Castlegar

Fireside Inn $$ *1810 8th Ave; tel: (250) 365-2128; tollfree reservations (800) 499-6399.* Convenient and central.

Flamingo Motel $ *1660 Columbia Ave; tel: (250) 365-7978; e-mail: info@flamingomotel.ca.* Has a park-like setting.

CRESTON

ℹ **Creston Visitor Centre and District Chamber of Commerce** *1607 Canyon St (Hwy 3); tel: (250) 428-4342, tollfree (866) 528-4342; www.crestonbc.com/ chamber. Open Jul and Aug daily 0900–1700; Sept–Jun Mon–Fri 0900–1600.*

🏛 **Creston Valley Museum and Archives** $ *219 Devon St; tel: (250) 428-9262; e-mail: info@creston.museum.bc.ca; www.creston.museum.bc.ca. Open May–late Sept daily 1000–1530. Tours any time of year by appointment.*

Creston Valley Wildlife Management Area and Centre $ *Hwy 3, 10km northwest of Creston; tel: (250) 402-6906; e-mail: askus@crestonwildlife.ca; www.crestonwildlife.ca. Open May and Jun Tue–Sun 0900–1600; Jul and Aug daily 0900–1600. Contact for autumn hours.*

A small farming town overlooks a plain where the Kootenay River once sprawled between the Purcell and Selkirk mountains in the 'Valley of the Swans'. The river has been dyked and channelled, creating fertile grain fields. Creston's rural past appears on murals in the town centre. Highlight of the **Creston Valley Museum and Archives** is a replica of a traditional Kootenay canoe, a 'sturgeon-nosed' craft with ends pointing down into the water. **Creston Valley Wildlife Centre**, the interpretation centre for the 6,800ha Creston Valley Wildlife Management Area, offers guided canoe tours of one of BC's richest wetland areas, also walking trails and educational displays. The area has the largest concentration of nesting ospreys in North America as well as massive bird migrations spring and autumn (fall).

Accommodation and food in Creston

Dellas Place $ *129 north 10th Ave; tel: (250) 402-0062.* Big selection of pizzas, steaks, etc.

Downtowner Motor Inn $$ *1218 Canyon St; tel: (250) 428-2238; reservations (800) 665-9904.* Central and good value.

Granny's Place $$ *1230 Canyon St; tel: (250) 428-3990.* Has great home-cooked western-style fare.

GRAND FORKS

ℹ **Visitor Info Centre** *7362 5th St; tel: (250) 442-2833, tollfree (866) 442-2833; e-mail: gfchamber@ sunshinecable.com; www.grandforkschamber.com. Open Jul and Aug daily 0900–1800; rest of year Mon–Fri 0900–1700.*

Named after its proximity to the convergence of the Granby and Kettle rivers, the attractive valley town boomed with the Granby Smelter, once the largest copper smelter in the British Empire. Russian is taught in schools, thanks to the large Doukhobor population who also influence menus of vareniki, holubtsi and borscht. **Boundary Museum** houses artefacts from aboriginals to Doukhobors, miners and railways. See the overview, then take a self-guided tour of some of the

Boundary Museum
$ *Hwy 3 and 5th St;
tel: (250) 442-3737; www.
city.grandforks.bc.ca/museum.
Open 0930–1630 daily in
the summer; Mon–Fri winter.*

**Mountain View
Doukhobor Museum $**
*3655 Hardy Mountain Rd,
north of Hwy 3; tel: (250)
442-2881. Call for hours,
but currently Mon–Fri. Two
tours a day.*

**Phoenix Interpretive
Forest $**
*136 Sagemore Rd, 19.5km
west of Grand Forks; self-
guiding map at museums
in Grand Forks and
Greenwood; tel: (250)
442-5411. Drivable year
round.*

300-plus heritage buildings from the mining and railway era with a free museum map. **Mountain View Doukhobor Museum**, in a 1912 Doukhobor communal home, overflows with period artefacts and records. Many other Doukhobor buildings are visible along Hardy Mountain Road as it twists back to Hwy 3. The **Phoenix Interpretive Forest**, a 22km, self-guided back-road route between Grand Forks and Greenwood, passes many of the former mines, towns and railways that made the Boundary rich in the early-20th century.

Accommodation and food in Grand Forks

Clydes Brew & Cue $ *7748 2nd St; tel: (250) 442-3913; www.clydespub. ca.* Friendly, relaxed spot to dine or play billiards. Ask how it got its name!

Grand Forks Hotel and Restaurant $$ *7382 2nd St; tel: (250) 442-5944.* Also has Doukhobor food and non-vegetarian choices.

Grand Forks Motor Inn $$ *2729 Central Ave; tel: (250) 442-2127.* Is central and good value.

Kocomo's Coffee House $ *7361 2nd St; tel: (250) 442-0500.* Great coffee house with attached art gallery.

GREENWOOD

 **Greenwood
Museum $**
*214 south Copper St; tel:
(250) 445-6355. Open May,
Sept & Oct 1000–1600;
Jun–Aug 0900–1700;
Nov–Apr by appointment.*

Lotzkar Park $
*Hwy 3, northwest side of
town.*

The smallest city in BC (pop. 800), Greenwood was a service centre for dozens of mines in the early 20th century, a wild town with noisy pianos and midnight gambling parties. When mining collapsed after World War I, Greenwood became a ghost town. Japanese-Canadians were interned in the empty buildings during World War II and many stayed on. Many historic buildings have been restored. **Greenwood Museum** is small but speaks with emotion of the stories of grief and joy and the Japanese community. At **Lotzkar Park**, the best-preserved smelter ruins in North America rise above a barren ridge of black smelter slag that once glowed red-hot, even at noon. Locals call it a 'corner of hell gone mad'.

Right
Historic buildings, Greenwood

KASLO

ⓘ Kootenay Lake Historical Society
324 Front St; tel: (250) 353-2525; www.kin.bc.ca/archives/klhs. Open mid-May–mid-Oct.

ⓝ SS Moyie National Historic Site $
Front St; tel: (250) 353-2525. Open mid-May–mid-Oct for self-guiding tours.

The 'Little Switzerland of the Americas', Kaslo was a lumber town before lead and silver strikes brought miners flooding onto the Kootenays. Tourism is number one today, thanks to the restored Victorian-era homes, commercial buildings and heritage sites, and a departure point for boating, fishing and mountaineering. The meticulously restored 49m SS *Moyie*, beached at the **SS *Moyie* National Historic Site**, sailed Kootenay Lake until 1957, the last sternwheeler in regular passenger service in Canada.

KOKANEE CREEK PROVINCIAL PARK

ⓝ Kokanee Creek Provincial Park $
4750 Hwy 3A, 20km northeast of Nelson; tel: (250) 825-4212; www.westkootenayparks.com/park-info/kokanee. Open May–Sept.

Built on a site of a former lakeside estate, the park offers hiking, boating, camping, fishing and Redfish Creek spawning channel, an artificial spawning channel for kokanee salmon. The best time to see the bright-red fish is mid-August–mid-September. The park also shelters a major osprey population.

KOOTENAY LAKE

ⓘ Kootenay Lake Chamber of Commerce *Box 120, Crawford Bay; e-mail: info@kootenaylake.bc.ca; www.kootenaylake.bc.ca*

ⓝ Glass House $
Hwy 3A, 25km north of Creston; tel: (250) 223-8372. Open May–Oct.

Lockhart Beach Provincial Park $ *Hwy 3A, north of Creston; www.kootenayrockies.com*

Ⓖ Kokanee Springs Golf Resort $$
Crawford Bay; tel: (250) 227-9226; www.kokaneesprings.com. Open mid-Apr–Thanksgiving.

This long (100km), narrow (2–6km wide) lake between the Purcell and Selkirk mountains was a major navigation route long before it became a prime recreation area. Facilities lie along Hwy 3A, north from Creston to Kootenay Bay. There you can link to Balfour by BC Ferries, with more facilities along Hwy 3A west into Nelson. **Crawford Bay** (*Hwy 3A, 78km north of Creston*). is a collection of artisans producing woven brooms and metalwork in a traditional blacksmith shop. There is also an 18-hole championship golf course, **Kokanee Springs Golf Resort** (*www.kokaneesprings.com*). Mortician David Brown built the **Glass House**, a scenic lakeside house, from half a million embalming fluid bottles in the 1950s, as he explained, 'to indulge a whim of a peculiar nature'. There is excellent camping and hiking in **Lockhart Beach Provincial Park**. Farther east is the larger but undeveloped Kianuko Provincial Park which protects the headwaters of Kianuko Creek.

NELSON

ℹ Nelson and District Chamber of Commerce and Visitors Centre *225 Hall St; tel: (250) 352-3433, tollfree (877) 663-5706; fax: (250) 352-6355; www.discovernelson.com. Open summer 0830–1900; after 1 Sept 0830–1700 Mon–Fri.*

🏛 Chamber of Mines Eastern BC Museum $ *215 Hall St; tel: (250) 352-1933. Open Mon–Fri 1000–1600. Closed public holidays.*

Lakeside Park $ *Foot of the Nelson Bridge.*

Nelson Museum $ *502 Vernon St; tel: (250) 352-9813. Open afternoons year round.*

Streetcar No 23 $ *Downtown to Lakeside Park.*

Set on the slopes of the Selkirk Mountains overlooking Kootenay Lake, Nelson's steep streets and hundreds of handsome heritage buildings provided the scene for the 1986 Steve Martin film *Roxanne*. Local painters have enshrined the film star on a mural at the end of Vernon Street. Film publicity helped Nelson reinforce its incarnation as a rural refuge for urban professionals who expect high-speed Internet connections and the perfect *latte* after a tough day at the computer. The impressive **Court House** and **City Hall** were designed by Francis Rattenbury, the architect who designed the Empress Hotel and Legislature Building in Victoria. Guides in period costumes from the Chamber of Commerce lead walking and driving tours of the town's 355 heritage buildings in summer, or follow self-guiding maps in any season. A dozen galleries stage monthly shows by 75 local artists. Maps of Artwalk are available at the Info Centre. The **Chamber of Mines Eastern BC Museum**, run by the provincial mining association with a strictly local collection, emphasises steamboats and mines. **Streetcar No 23** is BC's only operating historic streetcar, making regular runs the length of the town along the lakeshore.

Previous page
Husky-drawn sled in the Kootenays

Right
Nelson

Accommodation and food in Nelson

All Seasons Café $$ *620 Herridge Lane; tel: (250) 352-0101.* Offers outstanding Northwest cuisine and an outstanding wine list.

Garden Inn $$ *408 Victoria St; tel: (250) 352-3226, tollfree (800) 596-2337; www.innthegarden.com.* A pleasant B&B in a historic home.

Hume Hotel $$ *422 Vernon St; tel: (250) 352-5331, tollfree (877) 568-0888; www.humehotel.com.* Has been Nelson's landmark hotel since the 1890s.

Main Street Diner $$ *616 Baker St; tel: (250) 354-4848.* Offers solid Greek meals.

Max and Irma's Kitchen $$ *515A Kootenay St; tel: (250) 352-2332.* Serves Nelson's best pizza and Italian dishes.

Prestige Lakeside Resort $$$ *701 Lakeside Dr.; tel: (250) 352-7222; www.prestigeinn.com.* Nelson's most luxurious hotel.

Suggested tour

Total distance: 300km.

Time: Greenwood to Creston can be driven in one day, however 2–3 days allows time to enjoy and explore.

Links: Hwy 3 leads to the Crowsnest (*see page 104*). To the west of Greenwood on Hwy 3 are the Cascade Mountains and the Okanagan Valley (*see page 198*).

Route: Only east–west road in the southern BC interior, Hwy 3 passes through the smallest city in BC, **GREENWOOD ❶**, a one-time mine boom town. Continue over Eholt Summit, named after an abandoned mining town, to **GRAND FORKS ❷**, the commercial hub of Boundary Country, an agricultural town that boomed with mineral strikes in nearby hills.

Hwy 3 continues eastbound through Boundary Country, a transition zone between the drier, fertile Okanagan Valley to the west and the high Kootenay peaks, while Hwy 395 near the lake leads south into Washington.

Hwy 3 goes along Christina Lake, then leaves Boundary Country and descends into the Kootenays, over Bonanza Pass and on the downhill leg to **CASTLEGAR ❸**. Take Hwy 3A and cross over the Kinnaird Bridge. A layaway (lay-by) 2.5km northeast of Castlegar overlooks the disused Brilliant Suspension Bridge and Brilliant Dam. The highway passes Bonnington Falls and four hydroelectric dams along the Kootenay River, built to take advantage of the 200m fall from Kootenay Lake at **NELSON ❹** to the Columbia River at Castlegar.

After exploring the pretty town of Nelson, return to the junction of Hwys 3A and 6, turn south on Hwy 6, cross over the bright orange Nelson Bridge and skirt the Selkirk Mountains in the direction of Salmo, the Latin word for salmon. At Burnt Flat Junction, turn east on Hwy 3 and continue over the 'The Skyway', at 1,774m one of the highest paved roads in Canada, past the Creston Valley Wildlife Centre and on into **CRESTON** ❼.

Scenic alternative: The more interesting 150km route to Creston follows Hwy 3A east of Nelson to Balfour. The 30-minute crossing is free but the line-up (queue) can take most of the day, especially in summer. Hwy 3A follows along the shores of **KOOTENAY LAKE**, passing Crawford Bay, Lockhart Beach Provincial Park and Glass House.

Detour: From Balfour, turn north on Hwy 31 to **AINSWORTH HOT SPRINGS** ❺ and Cody Caves Provincial Park on the way to **KASLO** ❻. The charming village has more than 60 heritage buildings, including the dry-docked SS *Moyie*, a sternwheeler that once carried passengers on the lake. Return to Balfour.

The Doukhobors

A sect of radical Russian dissenters, persecuted in the 18th century for their heresy and pacifism, was called Doukhobors or 'wrestlers against the Holy Spirit' by an Orthodox archbishop. Assisted by British and American Quakers, over 7,000 emigrated to Canada in 1898–9 in what was to become southeastern Saskatchewan. Exiled spiritual leader Peter (Lordly) Verigin joined the group, and in 1908 led the Doukhobors to southern BC after their homesteads were cancelled when they refused to swear an oath of allegiance demanded by the new minister of the interior. They settled on flat land across the Columbia River from Castlegar, and built many of the earliest bridges when authorities refused their request, including the graceful Brilliant Suspension Bridge over the Kootenay River.

The new immigrants planted orchards, grain and vegetables while building sawmills, jam factories, pipe works and similar enterprises. Their communal living arrangements, outspoken pacifism and vocal opposition to meat, tobacco and alcohol won few friends locally. Many were imprisoned for nude protest parades. Communal villages have disappeared but thousands of Doukhobors still live in Boundary Country from Castlegar to Grand Forks. Many of their distinctive farm buildings are still visible along country roads, and Russian restaurants – invariably Doukhobor – are local institutions, though the 'no meat, no booze, no smoking' slogan is a distant memory.

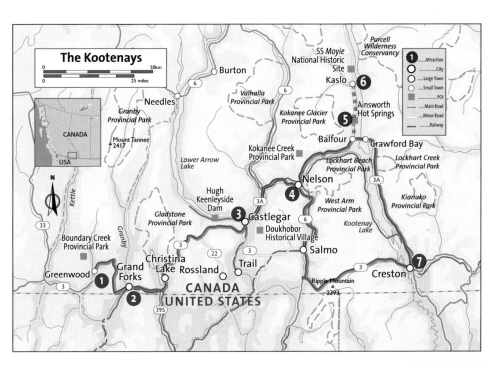

Right
Artefacts at Doukhobor
Historical Village

Columbia River

Ratings

Mountains	●●●●●
Nature	●●●●●
Outdoor activities	●●●●●
Parks	●●●●●
Scenery	●●●●●
Wildlife	●●●●●
Geology	●●●●○
Food and drink	●●●○○

Cutting deep gorges along its 2,044km course, the powerful Columbia River was named by Boston explorer-trader Robert Gray after his ship the *Columbia* and after which British Columbia is named. The Columbia begins its much dammed and serpentine route to the Pacific Ocean near Portland, Oregon from Columbia Lake. Bird migration along the Columbia Valley is breathtaking in spring and autumn (fall). Migration of humans over one of the world's snowiest mountain areas at Rogers Pass is almost as awe-inspiring because of the technical expertise it takes to keep the route open against avalanches. This is railway country, from the hub at Golden at the north end of the Columbia Valley, to Revelstoke west of the Selkirk Mountains along the Columbia River, west of Golden over Rogers Pass. Glaciers, old-growth cedars and wild-flower meadows lie in-between the towns, each claiming the distinction of Gateway to the Columbia.

BUGABOO PROVINCIAL PARK

 **Bugaboo Provincial Park $**
45km west of Hwy 95 at Brisco;
www.env.gov.bc.ca/bcparks/explore/parkspgs/bugaboo.
Commercial heli-skiing lodge near park entrance.

An alpine wilderness, Bugaboo Provincial Park is a rugged, breathtaking landscape that attracts serious mountain climbers and heli-skiers from around the world. The park can be reached by a good gravel logging road, 45km west of Hwy 95 at Brisco. The 13,646ha park is home to a variety of wildlife such as pikas, marmots, ground squirrels and mountain goats. There are 20 wilderness campsites but no services.

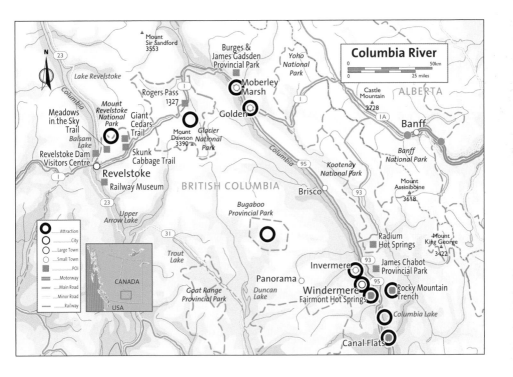

CANAL FLATS

→ Canal Flats
Historic Point, Hwy 93/95 at south end of Columbia Lake.

Sitting on a 2km strip of land that separates the southward-flowing Kootenay River and the northward Columbia River, Canal Flats originates from an 1889 canal built to divert the Kootenay away from valley farms. Too narrow locks were the canal's downfall. The *North Star*, only the second vessel to pass through, wrecked the locks and system in 1902. Look for skeleton sculptures on the east side of Hwy 95 at Canal Flats. Doug 'Up' Bonz is a skilled bone and fossil finder with a gift for humour and sculpture. The bones of birds and small animals become skeletons of impossible creatures, shown off around the property and in the trailer that is his workshop and sales gallery.

COLUMBIA LAKE

Columbia Lake
South of Fairmont Hot Springs on the east side of Hwy 93/95.

A sign at a lay-by on the east side of Hwy 93/95 states 'Columbia Lake – Source of Columbia River which empties into Pacific Ocean at Astoria – Oregon', that is, 2,044km southwest of the headwaters. Spiky golden hoodoos (eroded columns of rock) rise sheer above Dutch Creek at the lake's north end.

Above
Columbia River

FAIRMONT HOT SPRINGS

Ski Hill $$
Open year round.

Hot Pools $
Open daily 0800–2200.

Mountainside Golf Course $$$ *Tel: (250) 345-6311, tollfree (800) 663-4979.* One of two 18-hole courses, offering magnificent views over the Columbia River Valley.

Soak in the 43–48°C (109.4–118.4°F) hot springs, Canada's largest odourless natural hot pools which have been long used by Ktunaxa (Kootenay) people. From several vantage points, including the Mountainside Golf Course, the forest-bound Fairmont Hot Springs Resort (*midway between Canal Flats and Invermere on Hwy 93/95; tel: (250) 345-6311, tollfree (800) 663-4979; www.fairmonthotsprings.com*) looks westward to the craggy line of the Purcell Mountain Range. Hiking, biking, horse riding and winter skiing supplement the pools' attraction for the lodge guests and another 750,000 visitors who make an annual pilgrimage to the resort.

GLACIER NATIONAL PARK

⟳ Rogers Pass
69km east of Revelstoke, 72km west of Golden, on Hwy 1 in Glacier National Park.

🛈 Glacier National Park $
Mount Revelstoke and Glacier national parks HQ, 3rd St and Campbell Ave, Revelstoke; tel: (250) 837-7500; www.glacier.nationalpark.com

Rogers Pass Centre
Rogers Pass; tel: (250) 814-5232. Call for opening hours. Free.

The northern Selkirk Mountain Range, the birthplace of North American technical climbing (mountaineering) in 1888, is a land of snow and over 400 active glaciers and icefields, including Illecillewaet Glacier, visible from the Trans-Canada Highway on a clear day. Waterfalls and wild flowers are abundant in season. If travelling east, you will see the 14.5km Mount Macdonald Tunnel, North America's longest railway tunnel, built after hundreds died between 1885 and 1911 trying to keep Rogers Pass open. **Rogers Pass.** Many peaks poke the sky at 3,700m, catching shrouds of snow which slide dangerously below. **Rogers Pass Centre** offers excellent explanations of the Snow Wars waged by the CPR and more currently by Parks Canada and the Royal Canadian Horse Artillery to keep the Trans-Canada Highway open. Abandoned Rails Trail follows Hwy 1 past side-paths and snowsheds 1.3km to the Rogers Pass Monument, which commemorates completion of the Trans-Canada Highway in 1962, the first alternative to rail travel over the pass.

Accommodation and food in Glacier National Park

Best Western Glacier Park Lodge $$$ *Rogers Pass; tel: (250) 837-2126, tollfree (800) 528-1234; e-mail: info@glacierparklodge.ca; www.glacierparklodge.ca.* The only non-camping accommodation in the park provides 50 rooms next to the Rogers Pass Centre, with a restaurant, 24-hour cafeteria and petrol station.

GOLDEN

🛈 Kicking Horse County Chamber of Commerce
900 10th Ave N; tel: (250) 344-7125, tollfree (800) 622-4653; fax: (250) 344-6688.

Trains, lorries, rivers, an active sawmill, tourists, skiers and outdoor enthusiasts (hang gliders, rock climbers, whitewater kayakers and rafters, mountain bikers, hikers and anglers) all use Golden as a convenient valley-floor base. Here is the confluence of the Columbia and Kicking Horse rivers and access to Yoho National Park (*see page 91*) or Glacier National Park. Mountains rise along both sides of the valley, causing spectacular sunsets over the Purcells.

Accommodation and food in Golden

Golden Rim Motor Inn $$ *1416 Golden View Rd; tel: (250) 344-2216, tollfree (877) 311-2216; fax: (250) 344-6673; www.goldenrim.ca.* Views of the Columbia valley.

Legendz $ *1405 west Trans-Canada Hwy; tel: (250) 344-5059.* Serves delicious steaks and creamy eggs, with other Marilyn Monroe and James Dean-era specialities.

Sportsman Lodge $$ *1200 12th St north; tel: (250) 344-2915, tollfree (888) 989-5566; www.sportsmanlodge.ca.* Quiet and away from the highway.

INVERMERE

ⓘ **Invermere Columbia Valley Chamber of Commerce Visitor Info Centre**
651 Hwy 93/95 Crossroads, Windermere; tel: (250) 342-2844; fax: (250) 342-3261; www. columbiavalleychamber.ca. Open Labour Day–Jun Mon–Fri 0900–1700; Jul–Labour Day daily 0900–1700.

At the northwest corner of Windermere Lake, the area's commercial centre south of Golden boasts September–October kokanee salmon spawning in its end of the 15km lake and lakeside **James Chabot Provincial Park** with a swimming beach and watersports.

🏛 **James Chabot Provincial Park $**
North end of Windermere Lake; www.env.gov.bc.ca/ bcparks/explore/parkspgs/ james

Right
Ranch house near the Columbia River

Opposite
Decorative window, Revelstoke

MOBERLY MARSH/BURGES AND JAMES GADSDEN PROVINCIAL PARK

Most drivers do not stop in the rush to and from Golden, but migratory waterfowl do along this stretch of marsh between the Trans-Canada Highway and the Columbia River. Spot muskrats and ospreys from a 3.5km river-bank Dyke Trail.

MOUNT REVELSTOKE NATIONAL PARK

ⓘ **Revelstoke Info Centre** *Grizzly Plaza on McKenzie Ave; tel: (250) 837-3522. Open May and Jun 0830–1500; Jul 0830–2200; Aug 0830–2130.*

Unlike the Rocky Mountain National Parks, which were spurred on by the CPR and the need for an all-weather automobile route (Kootenay), this park was a result of City of Revelstoke citizens building a trail to the mountain's summit and lobbying for a road. That road, Meadows in the Sky Parkway, draws thousands of mid-summer visitors to the rich displays of wild flowers.

Revelstoke Chamber of Commerce *204 Campbell Ave; tel: (250) 837-5345, tollfree (800) 487-1493; fax: (250) 837-4223; www.revelstokecc.bc.ca. Open Mon–Fri 0830–1200, 1300–1630; summer open through lunch. For snow sports, www.seerevelstoke.com/snow*

🅘 **Mount Revelstoke National Park $** *Mount Revelstoke and Glacier national parks HQ, 3rd St and Campbell Ave, Revelstoke; tel: (250) 837-7500; www.pc.gc.ca. Wardens at Meadows in the Sky Parkway have park information.*

Giant Cedars Trail $ *1km west of east boundary of Mount Revelstoke National Park.*

Meadows in the Sky (Parkway) $ *3km east of Revelstoke in Mount Revelstoke National Park. Trailers are prohibited beyond the parkway trailer parking area 0.5km from Hwy 1.*

Revelstoke Dam $ *5km north of Revelstoke; tel: (250) 814-6697, tours off-season (250) 814-6600; open mid-Apr–mid-Oct daily 0900–1700.*

Revelstoke Railway Museum $ *Victoria Rd, Revelstoke; tel: (250) 837-6060, tollfree (877) 837-6060; www.railwaymuseum.com. Open Jul and Aug daily 0900–2000; Sept, Oct & Mar–Jun 0900–1700 (closed Wed Mar and Apr); Nov–Feb Fri–Tue 1100–1600.*

Giant Cedars Trail. Rainforest in the interior of BC? Eight-hundred-year-old Western red cedars along a half kilometre boardwalk tell the tale. The damp, mossy streambed is dim but vibrant with many hues of green. **Meadows in the Sky.** Stop at the elaborate archway Welcome Station entrance to the 26km Meadows in the Sky Parkway for information. Depending on the severity of the past winter, the parkway may be closed part of the way up, even though the route is normally open early July–late September. Enjoy the winding, 16-switchback drive past fine views of Revelstoke and the Columbia River. Park at Balsam Lake and take the Summit Shuttle to the wildflower meadows or hike the colourful carpet by way of the 1km Summit Trail to the top.

BC Hydro operates **Revelstoke Dam** and generating station, a must for those fascinated by waterway engineering and the intricacies of changes to the Columbia River. It is not large but the **Revelstoke Railway Museum** is a good introduction to the challenges faced by CPR engineers and officials who encountered avalanches, difficult soil, steep grades, harsh winters and labour strife while constructing and maintaining the railway. Prized are the Business Car No 4 and Mikado P-2k class locomotive No 5468, on display in a replica of Victoria's E&N Roundhouse.

Accommodation and food in Revelstoke

Many Revelstoke motels are near the noisy railway tracks at the west end of town.

112 Restaurant & Lounge $$$ *112 E First St; tel: (250) 837-2107, tollfree (888) 245-5523.* Called one of the best restaurants between the Rockies & the Pacific.

Canyon Motor Inn $$ *1911 Fraser Dr., off Hwy 1 at Columbia River Bridge; tel: (250) 837-5221, tollfree (877) 837-5221; e-mail: canyonmotorinn@rctvonline.net; www.canyonmotorinn.ca.* Has small, very clean rooms in a quiet spot near the river.

Minto Manor B&B $$ *815 Mackenzie Ave; tel: (250) 837-9337, tollfree (877) 833-9337; fax: (250) 837-9327; e-mail: mintomanorb&b@telus.net.* An elegant B&B in a fine old heritage home.

ROCKY MOUNTAIN TRENCH

Astronauts say this depression between mountain ranges which extends from Alaska along the western side of the Rocky Mountains into the Central US is one of the most prominent features on earth. The rift valley separates the ancient Columbia Mountains from the craggier, younger Rocky Mountains on the eastern side, with lush wetlands and cultivated farmland in-between. Rocky Mountain Trench, dividing the Rocky and Cascade mountain ranges from Alaska to the Central US, has the Columbia River at its bottom in this area.

WINDERMERE

St Peter's Anglican Church $ *Kootenay St; tel: (250) 342-6644.*

The town and its namesake lake are a resort getaway for locals and people from colder climes. **St Peter's Anglican Church** was stolen in 1897, removed via a railway flatcar from Donald, 210km north, by residents who wanted a ready-made church when most Donald inhabitants moved to Revelstoke along with the CPR operations.

Suggested tour

Total distance: 310km.

Time: 2 days.

Links: From Revelstoke, continue west on the Trans-Canada Highway (Hwy 1) to the Shuswap Lakes (*see page 160*). At Golden, go east to Yoho National Park in BC Rockies or at Radium Junction, go east to Kootenay National Park in the UNESCO Trail North (*see page 84*). South of Canal Flats on Hwy 93/95 to the Crowsnest (*see page 104*).

Route: At **Revelstoke ❶**, the pretty city called 'Home of the World's Largest Sculpted Grizzly Bears', visit the Revelstoke Railway Museum, Revelstoke Museum and the amazing collection at Piano Keep Gallery. Travel east on the Trans-Canada Highway and enter **MOUNT REVELSTOKE NATIONAL PARK ❷**, and take the park's jewel, the

Opposite
Sinclair Canyon, Kootenay National Park

Meadows in the Sky Parkway, a 42km drive to Balsam Lake parking and a 2km shuttle ride or walk to Mount Revelstoke's summit, carpeted with wild flowers in mid-summer. Return to Hwy 1 and stop and take the short 0.5km Giant Cedars Trail for a view of BC rainforest; look for bats in summer. In May, walk the 1.2km Skunk Cabbage Trail for views of birds and the odiferous plants flowering yellow along the Illecillewaet River.

In **GLACIER NATIONAL PARK** ❸, the Illecillewaet Glacier ('The Great Glacier') campground and trail head to a series of trails near the glacier, accessible from Hwy 1. Rogers Pass Monument (1,382m), memorial arch to the 1962 Trans-Canada Highway completion, is 1km from Rogers Pass Centre with a roaring fire, excellent exhibit and film depictions of avalanche control and snow management, and a well-stocked bookstore. Tunnels covering the Trans-Canada Highway are snowsheds, built to deflect the violent impact of avalanches. Before leaving the park, Beaver Valley has a lovely picnic spot and wild flowers in summer. Continue past **BURGES and JAMES GADSDEN PROVINCIAL PARK** ❹ at **MOBERLEY MARSH** and Donald, where the CPR line first crossed the Columbia River.

At the junction of the Trans-Canada Highway in **GOLDEN** ❺, continue south on Hwy 95 along the Columbia River Valley, through the Great Blue Heron Rookery, the second largest population in Western Canada. At **Radium Hot Springs** ❻, Hwy 93 splits off east from Hwy 95 to Radium Hot Springs and Kootenay National Park.

Travel south on Hwy 95 to **INVERMERE** ❼ on the west side with views of the Purcell Mountains and **WINDERMERE** ❽ on the highway side. Continue along Windermere Lake to **FAIRMONT HOT SPRINGS** ❾, an oasis for soaking, swimming, golfing, hiking and winter skiing. Looming mysteriously to the right are the Dutch Creek Hoodoos. Travel south on the west side of **COLUMBIA LAKE** ❿, headwaters of the Columbia River. The wetlands that begin here are the most extensive and richest on earth, 26,000ha of protected space. Continue along the Rocky Mountain Trench and on into **CANAL FLATS** ⓫.

Detour: To Panorama Mountain Village. Follow the signs and turn right into the town of Invermere, then turn right again at the sign near the top of the hill. Follow the winding, hilly road for 18km to Panorama Mountain Village, a year-round retreat for golf, hot pools, hiking and skiing.

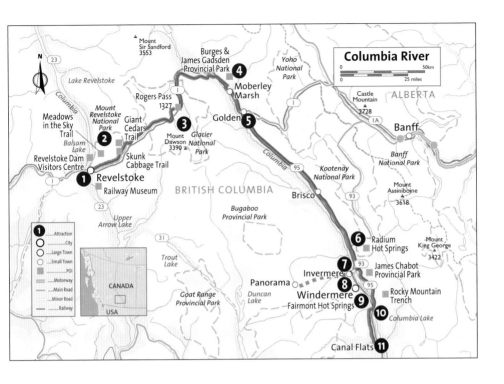

The man behind Rogers Pass

A railway engineer and surveyor, Albert Bowman Rogers is described by Parks Canada as 'short, sharp and rough-tongued'. A native of Massachusetts, Rogers graduated from Yale University and was hired by the CPR to find a southerly route through the rugged Selkirk Mountains, a route that would be closer to the Canada–US border. In 1881, he tried the Pass's west side, and 'many a time I wished myself dead'. He approached from the east the following year and 'felt like a piece of liver' after finding a viable pass through the mountains. The incentives were a $5,000 bonus and the naming of the pass after him, yet in his typically stubborn style, Rogers never cashed the cheque.

Cariboo Country

Ratings

Geology	●●●●●
Nature	●●●●●
Outdoor activities	●●●●●
Scenery	●●●●●
Children	●●●●○
History	●●●●○
Mountains	●●●●○
Wildlife	●●●●○

A semi-wilderness of forests, mountains, lakes and prairie, the Cariboo is a land where towns are small, few and far between. What many call the Real West is a land where cattle outnumber people and dreams grow as big as the sky is broad. East of the Fraser River lie lakes and dense evergreens that stretch to the Cariboo Mountains. West lies the Chilcotin ('people of the young man's river' in Tsilhqot'in), a vast rolling plain rising from the mighty Fraser and running to the foothills of the Coast Mountains. The region contains vast tracts of protected parkland that are barely mapped. Farther west is the glacial crown of the Coast Range, dropping precipitously into deep fiords which cut inland up to 70km from the Pacific Ocean. This land called Cariboo Country conjures up images of those brave early explorers who travelled along the rugged Grease Trail.

ALEXIS CREEK

 Alexis Creek
112km west of Williams Lake.

With nearly 250 residents, this Chilcotin community has petrol, an RCMP detachment, post office, grocery store and a BC Forest Service office.

Accommodation and food in Alexis Creek

Chilcotin Hotel $ *7676 Hwy 20; tel: (250) 394-7500, tollfree (877) 394-7500; e-mail: chilcotinhotel@gmail.com; www.chilcotinhotel.com.* The only hotel and restaurant in town.

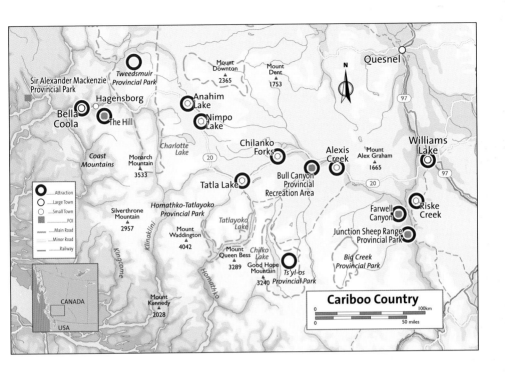

Cariboo Country

ANAHIM LAKE

❶ MacLean Trading
tel: (250) 742-3266.
The best source for area
information and supplies.

❶ Anahim Lake
Resort $$ Hwy 20;
tel: (250) 742-3242, tollfree
(800) 667-7212;
www.anahimlakeresort.com

This aboriginal village is the largest in the West Chilcotin and a centre for fishing the Dean and nearby rivers. Anahim Lake Resort offers fishing, air taxi service, hiking, riding and general relaxation. The locally renowned August Stampede is authentic here, much less commercial than early July's Calgary Stampede.

BELLA COOLA

❶ Tourism Bella
Coola Coop Bldg,
Mackenzie St; tel: (250) 799-
5202, tollfree: (866) 799-
5202; www.bellacoola.ca.
Open Jun–Aug 0900–1730.

British Capt George Vancouver sailed up fiord-like North Bentinck Arm to Bella Coola in 1793, just weeks before Alexander Mackenzie walked down the narrow valley to the Pacific. Norwegian farmers arrived in 1894 to share the valley with Nuxalk (Bella Coola) aboriginal people. Town and fiord are ringed by sheer mountains, providing endless opportunities for fishing, hiking and outdoor adventure.

ℹ Quesnel Forest Office *322 Johnston Ave, Quesnel; tel: (250) 992-4400 or 4433. For information on travelling the Alexander Mackenzie Heritage Trail/Nuxalk–Carrier Grease Trail.*

⊝ Hagensborg *Hwy 20, 18km east of Bella Coola.*

🔟 Acwsalcta Nuxalk Nation School $ *4km east off Hwy 20.*

Sir Alexander Mackenzie Provincial Park and Mackenzie Rock $ *60km west on Dean Channel, no land access. Ask about transport at the museum.*

Thorsen Creek Petroglyphs $ *Off Hwy 20, east of Bella Coola. Ask for directions at the museum.*

The **Acwsalcta Nuxalk Nation School** has some of the finest aboriginal artwork on public display along the coast. **Bella Coola Valley Museum** (*269 Highway 20; tel: (250) 799-5767; open Jun–Sept Mon & Wed–Sun 0900–1700*), in a 19th-century schoolhouse and surveyor's cabin, has Hudson's Bay Company relics and Norwegian goods. Norwegian farmers at **Hagensborg** were Bella Coola's first non-aboriginal residents in modern times. Many of the century-old homes and barns show adze marks produced by the original builders. Mackenzie Rock in **Sir Alexander Mackenzie Provincial Park** was the final stop of Mackenzie's 1793 trek across Canada. He painted a message in vermilion and bear grease: 'Alexander Mackenzie, from Canada, by land, the twenty-second of July, one thousand, seven hundred and ninety-three', which was later chiselled into the rock. The **Thorsen Creek Petroglyphs** are dozens of carvings lining rocks along the creek.

Accommodation and food in Bella Coola

Bella Coola Valley Inn $$ *Corner of Dean and Mackenzie St; tel: (250) 799-5316, tollfree (888) 799-5316; www.bellacoolavalleyinn.com.* The best motel in town and the closest to the BC Ferries dock.

Tallheo Cannery $$ *Across the harbour from Bella Coola; tel: (250) 982-2344; e-mail: tallheocannery@centralcoastbc.com.* Rooms in a restored bunkhouse, home-cooked meals and adventures.

BULL CANYON PROVINCIAL RECREATION AREA

🔟 Bull Canyon Provincial Recreation Area $ *Hwy 20, 6km west of Alexis Creek; www.env.gov.bc.ca/bcparks/explore/parks*

This pleasant picnic and camping stop along the grey-green Chilcotin River was a cattle roundup point and the site of a decisive battle between Tsilhqot'in and Secwepemc bands.

Right
Cariboo Country's rolling plains

CHILANKO FORKS

→ Chilanko Forks
62km west of Alexis Creek.

Chilanko Forks is a traditional Chilcotin town with a general store and petrol station. A marsh by the airport access road is good for beaver and muskrat spotting.

FARWELL CANYON

→ Farwell Canyon
19km south of Hwy 20 from Riske Creek.

The Chilcotin River has cut a deep canyon through soft golden cliffs, creating flat-topped hoodoos (columns of rock formed by erosion) capped by sand dunes that shift with the wind.

THE HILL

→ The Hill
Hwy 20, east of Bella Coola.

The final barrier to land travel between Bella Coola and the rest of BC was finally breached in 1953 by local bulldozer operators who were tired of government highway engineers saying a road down the sheer western face of the Coast Range was impossible. Views from the single-track gravel road are stupendous but there are no verges or lay-bys.

JUNCTION SHEEP RANGE PROVINCIAL PARK

🅘 Junction Sheep Range Provincial Park $ *15km south of Hwy 20; www.env.gov.bc.ca/ bcparks*

This isolated park protects the world's largest herd of California bighorn sheep, as well as some 40 or so species of butterfly.

Right
Bighorn sheep

NIMPO LAKE

Dean River Resort
1145 Hwy 20;
tel: (250) 742-3332,
tollfree (888) 646-7655;
www.thedeanonnimpo.com

This 12km lake claims to be BC's float plane capital for the many daily charter flights to remote rivers and lakes. **Dean River Resort** is the most comfortable of several lake-front fishing resorts.

RISKE CREEK

Riske Creek
46km southwest of Williams Lake; tel: (250) 659-5646, tollfree (888) 659-5688;
e-mail: welcome@ chilcotinlodge.com;
www.chilcotinlodge.com

The tiny farming town of Riske Creek is named after a 19th-century Polish farmer, an early settler in the area.

Accommodation and food in Riske Creek

Chilcotin Lodge $$ *Riske Creek; tel: (250) 659-5646; www.chilcotinlodge.com.* A former hunting lodge turned B&B, restaurant and campground.

TATLA LAKE

Tatla Lake $
109km west of Alexis Creek.

Lake and town are the half-way point between Williams Lake and Bella Coola. Nordic skiing is a popular winter activity, rivalling lake diving in summer.

TS'YL-OS PROVINCIAL PARK

Ts'yl-os Provincial Park $
100km south of Hwy 20 from Lees Corner;
www.env.gov.bc.ca/bcparks/ explore/parkspgs/ts.html

Lakes and streams in this undeveloped wilderness produce one-quarter of the entire Fraser River salmon run. Apart from two gravel roads off Hwy 20, the only access is by air, boat, horse or foot.

TWEEDSMUIR PROVINCIAL PARK

Tweedsmuir Provincial Park $
HQ on Hwy 20 east of Bella Coola.

Tweedsmuir is 980,000ha of wilderness outside a narrow corridor along Hwy 20. The best easy walks are on the Bella Coola side along the Atnarko River Spawning Channels, where grizzlies and black bears have the right of way.

WILLIAMS LAKE

① Cariboo Chilcotin Coast Tourism Association *118A 1st Ave north, Williams Lake; tel: (250) 392-2226, tollfree (800) 663-5885; e-mail: info@landwithoutlimits.com; www.landwithoutlimits.com*

Williams Lake and District Chamber of Commerce *1660 South Broadway (Hwy 97, south end of city); tel: (250) 392-5025; e-mail: info@ williamslakechamber.com; www. williamslakechamber.com. Open mid-Jun–Aug daily 0900–1700; Sept–mid-Jun Mon–Fri 0900–1600.*

⑪ Scout Island Nature Centre $ *1305A Borland Rd, west end of city, off Hwy 97, east of city centre; e-mail: shemphill@wlake.com*

Stationhouse Gallery $ *1 north Mackenzie Ave in old BC Rail Station; tel: (250) 392-6113. Open Mon–Sat 1000–1700; e-mail: curator@ stationhousegallery.com; www.stationhousegallery.com*

Museum of the Cariboo Chilcotin $ *113 north 4th Ave; tel: (250) 392-7404; e-mail: mccwl@uniserve.com; www.cowboy-museum.com. Open Jun–Aug Mon–Sat 1000–1600; Sept–May Tue–Sat 1100–1600.*

This is the only real town between Hope and Quesnel, a cowboy city that has expanded into forestry, mining, agriculture and tourism. Williams Lake's public gallery, the **Stationhouse Gallery**, concentrates on BC artists, while the **Museum of the Cariboo Chilcotin** focuses on the ranching, rodeo and cowboy history of the Cariboo region. **Scout Island Nature Centre**, a small marsh, has lakeside walking paths, wildlife watching and a summer nature centre.

Accommodation and food in Williams Lake

Fraser Inn $$ *285 Donald Rd; tel: (250) 398-7055, tollfree (800) 452-6789; e-mail: book@fraserinn.com; www.fraserinn.com.* The largest hotel in town.

Hearth Restaurant $$ *99 South 3rd Ave; tel: (250) 398-6831.* In the Cariboo Friendship Society, has open-beam aboriginal decor.

Overlander Hotel $$ *1118 Lakeview Cres; tollfree (800) 359-5672.* A busy, moderate hotel with a good restaurant.

Rowat's Waterside B&B $$ *1397 Borland Rd; tel: (250) 392-7395, tollfree (866) 392-7395; www.wlakebb.com.* A short walk from Scout Island.

Suggested tour

Total distance: 465km.

Time: Allow 10–12 hours to drive; 2–5 days to explore.

Links: From Williams Lake, Hwy 97, the Gold Rush Trail (*see page 140*) leads north towards Prince George or south towards Hope (*see page 223*). From Bella Coola, BC Ferries Discovery Coast route (*see pages 182–4*) leads south to Port Hardy and North Vancouver Island (*see page 226*).

Route: From **BELLA COOLA ❶**, sitting at the head of the North Bentinck Arm and mouth of the Bella Coola River, travel east on Hwy 20 which runs gently uphill through the Bella Coola Valley. Continue on to Hagensborg which still has many of the square-cut, hand-hewn buildings left by early Norwegian settlers from Minnesota a century ago. The highway runs through dense forest along the Atnarko and Bella Coola rivers.

Use low gear to creep up (or down) the steep 18 per cent grade as the paved road ends. There are no verges, no guardrails and no lay-bys to enjoy the spectacular views along the 9km of single-track, hairpin turns that climb 1,300m from the Bella Coola Valley to the Heckman

Alexander Mackenzie–Grease Trail

The 450km trail, stretching from the junction of the Blackwater and Fraser rivers near Quesnel to the Dean Channel north of Bella Coola, was a main trade route of the Bella Coola, Carrier and Chilcotin bands, a corridor used by aboriginal people for 6,000 years. The name given to the road, 'Grease', was taken from the processed oil of the oolichan (a small smelt-like fish that was dried or rendered into fat), a major trading commodity of the Bella Coola band.

Alexander Mackenzie, an explorer and fur trader with the North West Co., was advised by Indians to travel overland on his expedition to reach the Pacific. He was guided along the rugged Grease Trail, the first European to journey across North America. A national historic trail, the foot and horse track is made up of highways, forest access roads, local wagon roads, rivers and coastal waters.

Pass east of the top of **THE HILL ❷**, surveyed and built by local volunteers when government engineers said it was impossible.

The 1,524m Heckman Pass is the east entrance to **TWEEDSMUIR PROVINCIAL PARK ❸**. There are good views of the multicoloured Rainbow Mountains from the Tsulko River east of Heckman Pass. Local aboriginal bands mined obsidian from the Rainbows, a string of ancient volcanoes stained red, yellow and purple by mineral deposits.

The paved highway begins west of **ANAHIM LAKE ❹**, a small Tsilhqot'in community named after a prominent leader in the 1860s. Gravel roads lead north along the Dean River, but check locally for conditions before setting out. Beyond the last tyre tracks lies the Nuxalk–Carrier Grease Trail east to the Fraser and west to Bella Coola.

Hwy 20 crosses the Dean River east of Anahim Lake. A historical marker commemorates the 1864 Chilcotin War when Tsilhqot'in warriors, fearing a smallpox epidemic, clashed with men attempting to build a road across the Chilcotin to the Cariboo gold fields. A provincial inquiry in 1993 granted five posthumous pardons and a memorial was erected.

The paved road ends again at Nimpo Lake. The well-maintained gravel highway winds southwards through Coast Range foothills. Tatla Lake, western edge of the Chilcotin Plateau, is the midway point to Williams Lake. The gently rolling grasslands, also called the Fraser Plateau, stretch east to the Fraser River. It is a pleasant drive in summer but the weather is deceptively gentle. Winter temperatures can feel like −50°C (−58°F) with winds driving blinding blizzards. Pollywog Marsh is a pleasant lakeside rest stop. Best view of the entire Tatla Lake valley is from a lay-by 22km beyond the lake.

The paved road begins again 15km east, just west of **CHILANKO FORKS ❺**. The highway east is dotted with stunning views to the Coast Range.

BULL CANYON PROVINCIAL PARK ❻ is a pleasant picnic and camping spot in an aspen forest along the grey-green Chilcotin River. The canyon was the site of an epic battle between the Tsilhqot'in and Secwepemc bands, and a cattle roundup point. **ALEXIS CREEK ❼** is the main settlement in the eastern Chilcotin.

Detour: The road continues south and west to **TS'YL-OS PROVINCIAL PARK ❽**, created to protect traditional Aboriginal lands from logging.

One of the best views of the Chilcotin is from a rest area at the top of a long grade 12km east of Lee's Corner, named after an ill-fated attempt to drive 200 head of cattle 2,500km through the mountains to the Klondike gold fields in 1896. The town of Riske Creek, named after an early rancher, is 1.5km east at the log cabins painted bright yellow on the north side of Hwy 20.

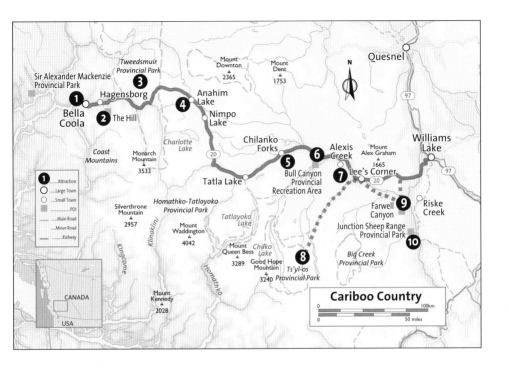

Detour: Follow the gravel road along the rolling curves of the almost treeless plain to **FARWELL CANYON** ❾ and a wooden bridge over the Chilcotin River. There are early aboriginal rock paintings on the overhang at the south end of the bridge. Local Tsilhqot'in fishers net salmon from the river in summer and autumn (fall), drying their catch on racks nearby. The road loops 50km back to Hwy 20 at Lee's Corner.

The enormous antennae rising from the prairie form part of the Loran-C navigation system. A good gravel road 9.5km west leads 16km east to the fairy tale hoodoos of Farwell Canyon and **JUNCTION SHEEP RANGE PROVINCIAL PARK** ❿, a reserve for California bighorn sheep.

Continue east across Becher's Prairie, rolling grassland strewn with boulders deposited by retreating glaciers. Nesting boxes on fenceposts attract bluebirds and tree swallows that feast on the mosquitoes that can plague the small lakes and ponds dotting the Chilcotin. The eastern edge of the plateau is the immense Fraser River trench. Watch slow-moving logging trucks on the steep grades at both ends of the Sheep Creek Bridge over the river. The mouth of the Fraser River is 500km south. Continue 25km east into **WILLIAMS LAKE**.

Cariboo Gold Rush Trail

Ratings

History	●●●●●
Nature	●●●●●
Outdoor activities	●●●●●
Scenery	●●●●●
Walking	●●●●●
Museums	●●●●○
Children	●●●○○
Food and drink	●●○○○

The Cariboo Gold Rush of the 1860s transformed BC from a distant source of furs into a major presence on the world stage. Nearly every product, place and attitude that is part of BC today has its roots in the Gold Rush. Most of the province's major highways exist because they once filled Gold Rush needs. Even timber, largest of BC's traditional industries, owes much to the insatiable Gold Rush demand for wooden buildings, railway sleepers and fuel. Who first discovered gold and where may never be known. Aboriginal traders brought small amounts to the Hudson's Bay Company for years but the fur-trading giant hid its secret, fearing that an influx of gold seekers would disrupt its profitable monopoly. When gold was discovered in the Cariboo Mountain region, the company began to relinquish its colonial responsibilities and controlling interest fell to the International Financial Society.

ASHCROFT

Ashcroft Manor $
10km south of Cache Creek on Hwy 1; tel: (250) 453-9983. Open May–Oct 0900–1700.

Built in 1862 as a roadhouse for the Cariboo Waggon Road, Ashcroft grew into a prosperous farm, ranch, mill and social centre in the sagebrush and cactus desert south of Kamloops. The manor also served as one of BC's earliest court houses. Most of the complex burned down in 1943, but a church and roadhouse, now a museum and tearoom, survived.

BARKERVILLE HISTORIC TOWN

For most of the 1860s, Barkerville was the biggest town north of San Francisco and west of Chicago. More than 100,000 hopeful miners and hangers-on travelled the Cariboo Waggon Road to Barkerville between 1862 and 1870. They turned what had been a shanty town

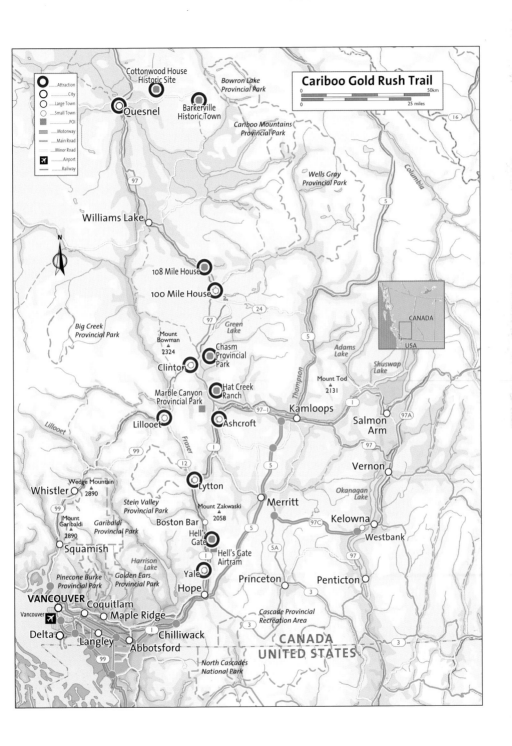

Cariboo Gold Rush Trail

0 .... 50km

0 .... 25 miles

⊕ Barkerville Historic Town $
Hwy 26, 8km east of Wells; tel: (250) 994-3302, tollfree (888) 994-3333; e-mail: barkerville@barkerville.ca; www.barkerville.com. Open daily 0800–2000 year-round; costumed interpreters, full services plus special programmes mid-May–Sept.

into a city so rich and so confident that it nearly outdid Victoria in a bid to become the capital of BC.

The gold along Williams Creek ran out in little more than a decade but the town survived to become a thriving heritage site. More than 125 buildings remain, most of them original, if heavily restored. The bordellos and dance halls never reopened, but restaurants, theatres, churches, stores, bakeries, photographers and a Chinese grocery are back in business during the summer months. In winter, the only residents are ground squirrels and park wardens.

For a better sense of just how far Barkerville lies from the rest of BC, walk (or ski in winter) that last 1.6km of the old wagon road west of Richfield with *Signage*, a self-guiding map to historic sites. The map is available at the Barkerville Visitor Centre. Most visitor facilities are in Wells.

CHASM PROVINCIAL PARK

⊕ Chasm Provincial Park $ *Hwy 97, 16km northeast of Clinton; www.bcadventure.com/ adventure/explore/ high-country/parks/chasm*

The Painted Chasm is an enormous river-carved gash through 120m and 15 million years of lava atop the Fraser Plateau. The 1.5km gorge shows multiple layers of reds and yellows that are especially brilliant in late afternoon sun.

CLINTON

ⓘ Clinton Info Centre
Located within the South Cariboo Historical Museum.

⊕ South Cariboo Historical Museum
$ 1522 Cariboo Hwy; tel: (250) 459-2442. Open daily May–Sept.

Straddling the junction of two wagon roads, Clinton was originally called Junction, a name discarded when Queen Victoria decided her Colonial Secretary needed a town named in his honour. Little has changed in the years since. Clinton remains a quintessential cowboy town where everyone knows everyone, and if you have to ask directions, you most definitely do not belong. Most of the horse-riding trails, hiking, rafting and other outdoor activities take place at guest ranches scattered in the hills and valleys to the west. **South Cariboo Historical Museum**, set in an 1890s school house, chronicles the transition from Gold Rush to cowboy country.

Accommodation in Clinton

Many area ranches have discovered that guests are more profitable (and less laborious) than huge cattle herds. The self-proclaimed Guest Ranch Capital of BC has facilities ranging from rustic to ritzy.

Big Bar Guest Ranch $$ *tel: (250) 459-2333; e-mail: contact@bigbarranch.com; www.bigbarranch.com.* One of the first and still among the best for families: horse riding, hiking, river rafting, backcountry camping trips, Nordic skiing and similar activities are geared for beginners.

Moondance Guest Ranch $$$ *tel: (250) 459-7775, tollfree (888) 459-7775; e-mail: info@moondanceguestranch.com; www.moondanceguestranch.com.* A luxury ranch with private cabins, gourmet meals and wood-fired saunas.

COTTONWOOD HOUSE HISTORIC SITE

Cottonwood House Historic Site $ *4660 Barkerville Hwy, Hwy 26, 28km east of Hwy 97; tel: (250) 992-2071 or (250) 983-6911; e-mail: edcoleman@sd28.bc.ca; www.cottonwoodhouse.ca. Open mid-May–Aug 1000–1700.*

Another of the roadhouses en route to Barkerville, Cottonwood was a family residence 1874–1951. Period buildings include the main house, root cellar and a double barn, all explained by costumed interpreters.

HAT CREEK RANCH

Hat Creek Ranch $ *Hwys 97 and 99; tel: (250) 457-9722 or (800) 782-0922; e-mail: hhcr@telus.net; www.hatcreekranch.com. Open May–mid-Oct daily 0900-1800; services and costumed interpreters May–Sept.*

Still a working ranch, Hat Creek is the last intact roadhouse on the Cariboo Waggon Road. The 20 heritage buildings include one of the largest barns in BC. Stagecoaches and wagon trains used ranch facilities until motor vehicles began using the road in 1916. Facilities include trail rides, ranching demonstrations, museum displays and a summer aboriginal village. See page 190 for more information.

Below
Hat Creek Ranch

HELL'S GATE

Hell's Gate (Airtram $$) *Trans-Canada Highway (Hwy 1), 10.5km from Alexandra Bridge Provincial Park; tel: (604) 867-9277; e-mail: visit@hellsgateairtram.com; www.hellsgateairtram.com. Open Apr–mid-May and Sept–mid-Oct 1000–1600; mid-May–Aug 1000–1730.*

Below
Hell's Gate cable car

An average of 850,000 cubic metres of water blasts through a space about the width of a city street every second. River rafters run the rapids daily in summer but only one steamboat, the *Skuzzy*, ever made it upstream, winching through the raging narrows with bolts driven into the rock. The rapids are more fearsome now. In 1913, a careless Canadian National Railway construction crew touched off a landslide that choked the river and blocked the salmon run for years. Fish ladders built in 1945–6 helped, but modern salmon runs are less than one-third the pre-1913 volume, even in the best of years.

For the best view of the rapids, ride the **Airtram** 152m down and across the canyon to a museum, restaurant, gift shop and viewing platform. A suspension bridge crosses the river just downstream, and railway trains pass every half-hour.

LILLOOET

Lillooet Visitor Centre *790 Main St; tel: (250) 256-4308; lillooet.com/visitor_info.php. Open May, Jun, Sept & Oct Tue–Sat 1000–1600; Jul and Aug daily 0900–1900.*

Lillooet Museum $ *790 Main St; tel: (250) 256-4308. Open May–Oct daily.*

Mile-0-Motel $$ *616 Main St; tel: (250) 256-7511, tollfree (888) 766-4530; www.mileomotel.com. Central and comfortable.*

The main streets of Lillooet are extraordinarily wide to allow the 20-team ox wagons that worked the Cariboo Waggon Road to turn around. The **Mile Zero Cairn** opposite the Visitor Info Centre is Mile 0 for the roadhouses and supply points north. **Lillooet Museum** shares a former Anglican church with the Visitor Info Centre and is a trove of mining and pioneer artefacts. A self-guiding museum map lists 14 historical sites on Main Street alone.

LYTTON

Lytton Visitor Info Centre *400 Fraser St;*
tel: (250) 455-2523; e-mail lyttoncc@telus.net;
www.lytton.ca. Open Jun–Sept daily; Oct–May as posted.

Lytton Museum $ *next to the Info Centre. Open daily in summer.*

Lytton lives by forestry, tourism including hiking and river rafting. Companies based here launch trips up and down the Fraser and Thompson rivers that last a few hours to a few days. Five kilometres of riverfront have also been set aside as a Gold Panning Recreational Reserve with hand-panning only. Ask for information and pans at the **Lytton Info Centre**. The museum is devoted to the Cariboo Waggon Road and mining history.

100 MILE HOUSE

South Cariboo Visitor Info Centre *422 Cariboo Hwy 97; tel: (250) 395-5353, tollfree (877) 511-5353; www. southcaribootourism.com. Open summer daily 0900–1900; winter Mon–Sat 0900–1700.*

This small town is the service centre for the Central Cariboo and a major Nordic skiing area in winter. It began as a Cariboo Road stage stop in the 1860s. Seventy years later, Lord Martin Cecil, Marquis of Exeter, began and headquartered his Emissaries of Divine Light here.

108 MILE HOUSE

Watson Clydesdale Log barn $ *Hwy 97, 13km north of 100 Mile House; tel: (250) 791-1971. Open May–Sept daily 1000–1700.*

Hills Health and Guest Ranch $$$ *13km north of 100 Mile House off Hwy 97; tel: (250) 791-5225, tollfree (800) 668-2233. A ranch with a first-class spa resort.*

Best Western 108 Resort $$$ *4816 Telqua Drive, 108 Mile House; tel: (250) 791-5211, tollfree (800) 667-5233. Borders on riding trails, two lakes and a CPGA golf course.*

The one-time roadhouse has become a museum with a collection of heritage buildings moved to the site, including one of the largest **log barns** in Canada.

Right
108 Mile House ranch

QUESNEL

ⓘ Quesnel and District Information Centre
Le Bourdais Park, 703 Carson Ave; tel: (250) 992-8716, tollfree (800) 992-4922; www.northcariboo.com. Open Tue, Thur & Sat 0900–2100, other days 0900–1800; winter closed Sun and Mon.

⮑ Heritage Corner
Carson and Front Sts.

ⓗ Quesnel and District Museum and Archives $
410 Kinchant St; tel: (250) 992-9580; www. quesnelmuseum.ca. Open May–Sept daily 0900–1800 (until 2100 Tue, Thur & Sat); winter Tue–Sat 0830–1630.

Sitting at the confluence of the Fraser and Quesnel rivers, Quesnel was the last river town before the final overland trek to the gold fields at Barkerville. There is still enough gold in the rivers to keep prospectors busy. Much of the river has been staked or claimed, but there is public panning at the river junction. **Heritage Corner** is the centre of town, marked by massive steamboat and mining machinery in the riverfront park and a scenic 1929 bridge across the Fraser River. Highlight of the **Quesnel and District Museum and Archives** is an extraordinary collection of area photographs from 1865 onwards.

YALE

ⓗ Historic Yale Museum $
31187 Douglas St; tel: (604) 863-2324; e-mail: ydhs@uniserve.com; www.historicyale.ca. Open mid-Apr–mid-Oct daily 1000–1700. By appointment in winter.

St John the Divine Church $ *next to the museum.*

A handful of people still live in this Gold Rush boom town, though most of the town centre is a pleasant historic district. The interior of the 1859 Anglican **St John the Divine Church** remains almost unchanged since its consecration. The oldest church in BC is filled with period photographs and exhibits concentrating on the two Sto:lo villages that were once here and Gold Rush memorabilia. Ask about gold panning at Foreshore Park on the riverfront. Costumed interpreters give guided tours in summer.

Suggested tour

Total distance: 600km.

Time: Allow 2 days to drive from Barkerville to Hope and a week to explore along the way.

Links: From Quesnel, Hwy 97 continues north to Prince George. At Cache Creek, the Trans-Canada Highway (Hwy 1) leads east to Kamloops (*see page 191*) and the Shuswap Lakes (*see page 160*). From Hope, Hwy 3 runs east through the Lower Fraser River Valley (*see page 218*) to Vancouver (*see page 268*) and west to the Cascades.

Above
Barkerville

Williams Lake

As the prominent mission in the area, Williams Lake should have shared in the Cariboo gold rush bonanza of the 1860s. Yet when Cariboo Road contractors asked Tom Manifee, who owned a thriving roadhouse in the heart of Williams Lake, for a short-term loan so they could pay their workers, Manifee refused. The contractors then re-routed the road through 150 Mile House, 14km to the east, where the roadhouse owner was more than pleased to lend them money. Manifee got no more business, and not until the Pacific Great Eastern Railway arrived in 1920 did Williams Lake, named after Secwepemc Chief William, get on its feet.

Route: From **BARKERVILLE ❶**, head west to **COTTONWOOD HOUSE HISTORIC SITE ❷**, another Gold Rush roadhouse, before arriving at **QUESNEL ❸**, midway point between Prince George and Williams Lake. Hwy 97 continues south through Kersley, past Australian Rest Area to Fort Alexandria Monument that marks the end of Alexander Mackenzie's journey down the Fraser. Continue on to Soda Creek, terminus of the Cariboo Waggon Road.

Williams Lake ❹, home of BC's largest rodeo, is at the junction of Hwy 20 west to Bella Coola (*see page 133*). Continue in an easterly direction towards 150 Mile House, once an important junction where passengers changed stagecoaches going west to the Chilcotin or east to the gold fields. Hwy 97 follows the eastern shoreline of Lac La Hache to **108 MILE HOUSE ❺**, an open-air museum of late 19th-century buildings, including a Watson Clydesdale barn, one of the largest log barns in Canada. The neighbouring town of **100 MILE HOUSE ❻** is a major producer of log houses for North American and Japanese markets.

South is **CHASM PROVINCIAL PARK ❼**, a vast gorge cut through 15 million years of lava eruptions. Just south is **CLINTON ❽**, a centre for cattle and guest ranches, and a point where green hills and conifers are replaced by sagebrush as the road leads to **HAT CREEK RANCH ❾** and the junction of Hwy 97 and Hwy 99.

Alternative route: To Lytton. From Hat Creek Ranch, travel in a westerly direction on Hwy 99 through Marble Canyon Provincial Park and through the hamlet of Pavilion and Pavilion General Store, one of the oldest buildings in BC still on its original site. Hwy 99 corkscrews down rolling semi-desert Fraser Benchlands along the original wagon track road. Head across the Bridge of the 23 Camels, named after the ill-fated freight carriers during the Cariboo Gold Rush, and on into **LILLOOET ❿**. Hwy 12 continues in a southeasterly direction towards **LYTTON ⓫**, a non-stop, exciting 65km drive as the roadway hugs the mountainside, while the yellow-brown waters of the mighty Fraser River rage far below.

From Hat Creek, continue south to Cache Creek, in the heart of desert country, where Hwy 97 ends as it meets the Trans-Canada Highway. Off the Trans-Canada Highway turn off to **ASHCROFT ⓬** and **Ashcroft Manor**. Dating from 1862, the manor was a ranch with grist and sawmills that served the Cariboo miners. Goldpan Provincial Park is a river-raft launch, and a popular site for steelhead fishing in autumn (fall). The highway continues along to Lytton, at the confluence of the coffee-coloured Fraser and the icy-blue Thompson rivers. By 1864, Royal Engineers had blasted the Cariboo Waggon Road through to Lytton, opening the interior to miners, loggers and settlers. Hwy 1 follows the same route, and usually the same roadbed.

The Trans-Canada Highway continues along to Siska, one of 11 Nlaka'pamux Nation communities along the Fraser Canyon. Several tribal artists are building world-wide reputations carving soapstone from traditional quarries nearby. Siska Art Gallery and Band Museum (*tel: (250) 455-2539*) displays and sells local art as well as CDs by the Siska Halaw Singers and Drummers. The highway snakes high above the Fraser River toward **Boston Bar ⓭** and continues to **HELL'S GATE ⓮**, the narrowest spot along an already narrow canyon.

The highway continues south to **YALE ⓯**, past Emory Creek Provincial Park to the city of **Hope ⓰**, a Gold Rush boomtown set in a dramatic amphitheatre of mountains.

Right
Sunflowers at Williams Lake

Margaret 'Ma' Murray

Threatened with lawsuits and horsewhipping for her biting 'that's fur damshur' editorials on economics, politics and morals, Margaret 'Ma' Murray delighted her readers and infuriated politicians with her acid, earthy wit. She and her husband George published the *Bridge River–Lillooet News* in Lillooet and the *Alaska Highway News* in Fort St John from the 1940s to the 1980s. 'The state of politics in Canada', wrote the feisty pioneer editor, 'is as low as a snake's belly in Arkansas but a snake never goes so low that he didn't have a pit to hiss in.' Quoted across Canada, the legendary editor who 'guaranteed a chuckle every week and a belly laugh once a month or your money back' died in 1982 at the age of 94.

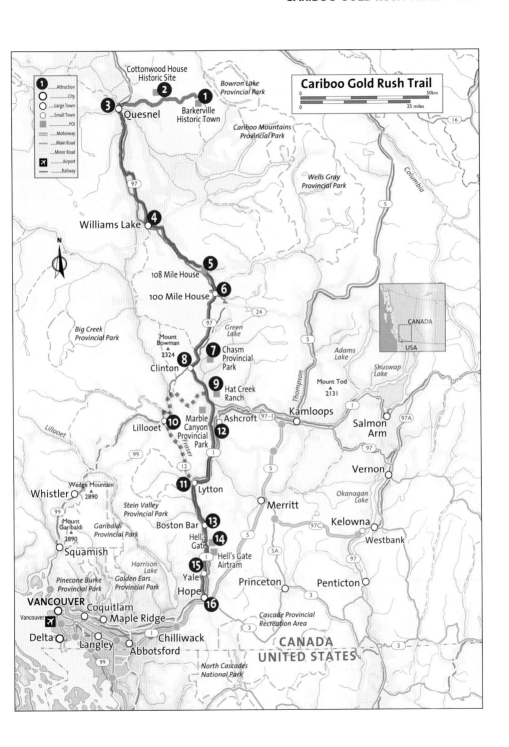

Cariboo Gold Rush Trail

Sea to Sky Highway

Ratings

Children	●●●●●
Mountains	●●●●●
Outdoor activities	●●●●●
Skiing	●●●●●
Entertainment	●●●●○
Food and drink	●●●●○
Nature	●●●●○
Villages	●●●○○

The Sea to Sky Highway, also called the Squamish Highway after the Squamish First Nations, is a spectacular drive. Yet by any name it is not a relaxing drive, the roadway curling and twisting along the glacier-carved shores of Howe Sound to the base of Whistler Mountain, one of North America's great holiday destinations. Much of the roadway is carved into the sheer cliffs hugging Howe Sound. The drive is scenic but the mountain terrain must be treated with care and respect: the frequent 'No Stopping' signs warn of rockfall and avalanche hazards. Nonetheless, the few lawful stopping spots provide picture-postcard views of BC Ferries navigating the protected waters of Howe Sound. Mountains rise just beyond the highway, some scarred with the remains of enormous mining operations, some never touched, and all cut by ice-cold streams rushing from the sky back to the sea.

BRACKENDALE EAGLE RESERVE

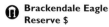 **Brackendale Eagle Reserve $**
Government Rd. Park at the dyke and walk to the viewpoint on the river. Best eagle viewing Dec–Feb.

The 600ha Eagle Reserve lies along both banks of the Squamish River north of Squamish, providing winter habitat and food for as many as 2,000 bald eagles in mid-winter. Eagles flock to the river to feed on spawning fish, a feeding frenzy that usually peaks around Christmas and tapers into mid-February, when the eagles disperse. Eagles can be observed from a riverside walk and observation point on the east bank or from the water with rafting and kayaking operators out of Squamish.

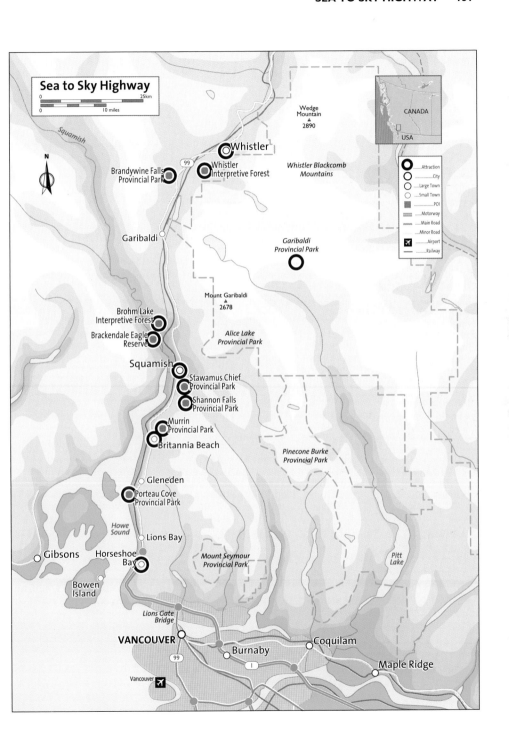

Sea to Sky Highway

0   25km
0   10 miles

N

CANADA
USA

Attraction
City
Large Town
Small Town
POI
Motorway
Main Road
Minor Road
Airport
Railway

Squamish

Wedge
Mountain
▲
2890

Whistler

99   Whistler
Interpretive Forest

Whistler Blackcomb
Mountains

Brandywine Falls
Provincial Park

Garibaldi

Garibaldi
Provincial Park

Mount Garibaldi
▲
2678

Brohm Lake
Interpretive Forest

Alice Lake
Provincial Park

Brackendale Eagle
Reserve

Squamish

Stawamus Chief
Provincial Park

Shannon Falls
Provincial Park

Murrin
Provincial Park

Pinecone Burke
Provincial Park

Britannia Beach

Gleneden

Porteau Cove
Provincial Park

Howe
Sound

Lions Bay

Gibsons

Horseshoe
Bay

Mount Seymour
Provincial Park

Pitt
Lake

Bowen
Island

Lions Gate
Bridge

VANCOUVER

99

Coquilam

Burnaby

1

Maple Ridge

Vancouver

BRANDYWINE FALLS PROVINCIAL PARK

Brandywine Falls Provincial Park $
Hwy 99, 47km north of Squamish; tel: (604) 986-9371; www.env.gov.bc.ca/bcparks/explore/parkpgs/brandywi.html. Open daily.

Brandywine Falls is the centrepiece of the park, an impressive smooth and wide 66m cataract erupting from atop an ancient lava bed. Viewpoint is an easy 10-minute hike through the forest from the highway. The name dates from a brandy versus wine bet over the height of the falls by two early railway surveyors: neither had cash, so one bet brandy and the other wine.

BRITANNIA BEACH

Britannia Beach
Hwy 99, 33km north of Horseshoe Bay.

BC Museum of Mining $$
tel: (604) 896-2223, tollfree (800) 896-4044; e-mail: general@bcmuseumofmining.org; www.bcmuseumofmining.org. Open May–Oct daily 0900–1630; year round for pre-booked tours.

Once a busy support and supply town for the Britannia Mine, the largest producer of copper in the British Empire 1930–5, the broad spot along Howe Sound is bustling again as a centre for arts and crafts shops, galleries, a general store and an ever-changing list of restaurants and bistros. The car park east of Hwy 99 is also a popular spot for RCMP radar speed traps.

During some 70 years of operation, the massive Britannia Mine employed over 60,000 persons who produced some 600 million kilos of copper. The facility closed in 1974 and re-emerged as the **BC Museum of Mining**, with nearly the entire plant battered but intact. A national historic site, the facilities include mining museum displays in the heritage support buildings just off the highway to the east. Outdoor displays include a 355-tonne 'Super Mine' truck and other massive equipment. Guided tours take visitors inside the mine and tunnels to see slushers, muckers, drills and one of the last surviving gravity-fed ore concentrators in the world. If the site looks familiar, it probably is. The spooky, rust-stained shop that seems to spill down the mountainside has starred in dozens of film and TV productions over the years.

BROHM LAKE INTERPRETIVE FOREST

Brohm Lake Interpretive Forest $
Hwy 99, 13km north of Squamish; tel: (604) 898-2100.

There is fishing in the shallow lake and swimming in the clear water that seldom warms to more than frigid. Eleven kilometres of trails lead through 400ha of forest with spreading views of the Tantalus Mountain Range and one the largest ice fields in North America.

GARIBALDI PROVINCIAL PARK

There is no road access into the wilderness park but well-developed trail systems lead to five of the most popular camping and hiking

Garibaldi Provincial Park $
east of Hwy 99, Squamish–Whistler; tel: (604) 898-3678; www.garibaldipark.com. Highway signs indicate trail access. Open daily but weather may make access difficult.

areas: Black Tusk/Garibaldi Lake, Cheakamus Lake, Diamond Head, Singing Pass and Wedgemount Lake. In summer, look for azure-blue lakes, vast meadows of wild flowers, untouched stands of Douglas fir, yellow and red cedar, mountain hemlock and lodgepole pine, depending on altitude. The entire park gets heavy snow in winter but Diamond Head is particularly popular with experienced Nordic skiers and snow campers. The park is also accessible via trails from Whistler.

HORSESHOE BAY

North Vancouver Info Centre
Suite 102, 124 West 1st St, North Vancouver; tel: (604) 987-4488; e-mail: tourism@nvchamber.bc.ca; www.nvchamber.bc.ca. Open daily in summer, Mon–Fri autumn (fall)–spring.

A terminus for BC Ferries to Nanaimo (*see map page 233*) as well as more local services, Horseshoe Bay lies at the entrance to Howe Sound. A dormitory community for Vancouver, the charming town offers restaurants, pubs, shopping and a pleasant park with views across the harbour from beneath spreading shade trees.

BC Ferries
end of Hwy 1; tel: (250) 386-3431 or (888) 223-3779; www.bcferries.bc.ca

MURRIN PROVINCIAL PARK

Murrin Provincial Park $
Hwy 99, 3km north of Britannia Beach; tel: (604) 898-3678; www.env.gov.bc.ca/bcparks/ recreation/stawamus. Open daily.

Donated by BC Electric Railway and named after its president 1929–46, the park is popular for walking, picnicking, swimming, fishing, sunbathing and novice to intermediate rock climbing up the steep, almost vertical cliffs. More experienced rock climbers head for the granite cliffs of Stawamus Chief, just up the road.

PORTEAU COVE PROVINCIAL PARK

Porteau Cove Provincial Park $
Hwy 99, 25km north of Horseshoe Bay; tel: (604) 689-9025; www.env.gov.bc.ca/bcparks/ explore/parkpgs/porteau. Open daily.

On the east shore of Howe Sound, the Cove was once an important ferry landing but today is better known for beachcombing, fishing and scuba diving. Several ships have been scuttled just off the beach to the north of the pier for divers to explore. The actual cove is at the more protected south end of the park, beyond the camping area.

SHANNON FALLS PROVINCIAL PARK

Shannon Falls Provincial Park $
Hwy 99, 7km north of Britannia Beach;
call Squamish Chamber of Commerce (see below);
www.squamishchamber.com.
Open daily.

Six times the elevation of Niagara, the 335m Shannon Falls is the third highest in BC. A 5-minute walk along a pleasant but well-worn forest trail, the falls can also be viewed from your car. Best time to visit is shortly after noon when the sun highlights the falls dropping from the cliff high above. Expect crowds in summer, including motorcoach tours en route to Whistler.

SQUAMISH

Chamber of Commerce Info Centre *38551 Loggers Lane; tel: (604) 815-4994; www.squamishchamber.com. Open daily 0900–1800.*

Soo Coalition for Sustainable Forests $
Tel: (604) 892-9001.

Squamish Estuary $
West from 3rd Ave beyond Vancouver St, just southwest of town.

West Coast Railway Heritage Park $$
39645 Government Road, Squamish; tel: (604) 898-9336; www.wcra.org. Open daily 1000–1700.

At the head of a narrow corridor on Howe Sound, 'squamish' means 'mother of the winds' in the language of the Coast Salish, an appropriate description of local weather. Squamish is surrounded by sheer rock faces that heat up in the daytime sun, creating afternoon updrafts that build into world championship windsurfing gusts.

Squamish is a timber town of two minds. Forestry jobs and incomes are slowly declining while hiking, kayaking, cycling, fishing, rock climbing and other outdoor activities are growing in economic importance, and luring outsiders who hate nothing so much as the sight of logging trucks, pulp mills and clearcuts. Outdoor recreation is winning but timber interests are stringing out their measured withdrawal as long and as gracefully as possible. **Soo Coalition for Sustainable Forests**, the timber industry advocacy group, arranges mill and forest tours.

The **West Coast Railway Heritage Park** is a must-see for rail buffs, with more than four dozen vintage railway carriages and locomotive engines. Highlights include a gleaming 1890 Executive Business Carriage panelled in hand-rubbed teak, a restored Colonist Car that once carried migrants across the prairies on hard benches, the only surviving steam locomotive engine from the Pacific Great Eastern Railway that once served Howe Sound, and a gargantuan orange snowplough. **Squamish Estuary** has excellent birdwatching, especially during the spring and autumn (fall) migrations.

Accommodation and food in Squamish

Howe Sound Inn and Brewing Company $$ *37801 Cleveland Ave; tel: (604) 892-2603, tollfree (800) 919-2537; www.howesound.com.* The only brewpub on the Sound concentrates on local seafood and seasonal vegetables. Hotel rooms upstairs.

Sunflower Bakery $ *38086 Cleveland Ave; tel: (604) 892-2231; www.sunflowerbakerycafe.com.* A good source for light lunches or picnic supplies.

STAWAMUS CHIEF PROVINCIAL PARK

Stawamus Chief Provincial Park $
just north of Shannon Falls and east of Hwy 99; tel: (604) 898-3678; www.stawamuschiefpark.ca. Open daily.

Hikers and rock climbers are drawn to the 652m Chief, the second biggest granite monolith after Gibraltar, sacred to Squamish First Nations. There are some 180 different ascent routes, including a rugged walking trail that gains 550m in just 2.5km. Best spot to watch climbers is from a lay-by on the eastern side of the highway, about 1km north of the park entrance.

WHISTLER

Above
Ski rack in Whistler Village

Created in the hope of luring the Winter Olympics to Canada in the 1960s, Whistler landed the Winter Games for 2010 from the International Olympic Committee. North America's most successful mountain development may have started as a ski resort but has become just as successful – and just as busy – in summer.

Two mountains, Blackcomb and Whistler, have been trimmed and groomed for just about every mountain activity known to man or estate developer: skiing, golf, hiking, mountain biking, fishing, kayaking, rafting, canoeing, shopping, eating, drinking, climbing and snowboarding are only the beginning. The ski season extends well into summer, thanks to lifts that access high-altitude glaciers. A few hundred metres below, families with hiking boots and backpacks can watch for deer, marmots, bears and other wildlife amid alpine meadows and open forest.

At the base is Whistler Village, an artificial and hugely successful European-style pedestrian village packed with hotels, restaurants, shops, cafés, clubs, plazas, bridges, creeks, gazebos, musicians and magicians, none of them more than a 10-minute stroll away. Relaxing? No, but Whistler was designed for excitement, glamour and glitz. The original activity centre was Whistler Village, at the foot of Whistler Mountain. The Village still has more restaurants, more shops and more variety than the rest of the resort. A short walk across the valley is Upper Village, a more expensive, more exclusive and less frenetic enclave surrounding Fairmont Chateau Whistler. Smaller valleys to the south are filled with condominium developments that rely largely on the Village for services and entertainment.

For activity information in any season, contact the Whistler Resort Association and the Whistler Activity and Information Centre in the Whistler Village Conference Centre. Shops near the gondola base in

Whistler Village hire out bikes, skates and other equipment in summer and skis or snowboards in winter. Summer is Whistler's value season, as well as its most active. At the base, five lakes are strung like turquoise and green beads on a necklace, woven together with 20km of mostly paved trails for easy walking, cycling and roller blading. Six lakeside parks offer broad lawns, sandy beaches and full picnicking facilities with sailing, windsurfing, boating and fishing.

Both Whistler and Blackcomb lifts remain open, except for short maintenance periods in autumn (fall), with summer skiing on Blackcomb and hiking or mountain biking on both mountains. Other possibilities include golf, climbing, backpacking, hang-gliding, heli-hiking, jet boating, 'flight-seeing' and hay rides. Winter is Whistler's raison d'être, with 200-plus named runs and three dozen lifts. Blackcomb has the longest lift-serviced vertical in North America, 1,609m, as well as the longest uninterrupted fall-line skiing on the continent. Whistler comes a close second, with 1,530m of vertical served by lifts. Then there is Nordic skiing on valley golf courses and trails, ice skating, snow shoeing and sleigh rides.

Below
Whistler

Even if you are spending the day at Whistler, check out Fairmont Chateau Whistler at the base of two mountains. The enormous castle-like resort beneath a copper-green roof still manages to feel comfortable, thanks to touches such as Mennonite hooked rugs and quilts, and First Nations-inspired twig furniture. The Great Hall and Mallard Bar are best for people-watching. Whistler is short on history but the Whistler Museum and Archives makes the best of skiing gear from the 1960s, fishing souvenirs from the 1920s and local logging paraphernalia.

Accommodation and food in Whistler

Most Whistler hotels, inns, condos and other accommodation have their own booking number, but it is easier to book through the *Whistler Resort Association; tel: (604) 664-5625, tollfree (800) 944-7853.* Expect 2–3-night minimum stays in high season (January–March), the lowest rates in April and November–December, and mid-range rates during the rest of the year.

Araxi Ristorante $$$ *Whistler Village Sq.; tel: (604) 932-4540; www.araxi.com.* Gets raves for its pasta and wine list.

Caramba $$ *Town Plaza; tel: (604) 938-1879.* The liveliest Italian restaurant in Whistler.

Executive Inn $$ *4250 Village Stroll, Whistler Village; tel: (604) 932-3200; www.whistler.com/executive.* One of the better mid-range hotels with kitchens and plenty of room for families.

Fairmont Chateau Whistler $$$ *4599 Chateau Blvd, Upper Village; tel: (604) 938-8000; www.fairmont.com/whistler.* The best address for visitors in town.

Ingrid's Village Café $ *102, 4305 Skiers Approach, Whistler Village; tel: (604) 932-7000.* Worth the out-the-door queues for vegetarian dishes.

Pan Pacific Whistler Mountainside $$$ *4320 Sundial Cres., Whistler Village; tel: (604) 905-2999, tollfree (888) 905-9995; www.panpacific.com.* Has full-kitchen suites and a few steps from both Whistler and Blackcomb gondolas.

Residence Inn $$ *4899 Painted Cliff Rd, Upper Village; tel: (604) 905-3400, tollfree (800) 331-3131; www.whistlerblackcomb.com.* Has a prime ski-in, ski-out location midway up the base of Blackcomb Mountain.

Thai One On $$ *4557 Blackcomb Way in Le Chamois Hotel, Upper Village; tel: (604) 932-4822.* A calm refuge with good Thai dishes.

Zeuski's Mediterranean Cuisine $ *Unit 40, 4314 Main St, Town Plaza; tel: (604) 932-6009; www.zeuskis.com.* Cheerful, cheap and always busy.

WHISTLER INTERPRETIVE FOREST

Whistler Interpretive Forest
$ *Hwy 99, 9km north of Brandywine Fall Provincial Park; tel: (604) 935-8398. Open daily.*

There is an extensive and well-marked network of hiking and mountain biking trails throughout a working forest between Hwy 99 and Garibaldi Provincial Park. Watch for logging trucks and be sure to park entirely off the roadway. Almost directly across Hwy 99 is Function Junction, a service area for Whistler Resort. There are bakeries, hardware stores, a brewery, plumbers and all the mechanical and service functions that resorts like to keep out of sight.

Suggested tour

Total distance: 120km.

Time: 2–4 hours, depending on traffic.

Links: The Squamish Highway (Hwy 99) connects to Vancouver (*see page 268*) to the south, or continue north on Hwy 99 to the Gold Rush Trail (*see page 140*) near Hat Creek Ranch (*see page 143*).

Route: From **WHISTLER ❶**, take Hwy 99, the Sea to Sky Highway, south to **BRANDYWINE FALLS PROVINCIAL PARK ❷** and Daisy Lake. Continue south towards **SQUAMISH ❸**, a timber town that is turning towards outdoor recreation.

Just south is **SHANNON FALLS PROVINCIAL PARK ❹** with one of the highest waterfalls in BC, a 5-minute walk from the car park, and Stawamus Chief, a massive peak that is a favourite with rock climbers. Continue south to **BRITANNIA BEACH ❺** and the Britannia Mine, a museum that was once the largest copper producer in the British Empire. Eight kilometres south is **PORTEAU COVE ❻**, a one-time ferry landing for Howe Sound ferry service that has become a popular park for beachcombing, boating, fishing and scuba diving.

The views become spectacular, and can be enjoyed from several lay-bys which are accessible only from the southbound lanes. Hwy 1, the Trans-Canada Highway, runs to the ferry line-up at **HORSESHOE BAY ❼**. Follow signs eastbound to West Vancouver and over the Lions Gate Bridge, built by the Irish brewing Guinness family in 1938 to link British properties on the North Shore to Vancouver.

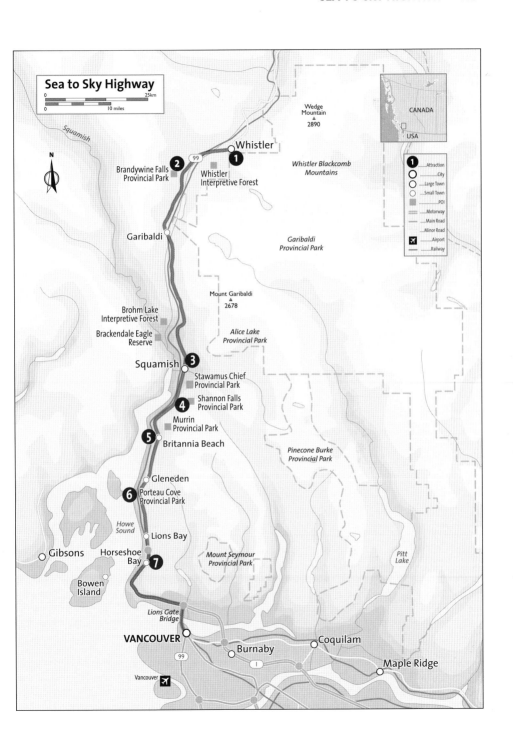

Sea to Sky Highway

0   25km
0   10 miles

Squamish

Wedge
Mountain
2890

CANADA

USA

Whistler
99
② Brandywine Falls
Provincial Park
Whistler
Interpretive Forest
①

Whistler Blackcomb
Mountains

N

① ......Attraction
○ ......City
○ ......Large Town
○ ......Small Town
■ ......POI
......Motorway
......Main Road
......Minor Road
✈ ......Airport
......Railway

Garibaldi

Garibaldi
Provincial Park

Mount Garibaldi
2678

Brohm Lake
Interpretive Forest
Brackendale Eagle
Reserve

Alice Lake
Provincial Park

Squamish ③

Stawamus Chief
Provincial Park
Shannon Falls
④ Provincial Park
Murrin
Provincial Park

⑤ Britannia Beach

Pinecone Burke
Provincial Park

Gleneden
⑥ Porteau Cove
Provincial Park

Howe
Sound Lions Bay

Gibsons Horseshoe
Bay ⑦

Bowen
Island

Mount Seymour
Provincial Park

Pitt
Lake

Lions Gate
Bridge

VANCOUVER
99

Coquilam

Burnaby
1

Maple Ridge

Vancouver ✈

Shuswap Lakes

Ratings

Children	●●●●●
Lakes	●●●●●
Mountains	●●●●●
Nature	●●●●●
Outdoor activities	●●●●●
Scenery	●●●●●
Parks	●●●●○
Food and drink	●●●○○

The scenic Shuswap lakes region contains an oasis of long, narrow lakes, linked to rivers that are home to some of the most amazing salmon runs in the world. The lakes, soaring mountains and sandy beaches are easy to reach from the Trans-Canada Highway. The Shuswap, a band of Salishan linguistic stock whose origin and meaning is unknown, have lived in the region for thousands of years. Some 5,000 Shuswap now live on reserves in the area, a region much smaller than their original vast hunting territory. Wild and historic, the Shuswap region is abundant with deer, osprey, golden eagles and black bears. Shuswap Lake is the magnet for fleets of houseboats which are drawn to the protected waters, and some 20 small marine parks. Highways skirt tiny historic towns, and follow rail lines which trace lakeshores and river canyons past rugged peaks and foaming waterfalls.

CHASE

ℹ Chase and District Chamber of Commerce
400 Shuswap Ave; tel: (250) 679-8432; www.chasechamber.com. Open Jul and Aug daily 0800–1700; Sept–Jun Mon–Fri 0800–1600.

 Chase Museum and Archives $
1042 Shuswap Ave; tel: (250) 679-8847. Open summer daily 1000–1600.

A carpenter from New York who was not lucky enough to strike gold in the Cariboo instead found fortune building a timber and cattle town. Chase is better known today for its outdoor recreation opportunities: canoeing down 55km of calm water to Kamloops, fishing, houseboating, hiking, swimming, golfing and winter skiing. The town is surrounded by calm pine forests at the head of Little Shuswap Lake. The municipal beach is particularly scenic and popular. **The Chase Museum and Archives**, the former Blessed Sacrament Church, is filled to the rafters with the town's first physician's office, the gleaming mahogany bar from an early hotel, an antique barber's chair and everything in-between. **Niskonlith Lake Provincial Park** (*8km northwest of Chase on Niskonlith Lake; tel: (250) 851-3000; www.env.gov.bc.ca/bcparks/explore/parkpgs/niskonli. Open Apr–Oct*) has camping, magnificent wild-flower displays in May and June and good rainbow trout fishing year round.

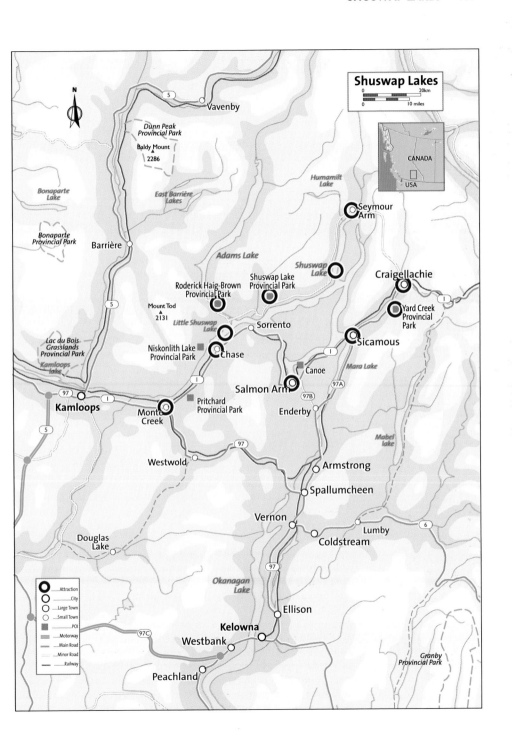

Shuswap Lakes

CRAIGELLACHIE

Craigellachie $
Hwy 1, east of Sicamous; tel: (250) 837-5345, tollfree (800) 487-1493. Gift shop open daily in summer.

A stone cairn, caboose and railway station-type souvenir shop commemorate the driving of the last spike to complete the Canadian Pacific Railway in 1885.

LITTLE SHUSWAP LAKE

Little Shuswap Lake $ *north and east of Chase to Adams River and Little River.*

Little Shuswap is the smallest of the Shuswap lakes but has the most accessible beaches from the Trans-Canada Highway.

MONTE CREEK

The hamlet and railway station at Monte Creek are best known as the site of an abortive railway robbery in 1906 by the infamous 'gentleman bandit', Bill Miner, who netted less than $15. Miner was captured, sentenced to life in prison, escaped, and eventually landed in a US prison for later robberies. A romantic Hollywood film about Miner, *The Grey Fox*, was filmed in the area.

RODERICK HAIG-BROWN PROVINCIAL PARK

Roderick Haig-Brown Provincial Park $ *North of Hwy 1 at Squilax; www.env.gov.bc.ca/bcparks/explore/parkspgs/roderick*

The park surrounds and protects 11km of the Adams River between Adams Lake and Little Shuswap Lake. The river has the largest sockeye run in North America, well over one million of the bright-red fish fighting their way up the Fraser and North Thompson rivers to spawn every fourth year (2010 is the next time). Off-years merely feature a few hundred thousand salmon plus attendant bears, eagles, ravens, mink, gulls and other wildlife. Observation decks provide a clear view of spawning, with naturalists on hand during the height of the late summer–autumn (fall) salmon runs.

SALMON ARM

Opposite
Salmon Arm golf course

The commercial centre of the Shuswap lakes region, Salmon Arm was born as a fruit and dairy town on the rich floodplain of the Salmon River, which enters Shuswap Lake here. The town and the south arm of Shuswap Lake were named 'salmon' because of the massive runs of salmon that made their way from the Pacific Ocean each year. The

ℹ️ **Salmon Arm and District Chamber of Commerce** #101, 20 Hudson Ave NE; tel: (250) 832-2230 or (877) 725-6667; www.sachamber.bc.ca. Open in summer daily 0800–1800; in winter Mon–Fri 0830–1630.

🏛️ **R J Haney Heritage Park and Museum** $ 751 Hwy 97NE, 4km east of Salmon Arm; tel: (250) 832-5243; e-mail:hpark@ jetstream.net; www.salmonarmmuseum.org. Open 1000–1700, see website for more information

Rotary Peace Park and Public Wharf $ Marine Park Dr. at the lake.

salmon disappeared when faulty railway construction blocked the Fraser River at Hell's Gate (*see page 144*) in 1912, destroying the fish run. Even without the salmon, Salmon Arm is a popular port to hire houseboats (like floating RVs) to explore the far reaches of Shuswap Lake. The **R J Haney Heritage Park and Museum** includes a historic church, farm buildings and schoolhouse. **Rotary Peace Park** and **Public Wharf**, a 250m pier and walkway, curves out from the park with excellent views of shorebirds and waterfowl. At least 150 different species of birds nest around the mouth of the Salmon River each spring. Best breeding displays are April–June.

Accommodation and food in Salmon Arm

Motels line the Trans-Canada Highway through the town, or to explore Shuswap Lake by water, hire a houseboat.

Salmon Arm Bay Houseboat Vacations $$ *tel: (250) 832-2745*. One of several local operators.

SEYMOUR ARM

 Seymour Arm
*North end of Seymour
Arm, the northern most arm
of Shuswap Lake, 47km
north of Anglemont by
logging road.*

A few old buildings still line the streets but the restaurant, pub, general store and a small hotel are all at the wharf on Bughouse Bay. The town is accessible by road in summer and by ferry from Sicamous all year.

SHUSWAP LAKE

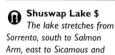 **Shuswap Lake $**
*The lake stretches from
Sorrento, south to Salmon
Arm, east to Sicamous and
north to Seymour Arm.*

The narrow, H-shaped lake is the most popular houseboating destination in BC. The 1,000km of shoreline tends to be steep with no shoals or reefs. Warm summer weather means few storms and no heavy waves. Nineteen species of fish keep anglers busy year round.

SHUSWAP LAKE PROVINCIAL PARK

 **Shuswap Lake
Provincial Park $**
*272 campsites;
www.env.gov.bc.ca/bcparks/
explore/parkpgs/shuswap*

The 149ha park has 272 campsites on the shores of Shuswap Lake, a huge area with 1,000km of shoreline. Depressions of a 3,000-year-old village, a reconstructed kekuli (pit house) and Copper Island 2km offshore are big attractions. Shuswap Lake Provincial Marine Park has 26 campsites on the shores of the lake, many accessible only by water. The sites are very popular with houseboaters.

SICAMOUS

**ⓘ Sicamous and
District Chamber
of Commerce**
*110 Finlayson St (near
Government Dock); tel:
(250) 836-3313;
www.sicamouschamber.bc.ca.
Open daily in summer
0900–1700; winter Mon–Fri.*

Ⓓ D Dutchman Dairy
*$ Hwy 1, 1km east of
Sicamous; tel: (250) 836-
4304. Open daily
0800–2100 (summer),
0800–1800 (winter).*

The name comes from a Secwepemc word that means 'narrow' or 'squeezed in the middle', a good name for the tiny narrows between Mara and Shuswap lakes. The one-time railway camp has become a resort town that is especially popular with houseboaters: local operators have more than 300 vessels to rent, no experience required. **D Dutchman Dairy** has an exotic game farm and 50 flavours of what aficionados call BC's best commercial ice cream. Even coach tours stop for a cone: highly recommended is the banana and black walnut.

Accommodation and food in Sicamous

Motels and restaurants line the Trans-Canada Highway and Hwy 97A from Vernon.

Sicamous Inn $$ *806 Trans-Canada Hwy E, Sicamous; tel: (250) 836-4117, tollfree (800) 485-7698; www.sicamousinn.ca.* The largest in town, with the best facilities.

Right
D Dutchman Dairy

Below
Houseboats at Sicamous

YARD CREEK PROVINCIAL PARK

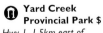 **Yard Creek**
Provincial Park $
Hwy 1, 1.5km east of
Sicamous; tel: (250) 851-
3000; www.env.gov.bc.ca/
bcparks/explore/parkpgs/yard

This wet, upland forest has excellent birdwatching and pleasant hiking trails beneath hemlock and cedars along a sparkling creek, and is a popular camping and picnic spot.

David Thompson

Born into poverty in Westminster, England in 1770, David Thompson apprenticed as a clerk with the Hudson's Bay Company, arriving on the shores of Hudson Bay at the tender age of 14. Thompson studied surveying and mapmaking while recovering from a broken leg, an incident that took most of a year to mend but changed his life. After a frustrating stint with the Hudson's Bay Company, he left to join the rival North West Co. to map their outposts and waterways. Using Rocky Mountain House as a base, Thompson mapped the fur-trading territories east of the Rocky Mountains, the uncharted Columbia River basin, and present-day British Columbia, Washington, Oregon, Idaho and Montana. Over his career, Thompson travelled by foot, horse and canoe an amazing 88,000km. Thompson's precise maps were used well into the 20th century, yet when Canada's greatest geographer died near Montreal at the age of 87, he passed away in poverty and virtual obscurity.

The Last Spike

The carrot to lure BC into Confederation in 1871 was a promise by the government in Ottawa to provide a transcontinental railway linking the British colony with the rest of Canada. After a scandal that brought down the Government, the contract was awarded to the Canadian Pacific Railway. One of the great engineering projects of the day, it was nevertheless an enormous financial burden for a young country of only 3.5 million. Five years later and fifteen impatient years after signing the accord 'The Last Spike' was driven by Lord Strathcona on 7 November 1885 at Craigellachie, 25km northeast of Sicamous, a tiny village where crews from the east and west met. Craigellachie was named by fur trader and CPR financier Lord Strathcona (Donald Smith) after a rocky crag near his home town in Morayshire, Scotland.

Suggested tour

Total distance: 160km.

Time: 2 hours to drive; 2–5 days to explore.

Links: Columbia River (*see page 122*) and Revelstoke are just east on the Trans-Canada Highway (Hwy 1); Kamloops (*see page 191*) is just west.

Route: The Trans-Canada Highway (Hwy 1) passes by **CRAIGELLACHIE ❶**, the village where the 'last spike' was driven in 1885 for the transcontinental Canadian Pacific Railway. The highway continues on to **YARD CREEK PROVINCIAL PARK ❷**.

Just beyond is **SICAMOUS ❸**, appropriately named by Secwepemc (or Shuswap) 'in the middle', straddling the narrow junction of Shuswap

Opposite
Shuswap Lake

Lake and Mara Lake, where Hwy 97A stretches southwards to Vernon and the Okanagan Valley (*see page 198*). The best place to admire Shuswap Lake, a vast lake system that extends north, south and west, is the Shuswap Rest Area, a picnic area east of Canoe on the north side of Hwy 1.

Continue along the Trans-Canada Highway past the junction with Hwy 97B, another artery which leads south to Vernon and the Okanagan Valley. If the valley seems hazy, blame the lumber mill at Canoe, which still burns sawdust and other waste. Hwy 1 leads to **SALMON ARM ❹**, a small picturesque town at the end of one of Shuswap Lake's four long arms.

Continue on to Sorrento, named after the romantic Italian town, a tiny community that swells to more than 4,000 in summer when motels, resorts, RV parks and campsites fill up. Hwy 1 continues west to Squilax and the turnoff just beyond to **SHUSWAP LAKE PROVINCIAL PARK ❺**, a favoured family holiday area. Continue west across the North Shuswap (Squilax) Bridge over the Little River. The 4km river between the two Shuswap lakes was once a thriving trade centre for Secwepemc. The river is better known today for trout fishing in February, March and October. Jade Mountain Lookout offers broad views of Little Shuswap Lake.

The Trans-Canada Highway and South Thompson River descend to **CHASE ❻**, a ranching and lumber town on the south shore of Little Shuswap Lake. The earliest known human remains in BC, a man trapped in a mudflow about 8,000 years ago, were found along Gore Creek, near the north end of the bridge at Pritchard.

The high cliffs on the north side of the river have been eroded into an irregular series of columns and buttresses that can take on fantastic shapes in the late afternoon light. Hwy 1 follows the river west to **MONTE CREEK ❼**.

Detour: From Craigellachie, take the gravel logging road north to **SEYMOUR ARM ❽**, a village that was once a boomtown during the 1880s Big Bend Gold Rush; the general store still has a working old glass hand pump for petrol. Continue in a southwesterly direction on the Squilax–Anglemont Road through the hamlets of Anglemont, Magna Bay, Scotch Creek and Lee Creek, and **Shuswap Lake Provincial Park**. The road angles northwest to **RODERICK HAIG-BROWN PROVINCIAL PARK ❾** and the Adams River.

Little Shuswap Lake Road runs to Quaaout Lodge, a resort and outdoor recreation centre owned by the Squilax/Little Shuswap Lake First Nation. The popular resort is jammed mid-July when the Nation hosts the annual Squilax Powwow, drawing attendees from across North America. Continue on to the Trans-Canada Highway and Squilax.

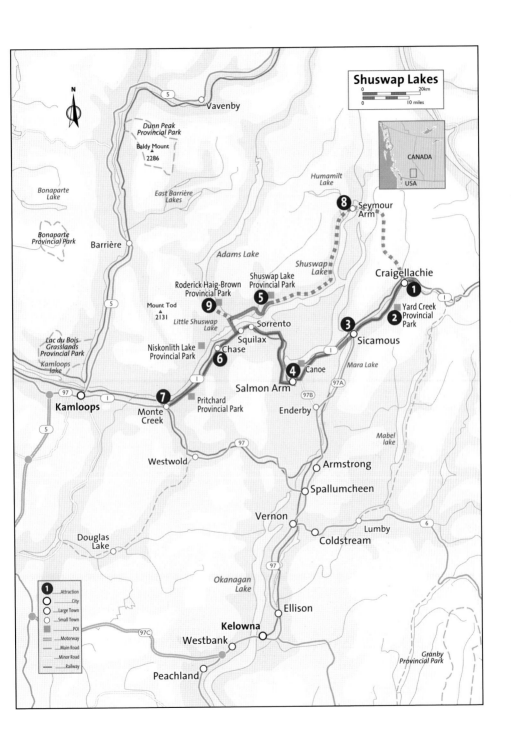

Train travel

Ratings

Heritage	●●●●●
Mountains	●●●●●
Nature	●●●●●
Railways	●●●●●
Scenery	●●●●●
Children	●●●●○
Food and drink	●●●●○
Entertainment	●●●○○

'Bonds of steel': railways influenced the development of Canada and especially Alberta and BC like no other industry. When settlers, miners, gold rush prospectors and immigrants raced west to claim land or resources, many took the train. Returning by rail to Eastern Canada were the raw materials from the land, forest, ocean and rivers, along with cattle and cultivated crops. BC was lured into Confederation as a province in 1871 with the assurance by the Government that a transcontinental link would be built within a decade. The completion of the Canadian Pacific Railway was formalised with the Last Spike driven in 1885, followed the next year by the first CPR passenger train from Montreal which arrived at the Vancouver suburb of Port Moody. Passenger routes today wind leisurely along craggy mountain massifs, crawl through river canyons, skirt shimmering lakes, and traverse deserts, ranchlands and golden grainfields.

ALBERTA PRAIRIE RAILWAY EXCURSIONS

Alberta Prairie Railway Excursions
$$$ PO Box 1600, Stettler, AB T0C 2L0; tel: (403) 742-2811 (Stettler); tollfree in Canada (800) 282-3994; e-mail: info@absteamtrain.com; www.absteamtrain.com. Open mid-May–mid-Oct. Trips vary in length from 4–8 hours; reservations recommended by phone.

Route: 67km from Stettler–Big Valley–Stettler.

Just as the train leaves the station, it comes to a screeching halt when the dreaded Bolton Gang holds up the train. After Gabriel Dumont arrests the bandits and donates the loot to children's charities, the train continues on to Big Valley, a divisional point for the former Canadian Northern Railway. On the return trip, actors in period costume sing and reminisce about the 'good ole days'. On most trips, all the excitement concludes with a hearty Alberta roast beef dinner.

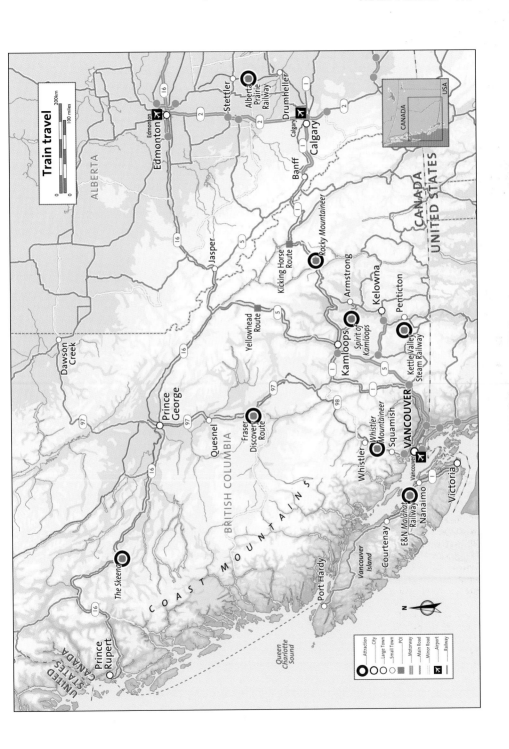

E&N *MALAHAT* RAILWAY

 E&N *Malahat*
Railway $$
VIA Rail Canada; tel: tollfree
(888) 842-7245;
www.viarail.ca. Runs daily.

Route: Victoria–Duncan–Nanaimo–Parksville–Courtenay.

There is only one class on the *Malahat* yet everyone can get on and off as many times as they wish and can order stops on request, a fine way to venture leisurely beyond Duncan's totem poles, Nanaimo's Bastion near the marina and Parksville's swimming beach. The Chemainus murals are worth a stop, a wallside composite history of First Nations, first settlers, Chinese merchants, lumberjacks, fishers and the railway. Unlimited stopovers are permitted but there is no provision for left luggage so travel light.

FRASER DISCOVERY ROUTE

 Rocky Mountaineer
$$ *Rocky Mountain*
Vacations, Pacific Central
Station, 1755 Cottrell St,
Vancouver; tel: (604) 606-
7245, tollfree (Canada and
US) (877) 460-3200, tollfree
(UK) 0800 0606 7372;
e-mail: reservations@
rockymountaineer.com;
www.rockymountaineer.com.
Operating hours Mon–Fri
0600–1900, Sat and Sun
0800–1600.

This new two-day all-daylight train journey made its debut May 2005 to provide a vital link between Canada's West and the Rockies. Dubbed in recognition of Simon Fraser who explored the region in the early 1800s, modern guests get to travel in considerably more comfort than the explorer did. Linking up with the *Whistler Mountaineer* in the resort town of Whistler, the premium GoldLeaf Service boasts exemplary personal service in bi-level glass domed coaches and an elegant private dining room. The more economical RedLeaf Service has assigned spacious reclining seats with at-your-seat meal service. The train moves from the lush farmland of the Pemberton Valley to the desert-like conditions of the Fraser Canyon where the turbulent waters of the Fraser River (one of the world's largest salmon rivers) provide dramatic views. Passing through the rolling hills and forests of the Cariboo, the open ranch lands in the Chilcotin and Prince George, the main cheering squad now consists mainly of moose, bear, elk, eagles and deer.

Opposite
The train is dwarfed by the natural landscape

KETTLE VALLEY STEAM RAILWAY

 Kettle Valley
Steam Railway $
Prairie Valley Station, west
side of Summerland; tel:
(250) 494-8422, tollfree
(877) 494-8424;
www.kettlevalleyrail.org.
Open mid-May–Jun and early
Sept–mid-Oct Sat–Mon,
Jul–early Sept Thur–Mon;
departs 1030 and 1330.

Route: 10km route from Prairie Valley Station to Canyon View Siding.

One of BC's few operational steam trains takes passengers on a 2-hr journey along a preserved section of the Kettle Valley Railway. Part of the CPR-owned 500km Coast-to-Kootenay line, the KVR crosses the Trout Creek Bridge (the highest bridge built on the original KVR line) over a canyon 73m above Trout Creek and chugs along hillsides overlooking beautiful orchards and vineyards in the Okanagan Valley. Well-informed guides bring the history of the railway to life.

ROCKY MOUNTAINEER VACATIONS

Rocky Mountaineer Vacations $$$
1755 Cottrell St, Vancouver;
tel: (604) 606-7245, tollfree
(Canada and US) (877) 460-
3200, freephone (UK) 0800
0606 7372; e-mail:
reservations@
rockymountaineer.com;
www.rockymountaineer.com.
Runs May–early Oct, with
Dec winter trips.

Route: Calgary–Banff–Kamloops–Vancouver or Jasper–Kamloops–Vancouver.

The *Rocky Mountaineer* (*RM*) tours live up to their billing as the 'Most Spectacular Train Trip in the World', travelling a route abandoned by VIA Rail. The heavily booked tourist train offers good steward service, food and, above all, stunning scenery. Expect occasional stops or slow-downs for wildlife spotting. The *RM* waits for commercial traffic, so schedules are not precise, enhancing the feeling of travelling back in time when nature (avalanche, flood or rockslide) or business (a freight train with more priority) could affect railway operations.

GoldLeaf Service, with roomy seats, has much-coveted dome car views, whose windows are kept clean despite often misty or rainy weather. White linen and flower-vase dining is below the dome car level. RedLeaf Service passengers benefit from access to landings between cars, a spot favoured by photographers. Meals served at your seat are box lunches of excellent quality. Snacks are non-stop.

Below
The *Rocky Mountaineer*

The *RM* provides a tabloid newspaper upon boarding, a Mile Marker by Mile Marker key to the routes, scenery, engineering feats, commercial development and ethnology the train passes through. With the tabloid guide, it is impossible to be lost even though the *RM* traverses about 1,000km and seven (roughly) 200km divisions over track controlled by two railway companies – Canadian National and Canadian Pacific.

The *RM* trains from Calgary and Jasper follow the same route to Vancouver from Kamloops. As the train leaves Kamloops and criss-crosses the Fraser and Thompson river canyons, who can resist the sight of an occasional raft upriver from Suicide Rapids or the evocatively named Jaws of Death Gorge? The *RM* travels down the Fraser River Canyon, gathering a collective gasp at gondolas moving across the river almost into the train at Hell's Gate Gorge. The train continues west through the sprawling suburbs, across the Alex Fraser Bridge and into Vancouver's Pacific Central Station.

Calgary–Kamloops: the *RM* leaves urban density behind for the rolling foothills as the Rocky Mountains loom larger with each passing mile. The train pulls into Banff townsite where passengers may continue on or take an exhausting but rewarding all-day motorcoach tour to the Columbia Icefields, with stops at Athabasca, Sunwapta Falls, Peyto Lake and Lake Louise. The tour is also available from Jasper. Return to the train and continue on to Kamloops.

Jasper–Kamloops: Mount Edith Cavell is on the left as the train leaves Jasper townsite. Yellowhead Pass, used by the Grand Trunk Pacific and Canadian Northern Railway (predecessors to Canadian National Railway), is the crossing rejected by the CPR as not southerly enough to protect Canadian interests against American railways. The *RM* stops briefly for photographers at lovely Pyramid Falls and follows the North Thompson River to Kamloops where passengers disembark. The major routes are the Fraser Discovery, the Yellowhead and the Kicking Horse.

THE SKEENA

The Skeena $$$
VIA Rail Canada; tel: tollfree (888) 842-7245; www.viarail.ca. Runs three times weekly. During peak season (mid-May to late Sept), a fourth is added.

Route: Prince Rupert–Jasper.

An overnight stop in Prince George is a welcome pause along the 2-day 1,160km route that follows the track of the early 20th-century Grand Trunk Pacific Railway. *The Skeena* leaves Prince Rupert, threading through its namesake canyon, often giving credence to the Skeena's name, 'river of mists', continuing east through the land of First Nations and the Gitxsan, preserving the world's largest collection of standing totem poles. After Prince George, the *Skeena* passes by the landmark Mount Robson on the left, over the Yellowhead Pass and into Jasper National Park and the townsite.

THE SPIRIT OF KAMLOOPS

 Spirit of Kamloops
$ 6–510 Lorne St, tel:
(250) 374-2141; e-mail:
info@kamrail.com;
www.kamrail.com. Operates
Jul and Aug Mon and Fri
1900, Sat 1100, 1900.

Route: From Kamloops to Armstrong, 115-mile round trip.

The fully restored steam locomotive 2141 *Spirit of Kamloops* offers passengers a journey back to the golden age of steam-powered railway travel while seated in open-air hayrack cars or in the comfort of the 406 Pioneer Park 1930 heritage coach. Departing from the historic CN Station at 510 Lorne Street, passengers can take in the sights and sounds of steam as they journey through grasslands, tunnels, lakes and hill country. They even get to experience a little of a bygone era's danger when the notorious train robber, Billy Miner, stages a little train robbing courtesy of the BX Stagecoach Company.

WHISTLER MOUNTAINEER

 Whistler Mountaineer $$$
Rocky Mountain Vacations,
Pacific Central Station,
1755 Cottrell St, Vancouver;
tel: (604) 606-7245,
tollfree (Canada and US)
(877) 460-3200, freephone
(UK) 0800 0606 7372;
e-mail: reservations@
rockymountaineer.com; www.
whistlermountaineer.com.
Operates from May to Oct
with daily departures.

Launched in May 2006, *The Whistler Mountaineer*, is a new three-hour rail journey that follows the magnificent 'sea to sky' coastal highway linking up two world-class destinations: Vancouver and Whistler. With its unique perspective hugging the shore most of the route, passengers dine while passing a tableau of Pacific Ocean, forests and the snow-capped Coastal mountains. Two classes of service are available – Coast Classic where a light meal and beverage are served and Glacier Dome where passengers have maximum views through wide glass dome windows during breakfast service or classic high tea. Some scenic highlights include Shannon Falls, Mt Garibaldi rising 2,672m above sea level, Cheakamus Canyon where the river tumbles into a craggy gorge and Brandywine Falls.

Suggested tour

Time: 5–8 days, depending on connections and season.

Links: For major stations, see Vancouver (*page 268*), Victoria (*see page 248*), Kamloops (*see page 191*), Jasper and Banff (*see pages 84–89*), Prince George and Prince Rupert. Central Vancouver Island covers stops on the E&N *Malahat*. At Prince Rupert, disembarking *Skeena* passengers can take an Inside Passage Ferry Cruise (*see page 184*) to Port Hardy.

Route: The railway companies work together to offer combination packages that involve motorcoach and ferries where appropriate. Most tourist rail excursions run from approximately May–September, depending on route and snowfall. There are also regular routes such as

Opposite
Heading into the Rockies

VIA Rail's transcontinental *Canadian* from Vancouver to Toronto. A cross-Canada railway excursion provides an excellent introduction to geography before hiring a car and taking to the road. Rail buffs will want to take the train to see the two Western provinces with all their varied scenery and rolling stock.

Rockies to Coast Great Circle Route: (Eastern Loop). Take the motorcoach from Calgary to Banff and board the *ROCKY MOUNTAINEER* **(Kicking Horse Route)** ❶ from Banff to Kamloops. Overnight and re-board the *Rocky Mountaineer* to Vancouver ❷. The next morning, take the *WHISTLER MOUNTAINEER* ❸ to Whistler. Overnight in Whistler before climbing on board *Rocky Mountaineer's* **FRASER DISCOVERY ROUTE** ❹ from Whistler to Prince George. Overnight in Prince George. Board the next morning for the last leg to Jasper. From here, a good option is to see the highlights between Jasper and Banff via the Icefields Parkway ❺ on a guided motorcoach tour before returning to Calgary.

Alternate route: Starting in Vancouver, take the *WHISTLER MOUNTAINEER* to Whistler, continue on the *ROCKY MOUNTAINEER* (Fraser Discovery Route) to Jasper. Board the *ROCKY MOUNTAINEER* (Yellowhead Route) back to Vancouver via Kamloops.

Great Coast Circle: (Western loop, shown green on map). Take a BC Ferry from Vancouver to Victoria and board the E&N *MALAHAT* ❻ to Courtenay, then a motorcoach to Port Hardy at the north end of Vancouver Island. Catch a BC Ferry to Prince Rupert and board *THE SKEENA* ❼ going east and follow the curves of the broad, high-walled super-scenic Skeena River Valley to Prince George. Take the *ROCKY MOUNTAINEER* back to Vancouver.

The Silk Trains

Roaring across Canada in the early 20th century, Silk Trains transported bales of Chinese silk from the docks of Vancouver to the silk mills in New York City. The 'Silkers' set speed records that have yet to be broken as speed, security and safety were vital. Canadian Pacific freight trains carried the valuable cargo in up to 15 airtight boxcars. With preference over all trains, a Silker once had priority over Prince Albert, later King George VI, as he and his entourage waited on a siding for a racing train. Man-made fibres and the advent of air travel ended the exotic Silk Train era during World War II.

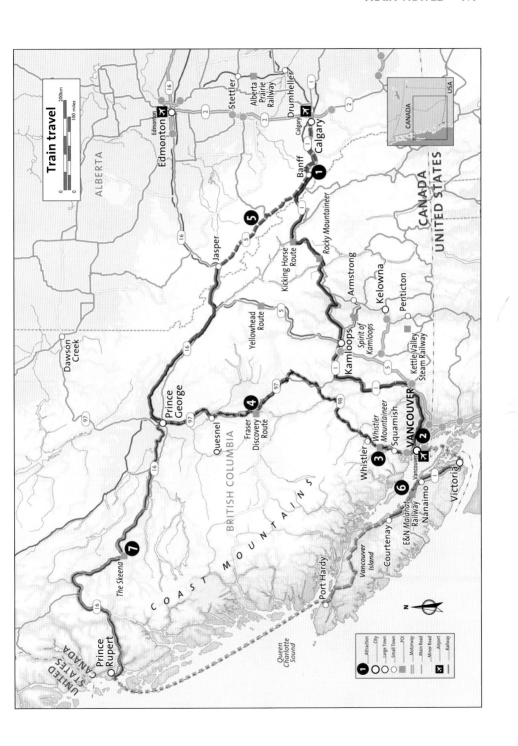

Train travel

200km
100 miles

Attraction ❶
City ◯
Large Town ◯
Small Town ◯
POI ■
Motorway
Main Road
Minor Road
Airport ✈
Railway

Ferry cruises

Ratings

History	●●●●●
Mountains	●●●●●
Nature	●●●●●
Scenery	●●●●●
Wildlife	●●●●●
Children	●●●●○
Food and drink	●●●○○
Villages	●●●○○

Operating one of the biggest fleets in the world, BC Ferries' 36 vessels navigate the province's varied waters with ferries ranging from the 34m *Nimpkish* to the jumbo 170m *Spirit of Vancouver Island*. Strictly speaking, the ferries are transportation for vehicles and passengers but even the most everyday ferry run can take on the air of a cruise when the sun shines bright and temperatures rise. On the north coast, a ferry trip is more adventure than transportation. Navigating the waters of the Inside Passage from Bella Coola, Prince Rupert and Port Hardy, a ferry voyage is the best way, and often the only route, to enjoy some of North America's most awesome coastal vistas. Expect to see snow-capped peaks dropping steeply into icy fiords lined with dark green forests, and do not be surprised to see nothing at all if a storm blows through.

BELLA BELLA/MCLOUGHLIN BAY

⊘ **Bella Bella/
McLoughlin Bay
Heiltsuk Band
Administration**
*Tel: (250) 957-2381. See
Quest Adventures, tel: (250)
957-2774.*

The Heiltsuk, based at Bella Bella (Waglisla), are opening the door to tourism slowly and cautiously. While hospitable, the Heiltsuk restrict tourists generally to McLoughlin Bay, 3km south of the village. The purser may say that Bella Bella is too far to walk during the short port call but it is not too far for several local artists to set up shop on the dock when the *Queen of Chilliwack* calls, including famed silversmith Peter Gladstone. McLoughlin Bay is also a popular stop for kayakers setting off for or returning from camping trips through the Hakai Recreation Area (*see page 182*). If the weather is reasonable, that is, anything blowing less than a full gale, walk a few hundred metres down the crushed shell beach to the traditional-style longhouse. Built by Heiltsuk carvers Frank and Kathy Brown, the longhouse is a combination of local history museum, Aboriginal art gallery and simple restaurant specialising in salmon roasted on cedar plants over

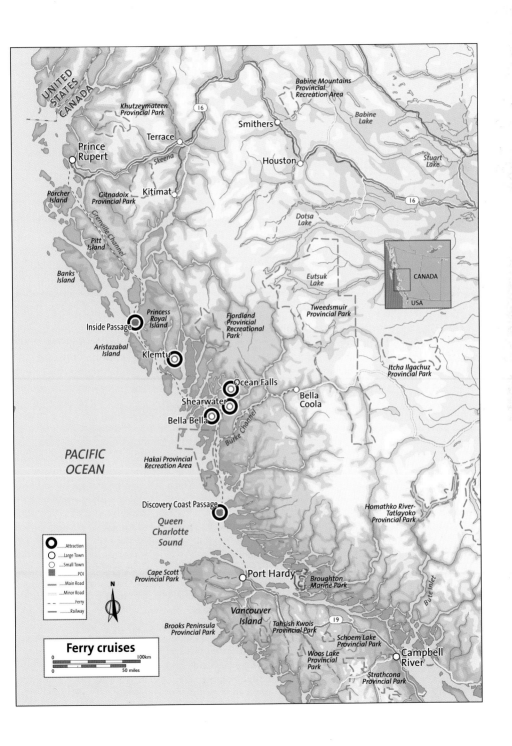

PACIFIC
OCEAN

UNITED
STATES
CANADA

Khutzeymateen
Provincial Park

Babine Mountains
Provincial
Recreation Area

Babine
Lake

Smithers

Terrace

Prince
Rupert

Skeena

Houston

Stuart
Lake

Porcher
Island

Gitnadoix
Provincial Park

Kitimat

Banks
Island

Pitt
Island

Grenville Channel

Dotsa
Lake

Eutsuk
Lake

CANADA

USA

Princess
Royal
Island

Inside Passage

Aristazabal
Island

Klemtu

Flordland
Provincial
Recreational
Park

Tweedsmuir
Provincial Park

Itcha Ilgachuz
Provincial Park

Ocean Falls

Shearwater

Bella Bella

Bella
Coola

Burke Channel

Hakai Provincial
Recreation Area

Discovery Coast Passage

Homathko River-
Tatlayoko
Provincial Park

Queen
Charlotte
Sound

Cape Scott
Provincial Park

Port Hardy

Broughton
Marine Park

Bute Inlet

Vancouver
Island

Brooks Peninsula
Provincial Park

Tahsish Kwois
Provincial Park

Schoem Lake
Provincial Park

Woos Lake
Provincial
Park

Campbell
River

Strathcona
Provincial Park

N

Attraction
Large Town
Small Town
POI
Main Road
Minor Road
Ferry
Railway

Ferry cruises

0   100km

0   50 miles

an open fire. Brown also takes passengers on a 1-hour paddle in the Glwa, a traditional Heiltsuk canoe carved from a single cedar log. The trip passes old totem poles, deserted fish canneries, ravens, eagles, orcas, herons, dolphins and often bear and deer before rejoining the *Queen of Chilliwack* in the next port, Shearwater. On ferry trips that stop at Shearwater but not McLoughlin Bay, Brown brings his authentically carved canoe out to meet the ship and take on paddlers. Seats on the canoe are limited and popular with repeat passengers, so sign up immediately after boarding the *Queen of Chilliwack*.

DISCOVERY COAST PASSAGE: BELLA COOLA TO PORT HARDY

Discovery Coast, Bella Coola–Port Hardy $$$
www.discoverycoast.bcferries. bc.ca. The summer-only route operates early-Jun–early Sept.

BC Ferries 1112 Fort St, Victoria; tel: (250) 386-3431 or (888) 223-3779; www.bcferries.bc.ca

Hakai Recreation Area
Tel: (250) 398-4414.

Unlike most BC Ferries that cater to commuters, commercial traffic and local residents, the Discovery Coast Passage route was created for tourists. The summer-only service aboard the *Queen of Chilliwack* was named 'Discovery' after Alexander Mackenzie, who, in 1793, was the first European to cross North America north of Mexico. Mackenzie emerged from the mountains at Bella Coola to discover that he had finally found the Pacific Ocean. There are more ghost towns than modern settlements along the route, but the often-narrow, always-scenic channels are seldom empty. Cruise ships and fishing boats make regular runs between Alaska, to the north, and Seattle and Canadian ports to the south. Pleasure craft throng the protected inlets and passages of the **Hakai Recreation Area**, a popular area for sea kayaking.

The entire voyage takes 15–33 hours, depending on how many of four potential port calls the *Queen of Chilliwack* makes. Allow about 50 hours for a return voyage from either Bella Coola or Port Hardy. The ship stays reasonably close to schedule but do not expect slavish devotion to the timetable. The 115m car ferry also carries kayaks and other small craft that can be dropped off and picked up at irregular stops along the trip. There may be detours when the captain spots a pod of orcas or a breaching humpback whale nearby. For the best sightseeing, sail the Discovery Coast southbound, Bella Coola–Port Hardy, to enjoy the panorama of mountains surrounding North Bentinck Arm (near Bella Coola) in daylight. For easier driving, take a northbound sailing, Port Hardy–Bella Coola. In Bella Coola, passengers board at the ferry dock but vehicles must check in at a staging area near the Cedar Inn, about 2km from the dock, to pick up a boarding pass before driving to the dock. In Port Hardy (*see page 229*), passengers and vehicles board at the Bear Cove ferry dock.

Check current procedures with BC Ferries when making your booking. Boarding starts 60 minutes before sailing at both ports but it is better to board early than late: early arrivals get the coveted seats next to the *Queen of Chilliwack*'s oversized view windows. Seating is first-come, first-served, so passengers in the know race aboard to drop a jacket or a backpack on their preferred window seat, usually in the forward lounge. Hotels, motels and B&Bs at either end of the route can arrange transportation to and from the dock for passengers on foot. Reservations are required for vehicles and are highly recommended for foot passengers: space is limited and the season short. There may be space on the first few and the last few sailings at the last moment, but book four to six months in advance for June–August trips. Reservations can be changed (if space is available on the new date) but each change costs $30 per segment. To check space availability and to make reservations, contact BC Ferries at *1-888-BCFERRY (223-3779)*.

Summer weather is usually good but the coastal climate is fickle. Rain, fog and wind are at least as common as sunshine, which comes and goes almost without warning. Stick to comfortable, layered clothing and flat shoes for walking about on deck, up and down outside stairways and on shore. Long trousers, long sleeves, closed shoes and a warm jacket with a hood are likely to be as useful as sunglasses and sun block, even if the weather forecast predicts nothing but sunshine. Seas will probably be calm no matter what the weather. Except for a short stretch of open water in the Queen Charlotte Sound north of Port Hardy, a maze of islands protects the entire route from ocean swells and large wind waves.

The Discovery Coast is a tourist cruise but the *Queen of Chilliwack* is no cruise ship; no disco, no casino, no swimming pool, no sauna, no beauty parlour, no dressy dinners. There is a gym, a couple of stationary bicycles on the solarium deck, as well as a full-service cafeteria, bar, lounge, laundry, showers, video arcade and gift shop. There is also plenty of outside deck space to enjoy the passing scenery while looking for orcas, humpback whales, eagles, seals, dolphins and passing vessels of all sizes. Binoculars and telephoto camera lenses are a must. The *Queen of Chilliwack* has no passenger cabins but the reclining seats are comfortable for night-long napping. Blankets, sheets and pillows can be hired on board, or bring your own. You can also pitch tents on board, or pitch your own on the outer decks (or perhaps indoors, depending on the weather). A popular option is to overnight in Klemtu, Ocean Falls or Shearwater and pick up the ship on a later sailing, but rooms on shore are limited. Book shoreside accommodation first (and explain that you are arriving aboard the *Queen*

Right
Killer whale breaching

of Chilliwack), then book passage to match your dates ashore. Port calls stretch from 30 minutes to half a day, depending on the port and day of the week.

Arrival and departure times are posted near the Purser's Office, forward of the cafeteria. There are shore excursions in most ports, usually walking tours, traditional dancing, salmon feasts or paddle trips. Buy shore tours as soon as possible after boarding. The better the weather, the earlier the excursions sell out. You can also explore ashore on your own, but watch the time. The *Queen of Chilliwack* does not wait for late returns. The only departure warning is a long whistle blast 15 minutes before pulling away from the dock.

INSIDE PASSAGE: PRINCE RUPERT TO PORT HARDY

Inside Passage, Prince Rupert–Port Hardy $$$
1112 Fort St, Victoria; tel: (250) 386-3431 or (888) 223-3779; www.bcferries.bc.ca

Eagles, whales and mouth-dropping scenery on all sides make this all-year car-ferry route the most popular 15-hour cruise in Canada. Look for sheer mountains cloaked with red cedar and Sitka spruce rising from glacier-carved channels, low islands swept clean by winter storms and lighthouses marking channels less than 250m wide. The entire trip takes place during daylight hours mid-May–end of September, when most sailings of the 117m *Northern Adventure* depart from Prince Rupert at 0730 and arrive at Port Hardy at 2230 the same day. Check with BC Ferries for off-season schedules. Vehicle spaces must be reserved in advance. Foot passengers should also book space, especially June–August when tour groups flock to north-coast ferry trips. Last-minute vehicle space may be available mid-September–mid-May but make reservations 4–6 months in advance for summer travel.

In Prince Rupert, follow Second Avenue (Hwy 16) to the ferry dock. In Port Hardy, board at Bear Cove, just south of town. Boarding starts 1 hour before sailing. In summer, be prepared to scramble for window seats in the forward cabins with the best views or opt for an outdoor seat. There is no rush to be first on board to scramble for window seats in winter, when there are few passengers. Weather is usually warm and clear (but not always sunny) in summer, while storms are common in winter. The Inside Passage is calm and well protected by dozens of islands off the coast, but rain, wind, fog and snow blast down from the Arctic in winter. In any season, most passengers opt to spend the trip in comfortable reclining chairs or in the many lounge areas set with tables and chairs. Private cabins are available at an additional charge. There is also a Coastal Café cafeteria, complete with white linen tablecloths in the evening and an outdoor BBQ to enjoy the wonderful scenery. Ferries also have a licensed lounge, video arcade, children's play area, lift, washroom for persons with disabilities, games, free videos in public rooms and a well-stocked gift shop.

KLEMTU

Klemtu Kitasoo Band Council
Tel: (250) 839-1255.

This is one of the most popular overnight stops on the Discovery Coast, thanks to a bed and breakfast operated by the Kitasoo Band: book accommodation first, then the Discovery Coast sailing that matches your stay. Most of Klemtu's 500 or so residents turn out to welcome the *Queen of Chilliwack*. Main street is among the longest boardwalks in Canada, skirting two sides of a bay that is alive with bald eagles, dolphins and orcas on the hunt for salmon and other fish. The most popular activity is a 3-hour walking tour of the town with stops at a busy carving shed and a traditional Aboriginal feast guaranteed to finish before the ship sails. BYOK – bring your own kayak – or charter a boat from band operators for fishing, sightseeing, hiking and camping on nearby islands.

Below
The *Northern Adventure*

OCEAN FALLS

BC Ferries
tel: (250) 386-3431 or
(888) 223-3779;
www.bcferries.bc.ca

Known for its world-class swimmers (1940s–1960s), Ocean Falls is also known for its mean annual precipitation of 4,386.8mm. Named after Link Falls, a waterfall that thunders directly into the sea, Ocean Falls was once a thriving pulp and paper mill-town at the head of Cousins Inlet. Three thousand people lived here in the mid-20th century, enough to fill a hospital, high school, hotel and Olympic-sized swimming pool. When the mill closed in 1980 and jobs evaporated, so did most of the people. A few families remain at the original townsite, which spreads uphill from the ferry dock, and a few more in nearby Martin Valley, but the population more than doubles when the *Queen of Chilliwack* passengers hit the streets on walking tours. Fishing and sightseeing boat charters are also available, as are a few B&B rooms: book onshore accommodation first, then matching sailing dates. There is home-made soup, ice cream and espresso at the only restaurant in town, Bernie Bashan's floating café. There are a fire hall, modern school and the mouldering remains of a long-closed hotel, but most of Ocean Falls is vanishing beneath a creeping carpet of alders, blackberry bushes and seedling pines. It is hard to miss the occasional splash of colour, usually a bright blue hydrangea in what was once a carefully tended front garden. Today's residents would not change much about their town. A hydroelectric dam built for the mill still churns out power, but with no logging and no toxic pulp waste pouring into the ocean, salmon, halibut, eagles, dolphins and other wildlife have returned.

Below
The *Queen of Chilliwack*

Inside Passage

The domain of basking seals, breaching killer whales and schools of playful dall porpoises, the Inside Passage is a majestic panorama of natural beauty protected by offshore islands and tempered by the *Kuroshio* (Japan Current). A vast archipelago of deep channels, quiet bays and forested islands makes up one of the most scenic and interesting waterways in the world. Sparsely populated, the area has been inhabited by Coast aboriginals for some 10,000 years. Fewer than 5,000 live on the coast, half of them at Bella Coola (*see page 133*) and another quarter in Queen Charlotte City in the Queen Charlotte Islands. Two hundred years ago, the waters and islands between Prince Rupert and Port Hardy were the realm of aboriginals who lived well off the bounty of the rich sea and the temperate coastal forests. A century ago, the same waters teemed with floating logging camps, pulp mills and fish canneries. Changing economic conditions closed most of the outside industries, leaving the Inside Passage once again a largely aboriginal area where humans are vastly outnumbered by the wildlife, and the scenery draws visitors from around the world.

Below
Prince Rupert harbour

SHEARWATER/DENNY ISLAND

Shearwater/Denny Island Shearwater Marine Resort
Tel: (604) 270-6204, tollfree: (800) 663-2370; www.shearwater.ca

Flying boats based at Denny Island, opposite Bella Bella, once patrolled the Queen Charlotte Channel during World War II watching for Japanese submarines. The base is long gone, as is an early 20th-century fish-packing plant, but with the newer name of Shearwater, the sheltered bay has become a base for tourism, sport fishing and maritime traffic. The Shearwater resort includes a small hotel, fishing charters, restaurant, pub, marina and B&B accommodation. Look for commercial fishing boats, sailing boats and luxury motor yachts tied up to the dock. Crew and passengers are most likely tied up to the bar inside, the only full-service stop between Bella Coola and Port Hardy. The *Queen of Chilliwack* ties up long enough for a meal or a drink at the resort. The alternative is to spend several days cycling and hiking the island or boating nearby waters.

Suggested tours

Time: Allow up to 15 hours to travel the Inside Passage between **Prince Rupert ❶** and **Port Hardy ❸**, or 33 hours to travel the Discovery Coast Passage between **Bella Coola ❷** and Port Hardy.

Links: Prince Rupert is the mainland terminus of the Yellowhead Highway, which continues westward to the Queen Charlotte Islands or eastward to the Rocky Mountains and Jasper National Park (*see page 87*). Both ferry routes meet at Port Hardy (*see page 229*), at the north end of Vancouver Island, for the drive south towards Victoria (*see page 248*). From Bella Coola (*see page 133*), it is possible to drive the Cariboo–Chilcotin to Williams Lake (*see page 137*) and either north to Prince Rupert or south towards Vancouver (*see page 268*).

Route: Both ferry trips fit into a circular driving tour from Vancouver, then north by mainland to Bella Coola or Prince Rupert, then south by ferry to Port Hardy on Vancouver Island, then south by highway to Victoria and by ferry to Vancouver. Allow 7–10 days for the entire route. It is possible to combine both ferry voyages by driving to either Bella Coola or Port Hardy, taking one ferry route into Port Hardy and then taking the second route back to the mainland. Allow 10–14 days for the two ferry trips, plus long-distance driving on the mainland and any excursions on Vancouver Island. Both routes are served by car ferries but do not take 'car' too literally. If it is street-legal in BC, BC Ferries will carry it: cars, vans, RVs, motorcoaches, motorcycles, bicycles, trucks and foot passengers. Both tours can be taken in either direction and both can be made with a combination of train, coach and air connections to avoid driving altogether.

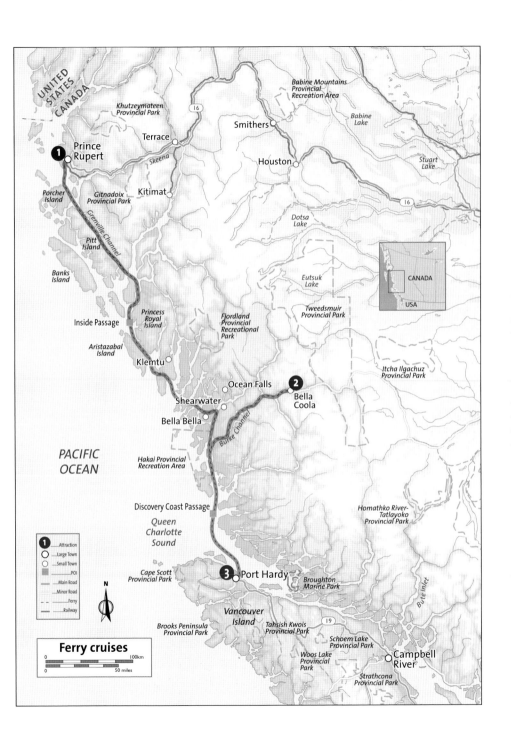

Ferry cruises

Cowboy Country

Ratings

Cowboys	●●●●○
First Nations	●●●●○
History	●●●●○
Outdoor activities	●●●●○
Scenery	●●●●○
Sport	●●●●○
Children	●●●○○
Museums	●●●○○

There's a kind of time warp in this arid region of rolling hills and grassland, like returning to a more rural existence when transportation meant a horse, not an RV or 4x4. There are certainly towns (and Kamloops is a large city in BC terms) but this is unquestionably 'cow country' as it was when the BC cattle industry was born in the 1860s. In its beginnings, the hot summers and open ranges seemed like a good fallback position after the gold rush petered out. Unlucky prospectors, too tired or poor to go home, purchased farmland and put down roots for new communities. Among the new settlers were English gentlemen farmers and remittance men who raised gamecocks and galloped about the hills to the sounds of hounds and hunting horns. Today, more than a thousand ranches give the area its dominating flavour.

CACHE CREEK

ℹ Cache Creek Info Centre *1270 Stage Rd; tel: tollfree (888) 457-7661.*

🏛 Historic Hat Creek Ranch $ *11km north of Cache Creek at junction of Hwys 97 & 99, then west 5km; tollfree (800) 782-0922; e-mail: hhcr@telus.net; www.hatcreekranch.com*

💎 Cariboo Jade Shoppe *1093 Todd Rd in downtown Cache Creek; tel: (250) 457-9566.*

With its large cattle ranches worked by real cowboys and its grasslands filled with grazing beef cattle, Cache Creek is the Wild West revisited. The **Historic Hat Creek Ranch** (*see also page 143*) is the last intact stopping house on the Old Cariboo Waggon Road and interpretive tours here provide a glimpse of what ranching was like from 1860 to 1915, along with a history of the area's First Nations people. This is still a working ranch but one that offers visitors nature walks, trail rides, wagon tours, gold panning, archery, 'powder shooting', blacksmith and farm machinery displays and a bunch of special events. Good sport fishing and a place to find jade which you can watch being cut and polished in the **Cariboo Jade Shoppe**.

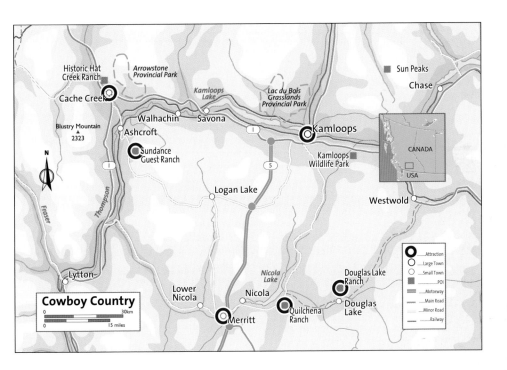

Cowboy Country

0 _____ 30km
0 _____ 15 miles

DOUGLAS LAKE RANCH

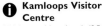 **Douglas Lake Ranch $$** *turn east off Hwy 5A at Douglas Lake Rd, continue 26km to ranch; tel: (250) 350-3344, tollfree (800) 663-4838; e-mail: info@douglaslake.com; www.douglaslake.com*

First set up in 1884, the Douglas Lake Ranch is the largest working cattle company in Canada and offers a well-established tour programme that looks at the rich history, traditions and lifestyle on the ranch. All of the tours take in the home ranch, the company town, general store, calving barn, quarter horse barn, feedlot and school.

KAMLOOPS

Kamloops Visitor Centre *1290 west Hwy 1; tel: (250) 372-8000, tollfree (800) 662-1994; fax: (250) 372-2121; e-mail: inquiry@ tourismkamloops.com; www.tourismkamloops.com. Open daily from May long weekend–Thanksgiving 0900–1800; rest of year Mon–Fri 0900–1700.*

This is BC's fifth largest city (and its biggest at least in terms of area) but there's still an Old West, cowboy feel to much of it. As it has for almost 150 years, Kamloops still serves as a watering hole for the area's ranch hands who come in from the 1,100 ranches largely near the city.

Kamloops takes its name from a Secwepemc native word meaning 'where the rivers meet', a place where the ancestors had their gathering place. Downtown, well-kept turn-of-the-century brick buildings rub shoulders with art galleries and theatres near the beaches on the low banks of the South Thompson River. The **Kamloops Museum and Archives** has three floors of displays that

Tranquille Marsh
10km west on Tranquille Rd from North Kamloops.

Kamloops Art Gallery *$ 5th & Victoria St; tel: (250) 377-2400; fax: (250) 828-0662; e-mail: kamloopsartgallery@ kag.bc.ca; www.kag.bc.ca. Open Mon–Sat 1000–1700, Thur 1000–2100, Sun 1200–1600.*

Kamloops Heritage Railway
See Spirit of Kamloops, Train Travel, page 176; e-mail: museum@kamloops.ca

Kamloops Museum and Archives *$ 207 Seymour St; tel: (250) 828-3576; www.kamloops.ca/museum. Open Mon–Fri 0930–1630 (until 1930 Thur Jun–Aug).*

Kamloops Wildlife Park *$ 15 minutes east of Kamloops city centre off Hwy 1; tel: (250) 573-3242; fax: (250) 573-2406; e-mail: campaign@bczoo.org; www.bczoo.org. Open Jun–Aug daily 0900–1700. Otherwise 0930–1600.*

Kamloops Cowboy Festival *Tel: (888) 763-2224; e-mail: cowboys@bcchs.com; www. bcchs.com. Held each March by the BC Cowboy Heritage Society, Canada's premier cowboy heritage event just keeps getting better.*

explore local Secwepemc First Nations history, local Chinese culture, Victoriana and natural history. The museum's collection of Secwepemc baskets is one of the best in the province. The exhibits include an 1842 log building from the Hudson's Bay Company fort on what is now the Kamloops Indian Reserve on the north bank of the South Thompson River, two Victorian-era house interiors and more. Just on the outskirts of town, the **Secwepemc Heritage Park and Museum** expands on the history of the First Nations people who have lived in this area for thousands of years. There is a 2,000-year-old archaeological site in the 5ha park and four reconstructed winter homes showing building styles over time. Summer dwellings, unique ethno-botanical gardens, and a wildlife marsh with many bird species are other features of the site. Outdoor performances are held from time to time. The museum exhibits archaeological and ethnographic materials of the Secwepemc (Shuswap people). There is a gift shop.

The **Kamloops Art Gallery** has undergone a facelift with a whole new design to enhance the largest public art exhibit in the interior of BC. Like many weekly markets, the **Kamloops Farmers Market** began as a produce outlet for local farms but has since expanded to include everything from rabbits and chickens to live music and square dancing. It's a great place to stock up on fragrant freshly baked breads, cheeses and vegetables for a weekend picnic to spots such as **Sun Peaks Resort**, a year-round mountain resort that offers good hiking, horse riding, mountain biking and more in the summer, and excellent skiing in the winter.

To the north of Kamloops, the **Tranquille Marsh** has its own beauty and attracts hundreds of birds to the delight of birdwatchers and hikers. Snow geese, herons and trumpeter swans are just a few of the species in this very active waterfowl habitat. The **Kamloops Wildlife Park** is the area's newest attraction and allows visitors to have an up-close and personal glimpse at some of the area's animal life. Kids will love riding the park's Wildlife Express, a steam locomotive-driven train that chugs along 1km of track.

Accommodation and food in Kamloops

The Brownstone Restaurant $$$ *118 Victoria St (1st Ave & Victoria); tel: (250) 851-9939; www.brownstonerestaurant.com. Open lunch and dinner Tue–Sat.* Terrific restaurant in downtown in former historic 1904 bank building.

Peter's Pasta $$ *149 Victoria St; tel: (250) 372-8514. Open Tue–Fri 1700–2200.* You can tell a restaurant that's popular with the locals by the length of the queue to get in. Run by a welcoming family, this has superb home-made pastas and breads.

The Plaza Heritage Hotel $$ *405 Victoria St; tel: (250) 377-8075; tollfree (877) 977-5292; fax: (250) 377-8076; e-mail: theplaza@telus.net;*

**Secwepemc
Heritage Park and
Museum $**
*355 Yellowhead Hwy;
tel: (250) 828-9779;
fax: (250) 372-1127;
e-mail: yvonne.fortier@
secwepemc.org;
www.secwepemc.org.
Open Jun–early Sept
Mon–Fri 0830–2000, Sat,
Sun & holidays 1000–2000;
otherwise Mon–Fri
0800–1630.*

Sun Peaks $$
*24.5km east of Hwy 5
via Heffley–Louise Creek Rd,
then 9km on Sun Peaks Rd;
tel: (250) 578-7222,
tollfree (800) 807-3257;
fax: (250) 578-7223;
www.sunpeaksresort.com*

Farmers Market $
*two locations: Victoria
St, between 4th–5th Aves,
Apr–Oct 0800–1200 (Wed);
St Paul and 3rd (Sat).*

www.plazaheritagehotel.com. This 1920s heritage building not long ago entertained bikers not barons and was definitely on its way to being seedy. After a total restoration, it now has charming, individually decorated rooms and exudes the warmth of a country inn.

Rick's Grill $$$ *downtown at 227 Victoria St; tel: (250) 372-7771.* As you'd expect in 'cattle country', beef is king in Kamloops and restaurants don't come any better for steaks and prime rib than this one.

The Swiss Pastry $ *359 Victoria St; tel: (250) 372-2625; open for lunch only.* Another spot with a heavy emphasis on home-made goodies: soups, sandwiches, breads and desserts.

Right
Cowboy country is cattle
country

MERRITT

ⓘ Merritt Chamber of Commerce Information Centre
2185B Voght St; tel: (250) 378-5634; e-mail: bic@merritt-chamber.bc.ca; www.merritt-chamber.bc.ca

◆ Merritt Mountain Music Festival
Tel: (604) 525-3330 or www.mountainfest.com

◑ Coldwater Hotel $
1901 Voght St; tel: (250) 378-2821; e-mail: info@coldwaterhotel.com; www.coldwaterhotel.com

This town sits in the valley at the confluence of the Nicola and Coldwater rivers and serves as a transportation hub for ranching country. It's a centre for five aboriginal communities and marks the spot where the territories of the Nlaka'pamux First Nation people and Okanagan First Nation people meet. For a nostalgic look at cowboy history, spend a little time in the shrimp-pink **Coldwater Hotel** with its balconies and copper-domed turret. When it was built in 1908 for $6,000 it was considered the finest hotel in the BC Interior since it boasted rooms with attached bathrooms. Couples could be married in the hotel and then rent a room for $1.50 including breakfast. On Saturday nights, cowboys would come in from the hills and sit on the balconies watching the women stroll by. The area is a major draw for fishermen, with 150 lakes filled with rainbow and cutthroat trout, kokanee and Dolly Varden char. The biggest event is a week-long **Merritt Mountain Music Country and Western Festival** in July.

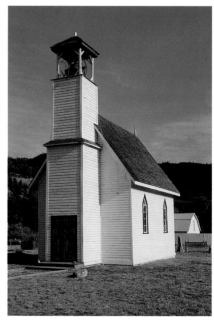

Right
Nicola Valley wooden church

Opposite
Looking over the valley at Sundance Guest Ranch

QUILCHENA RANCH

◑ Quilchena Hotel $$ on Hwy 5A north of Merritt; tel: (250) 378-2611; fax: (250) 378-6091; Ranch: (250) 378-4449; e-mail: info@quilchena.com; www.quilchena.com. Open end Apr–Thanksgiving weekend.

Like a lot of stories in BC, that of the Quilchena Ranch starts during the gold rush when four brothers named Guichon from Savoie, France, came to seek their fortunes. Ultimately, two of the brothers acquired land in the area and the Guichon Cattle Company was set up in 1890. The Quilchena Cattle Company today is one of the largest working cattle ranches in BC, runs about 4,500 head of cattle a year and is operated by the third and fourth generation of Guichon descendants. The **Quilchena Hotel** is set right in the heart of the ranch against a backdrop of gently rolling ranges and overlooks beautiful Nicola Lake. A full slate of activities (hiking, horse riding, biking) as well as excellent food in a Victorian house.

SUNDANCE GUEST RANCH

Sundance Guest Ranch $$–$$$ *take Hwy 1 to the Ashcroft turnoff and continue through the former gold rush town of Ashcroft onto Hwy 97C S, towards Logan Lake/Merritt. Sundance sign 10 minutes past Ashcroft; tel: (250) 453-2422, tollfree (800) 553-3533; fax: (250) 453-9356; e-mail: saddleup@ sundanceguestranch.com; www.sundanceguestranch.com*

Originally built in 1864 as a working ranch, for 30 years Sundance has been owned by the Rowe family who welcome guests keen to check out the cowboy lifestyle. With more than 100 horses available, it's not hard to get matched up with your ideal steed and take at least two rides into a vast Crown Land terrain all around the ranch. It says a lot that 70% of the ranch's business is repeat, with many clients still coming back after 30 years. The mood at Sundance is fun and relaxation, so guests are catered to with great food and wranglers who look after all the details (you can comb down your horse if you want to however). Riders are divided into beginner, intermediate and advanced groups, to make sure total dudes can walk before they gallop. This is true cowboy country with a near-desert climate, but the

landscape rolls and changes from sagebrush to pine forest and flower-filled mountain meadows. For non-riding time, there are excellent fishing lakes around, a chance to see black bear, coyote, deer, eagles and hawks, and a heated pool overlooking the exquisite valley.

Suggested tour

Total distance: 318km.

Time: 4 hours' driving time with up to 8 hours with stops.

Route: This is a circular driving tour starting and ending in KAMLOOPS ❶. Follow Hwy 5A to stay at the QUILCHENA RANCH ❷.

Detour: Just north of Quilchena on Hwy 5A, take the Douglas Lake Rd east for 26km and turn right into the main entrance of DOUGLAS LAKE RANCH ❸ for a complete look at Canada's largest working cattle ranch. Be sure to phone first since it's a gated ranch.

Continue on to MERRITT ❹. From Merritt, take Hwy 8 going west heading towards Lower Nicola. From here, swing north on Hwy 97C towards **Logan Lake**. This is an instant town created for employees of a vast copper mining operation 16km west of the community centre on Hwy 97C (heading towards Ashcroft). The big attraction here is the **Highland Valley Copper Mine** which is the largest copper mine in North America. The mine has tours and there's splendid photography of the lake. It's a beautiful drive west towards **ASHCROFT ❺** (*see page 140*). After a stop at historic **Ashcroft Manor** for tea, head over to **SUNDANCE GUEST RANCH ❻** or continue along Hwy 97C to join up with Hwy 1. Continue north to CACHE CREEK ❼.

Turn east here on Hwy 97 heading towards Savona. About 16km east of Cache Creek, you pass the tiny community of Walhachin with green-and-pink clapboard houses that's the site of a former town built by a group of English investors who dreamed of an orchard paradise in 1908. When the settlers returned home during World War II to enlist, storms destroyed the irrigation system and the orchards died. The few families who returned immediately turned around and went home again. All that's left of the dream is a dilapidated irrigation system. Continue on to Kamloops.

🅗 **Highland Valley Copper Mine**
Logan Lake; tel: (250) 523-3307.

Opposite
Exploring Cowboy Country

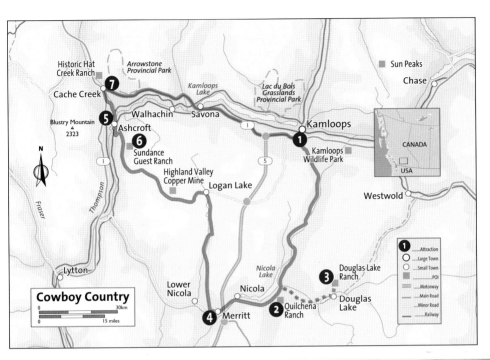

Okanagan Valley

Ratings

Beaches	●●●●
Children	●●●●
Food and drink	●●●●
Wineries	●●●●
History	●●●
Outdoor activities	●●●
Parks	●●●
Scenery	●●●

The Okanagan Valley is a 20km-wide strip that lies in the rain shadow of the Cascade Mountains creating a hot, sunny, dry climate and BC's most important fruit and grape-growing area. The Valley stretches from the US border and continues north following a series of lakes strung together like pearls on a string. Canada's only real desert is here, the most northerly tip of Mexico's Sonoran, but aside from cacti and a few scorpions it's a little hard to find. Only small patches remain because of farming and irrigation, hence the name 'pocket desert'. Lush orchards and burgeoning vineyards extend throughout the Valley, transforming what used to be hot sand into one of Canada's most fertile regions. For visitors, the lakes linked by the Okanagan River are a summer playground, and in winter the mountains offer dry snow and skiing called BC's 'best kept secret'.

OLIVER

ℹ **Oliver Info Centre**
36205 93rd St;
tel: (250) 498-6321,
tollfree (866) 498-6321;
fax: (250) 498-3156;
www.oliverchamber.bc.ca.
Open daily 0900–1700
summer; Mon–Fri winter.

➔ **Oliver Hiking and Bicycling Trail**
From the McAlpine Bridge where Hwy 97 crosses the river just north of Oliver to Osoyoos Lake.

This town of less than 5,000 people is surrounded by more than 9,000ha of such productive orchards south on Hwy 97, it's called 'the golden mile'. Some of the Okanagan Valley's most productive vineyards supply nine local wineries and you'd need a full day to visit the lot. Among the best are **Tinhorn Creek** with its flavourful reds and **Gehringer Bros** with their traditional German-style wines. Oliver, also known as the Cantaloupe Capital of Canada, has fruit and vegetable stands all along Hwy 97 with either picked or U-pick (pick-your-own) fruit available.

For hikers and mountain bike enthusiasts, the **Oliver Hiking and Bicycling Trail** provides dykes and an old railway right of way: 10km of paved trail and 8km of prepared road bed on the Okanagan River. **The Oliver and District Heritage Society Museum and Archives** is in a former 1924 headquarters of the BC Provincial Police and has exhibits on local agriculture and irrigation plus early mining artefacts

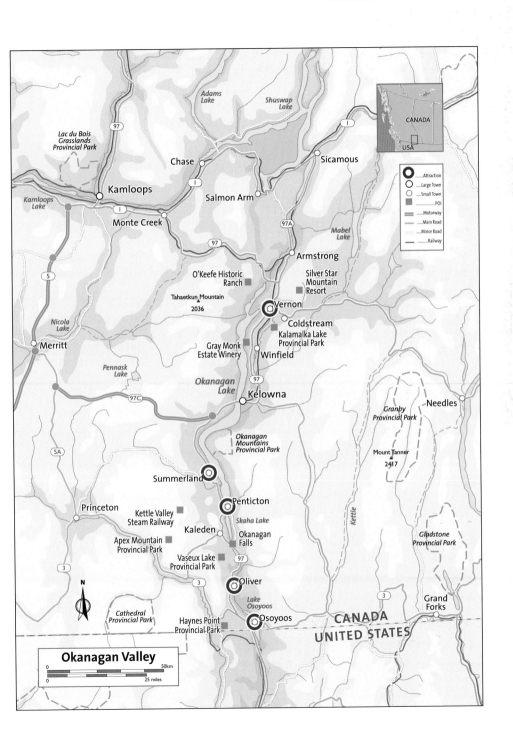

Okanagan Valley

Tinhorn Creek Winery $
Road 7; tel: (250) 498-3743, tollfree (888) 484-6467; fax: (250) 498-3228; e-mail: winery@tinhorn.com; www.tinhorn.com. Open 0900–1800 daily.

Gehringer Bros Winery $ Road 8; tel: (250) 498-3537, tollfree (800) 784-6304; fax: (250) 498-3510. Open Jun–mid-Oct daily 1000–1700; Mon–Fri until mid-May.

The Oliver and District Heritage Society Museum and Archives $ 9726 350th Ave; tel: (250) 498-4027; e-mail: (archives) odhs@cablerocket.com; (museum) museumdirector@cablerocket.com; www.oliverarchives.ca, www.olivermuseum.ca. Open Mon–Thur 0900–1600 (archives); museum open Tue–Sat 1000–1600.

Fairview 4.5km southwest of Oliver at the junction of Fairview Rd with White Lake Rd.

and the jail from a historical site called **Fairview**. There's not much left of a town that was said to be the biggest city north of San Francisco in 1893 with 500 people. In 1902 the grand Teepee Hotel burned down and by 1908 Fairview, once awash in gold, had become a ghost town.

OSOYOOS

Osoyoos Information
Info Centre at Hwys 3 and 97 junction (9912 Hwy 3); tel: (250) 495-5070, tollfree (888) 676-9667; fax: (250) 495-8081; e-mail: tourism@osoyoos.ca; www.destinationosoyoos.com. Open daily Jul and Aug 0800–2000; winter 0900–1700.

Above
Okanagan cowgirl and cowboy

As one of Canada's hottest spots, this little town in the fertile desert is both a fun place and a fruit basket with Canada's earliest fruit crops. In the summer, swimmers and water-skiers fill the four beaches in town and visitors come from all over to buy bushels of fruit and tomatoes at roadside stands. The name Osoyoos means 'narrows of the lake' and refers to **Lake Osoyoos** in the centre of town, a lake that stretches 17km from Canada into the US and is called Canada's warmest lake. To get a little background, the **Osoyoos Museum** (called the best small town museum in BC) has an excellent and eclectic collection that includes aboriginal artefacts, antique vehicles, period clothing, pioneer treasures, police archives, an original 1892 log schoolhouse and even liquor distilling apparatus from the bootlegging days. The museum gets rave reviews.

The Spotted Lake *8.8km west of Osoyoos on Hwy 3.*

Osoyoos Museum *$ On beach at end of Main St; tel: (250) 495-2582; www4.vip.net/ osoyoosmuseum. Open May long weekend–end Sept; afternoons until Jun then daily 1000–1600.*

Osoyoos (Pocket) Desert Centre *$ 146 Ave & Hwy 97; tel: (250) 495-2470, tollfree (877) 899-0897; e-mail: mail@ desert.org; www.desert.org. Open varying hours. Call for current times.*

Haynes Point Provincial Park *2km south of town on Osoyoos Lake; tel: (250) 494-6500 or (604) 689-9025.*

The Osoyoos Oxbows Fish and Wildlife Management Reserve *Near Oliver, 7.5km north of Osoyoos, turn east onto Road 22 and follow 1km to kiosk.*

Nk'Mip Desert Cultural Centre *$ 1000 Rancher Creek Rd; tel: (250) 495-7901, tollfree (888) 495-8555; fax: (250) 495-7912; e-mail: nkmipcentre.osoyoos.com; www.nkmipcentre.osoyoos.com. A new centre, creatively done, to interpret the desert and First Nations people.*

The dunes of the **Pocket Desert** are a bit hard to find but worthwhile for anyone interested in rare and endangered ecosystems. There are species here found nowhere else in Canada such as the pallid bat, shy night snake and the ground mantis. **The Osoyoos Desert Society** has guided boardwalk tours daily from Easter to the end of September. **The Spotted Lake** (8.8km west of Osoyoos) is another natural phenomenon that is on private property but is still visible and highly photographable from the highway. The lake has the world's highest concentration of minerals so that bizarre white-ringed circles form when the water evaporates under the hot summer sun. Ancient tribes were said to soak away aches and ailments in the healing mud and waters of 'Klikuk' as they called it.

Haynes Point Provincial Park is 2km south of town on Osoyoos Lake and is a popular swimming and camping site. Canada's tiniest bird, the Calliope hummingbird, can be seen buzzing around flowers, along with orioles, Eastern kingbirds and California quail. **The Osoyoos Oxbows Fish and Wildlife Management Reserve** provides a glimpse into what is left of crucial wildlife refuges. Road 22 continues on through vineyards and Inkaneep First Nation reserve land where there are real sand dunes and natural landscape.

Accommodation and food in Osoyoos

Campo Marina **$$** *5907 Main St, Hwy 3; tel: (250) 495-7650; www.campomarina.com.* Excellent Italian cuisine.

Newton Observatory B&B **$$** *3 Observatory Rd; tel: (250) 495-6745; e-mail: jack@jacknewton.com; www.jacknewton.com; open April–October.* This 4-star unusual B&B has a dramatic view of the lake and promises 'out of this world hospitality'. Owner Jack Newton is a passionate amateur astronomer so each guest gets a free lesson in astronomy along with a bed and breakfast.

Osoyoos Golf Club **$$** *12300 Golf Course Drive; tel: (250) 495-3355, tollfree (800) 481-6665; e-mail: mail@golfosoyoos.com; www.golfosoyoos. com.* Good food and good view.

Sonora Dunes **$$** *1300 Rancher Creek Rd; tel: (250) 495-4653; e-mail: info@sonoradunes.com; www.sonoradunes.com.* The area's latest golf addition.

PENTICTON

City boosters insist that the translation for the aboriginal name 'Penticton' means 'a place to live forever', and anyone visiting, particularly in the spring when thousands of fruit trees are in bloom, would be easily convinced. Like its sister cities in the Okanagan,

ℹ Tourism Penticton
553 Railway St;
tel: (250) 493-4055,
tollfree (800) 663-5052;
fax: (250) 492-6119; e-mail:
visitors@penticton.org;
www.tourismpenticton.com.
Open summer daily
0800–2000; winter
Mon–Sat 0900–1800,
Sun 0900–1700.

➲ Okanagan Lake
For access follow
Lakeshore Dr.

Skaha Lake *Is at end of*
Channel Parkway with access
via Lee Ave.

⦿ Skaha Climbing
Bluffs *South of town,*
left off South Main onto
Crescent Hill Rd.

⦿ Wonderful
Waterworld $
Skaha Lake Rd at Yorkton
Ave; tel: (250) 493-8121;
www.pentictonwaterslides.com

Penticton (AT
Atkinson) Museum and
Archives $ *785 Main St;*
tel: (250) 490-2451. Open
Sept and Jun Tue–Sat
1000–1700; Jul and Aug
Mon–Sat 1000–1700.

SS Sicamous $
On Okanagan Lake off
Lakeshore Dr.; tel: (250)
492-0403, tollfree (866)
492-0403; e-mail:
mail@sssicamous.com;
www.sssicamous.com. Open
mid-Jun–mid-Sept daily
1000–2100; Mon–Fri
offseason 1000–1600.

⦿ Apex Mountain
Resort $$ *32km*
southwest of Penticton
(about 45 minutes) to Green
Mountain Rd; tel: (250) 292-
8222, tollfree (877) 777-
2739; www.apexresort.com

Penticton has fruit and wine in abundance but its biggest appeal is to families who like active holidays. The city lies between the sands of two lakes joined by a narrow channel so beaches are everywhere. **Okanagan Lake** with its park and marina is joined to **Skaha Lake** by the 7km-long man-made Channel Parkway. Sun worshippers will bathe and swim in one lake and then 'tube' down the channel to the other. It's beach life at its best. For younger kids, there are water parks such as **Wonderful Waterworld** with everything from giant squirt guns to peach-shaped concession stands; older kids find an even longer list of activities: guided horse riding or overnight trips, mountain biking, parasailing, water skiing, jet skiing, kayaking and houseboating. In the winter **Apex Mountain Resort** has a quad chair that takes skiers and snowboarders up the slopes, and in the summer hikers ride up to alpine meadows. The **Skaha Climbing Bluffs** are a series of granite slabs, faces and overhangs that offer challenges to both amateur and experienced rock climbers as well as trails for hikers in the sage and ponderosa pine forests. For the more sedentary, the **Penticton (AT Atkinson) Museum and Archives** displays the history of First Nations people in the area, pioneer artefacts and military memorabilia. The **SS** *Sicamous* is in restoration and an example of the sternwheelers that once plied the lakes between 1914 and 1935. There's a good model of the Kettle Valley Railway here. Penticton is famous for its festivals all year round with everything from tributes to ale and Triathlons to Meadowlark and Square Dance Festivals.

Accommodation and food in Penticton

Chinese Laundry and Szechuan $ *123 Front St; tel: (250) 492-2828.* Good northern Chinese menu with antiques from historical Chinese laundries for décor.

Eden House B&B $$ *104 Arlayne Rd, Kaleden; tel: (250) 497-8382, tollfree (888) 497-3336; fax: (250) 497-8535; e-mail: info@edenhouse.ca; www.edenhouse.ca.* A gem of a B&B in a professionally decorated log home overlooking Skaha Lake about 10km south of Penticton. Bedrooms are themed, some have jacuzzi en suite and a swimming pool was recently added.

Granny Bogner's Restaurant $$ *302 Eckhardt Ave; tel: (250) 493-2711.* Northwest cuisine prepared by a European-trained chef. Serves a good list of local wines.

Grumpy's Place B&B $$ *192 Pineview Dr. (see website for driving instructions); tel: (250) 497-1120, tollfree (888) 747-8679; fax: (250) 497-1102; e-mail: grumpy@grumpysplace.com; www.grumpysplace.com.* Spectacular views of the lake from two decks. Two tastefully furnished rooms, gourmet home-made breads and jams and delicious breakfasts. Lots of amenities (pool table, etc).

Right
Enjoying an Okanagan beach

Lavender Lane Guesthouse $$ *3005 DeBeck Rd; tel: (250) 496-5740, tollfree: (888) 496-5740; fax: (250) 496-5741; www.lavenderlane.ca.* Nestled in the hills between orchards and vineyards, this beautifully decorated home has European antiques and modern amenities. Gourmet breakfasts served on a balcony overlooking the lake with the scent of roses and lavender.

Penticton Lakeside Resort and Casino $$ *21 Lakeshore Drive west; tel: (250) 493-8221, tollfree (800) 663-9400; fax: (250) 493-0607; e-mail: lakeside@rpbhotels.com; www.rpbhotels.com.* Lakeside resort with 204 rooms in several categories, fitness and business centre, in-room jacuzzis.

1912 $$$ *100 Alder Ave, Kaleden; tel: (250) 497-6868; www.1912bistro. com.* Specialises in excellent regional cuisine with fresh ingredients.

SUMMERLAND

ℹ Summerland Chamber of Commerce *15600 Hwy 97 (north end at Thompson Rd); tel: (250) 494-2686; fax: (250) 494-4039; e-mail: summerlandchamber@shaw. biz.ca; www. summerlandchamber.bc.ca*

🚂 Kettle Valley Steam Railway $ *Prairie Valley Station, west side of Summerland; tel: (250) 494-8422, tollfree in BC (877) 494-8424; www.kettlevalleyrail.org. Open mid-May–Jun and early Sept–mid-Oct Sat–Mon, Jul–early Sept Thur–Mon; departs 1030 and 1330.*

Summerland was the brainchild of a creative Baptist miner-turned-land developer looking to lure settlers from the more frigid parts of Canada. He subdivided lakeshore properties, put in irrigation and launched the slogan 'Heaven on earth with summer weather forever!' To ensure the prosperity of their community, settlers in Summerland fought long and hard to ensure that the Kettle Valley Railway (KVR) line from Nelson to Hope passed near town despite geographical obstacles. The result was the Trout Creek Trestle, the KVR's largest steel girder bridge and North America's third largest. Today you can board the **Kettle Valley Steam Railway** and see for yourself. Ride the train on a 1hr 45 minute journey through orchards and vineyards, through spectacular scenery and experience 'the Great Train robbery'. Today, Summerland rivals Kelowna as a major fruit-processing centre and is home to numerous fruit packing companies such as **Summerland Sweets** and the **Kettle Valley Dried Fruit Company**. **The Pacific Agri-Food Research Centre** is known locally as the Research Station Gardens and combines a good history of fruit development and experimentation in the area with a garden experience. The Interpretive Centre is surrounded by 6ha of English-style flower beds, lawns and wooden forest pathways. Also check out the **Summerland Museum** with its video presentations of Summerland history and the KVR.

Right
Okanagan Valley vineyards

Ⓘ Kettle Valley Dried Fruit Company $
14014 Hwy 97N; tel: (250) 494-0335, tollfree (888) 297-6944; e-mail: sales@kettlevalley.net; www.kettlevalley.net

The Pacific Agri-Food Research Centre $
4200 Hwy 97S (across from Sunoka Beach); tel: (250) 494-7711. Gardens open daily; interpretive centre weekday afternoons.

Summerland Museum $ 9521 Wharton St; tel: (250) 494-9395; www. summerlandmuseum.org. Open Tue–Sat afternoons year round; Jun–Aug Mon–Sat 1000–1600.

Summerland Sweets $
Canyon View Rd; tel: (250) 494-0377, tollfree (800) 577-1277; e-mail: ssweets@cnx.net; www. summerlandsweets.com. Open year round; summer 0900–2000.

Food in Summerland

Cellar Door Bistro $–$$ *located at Sumac Ridge Winery, 17403 Hwy 97 north of town; tel: (250) 494-0451 or (250) 494-3316; open daily.* Has a great menu of French-inspired regional dishes with wine sampling as a bonus.

VERNON

Ⓘ Tourism Greater Vernon 701 Hwy 97 south; tel: (250) 542-1415, tollfree (800) 665-0795; fax: (250) 545-3114; e-mail: info@vernontourism.com; www.vernontourism.com. Open daily.

At the northern edge of the great fruit belt running down to the US border, Vernon makes up for a slightly cooler climate (and therefore less fruit) with a more trendy, 'with it' kind of appeal. This is the oldest city in BC's interior with perhaps its most cowboy history thanks to Cornelius O'Keefe, a 19th-century cattle entrepreneur who drove his herds north to provide beef for hungry gold miners. You get the full story at **Historic O'Keefe Ranch** which began the year Canada became a nation. The ranch was the largest in the region and a town in itself with a church, general store and post office. The ranch is now

Floral Clock in Polson Park
25th Ave & 32nd St.

Historic O'Keefe Ranch $ *On Hwy 97, about 1km east of Westside Rd; tel: (250) 542-7868; e-mail: info@okeeferanch.ca; www.okeeferanch.ca. Open May–Oct daily 0900–1800; Jul and Aug until 2000.*

Greater Vernon Museum and Archives $ *3009 32nd Ave; tel: (250) 542-3142; e-mail: mail@vernonmuseum.ca; www.vernonmuseum.ca. Open year-round Tue–Sat 1000–1700.*

The Okanagan Science Centre $$ *2704 Hwy 6; tel: (250) 545-3644; www.okscience.ca. Open Tue–Fri 1000–1700, Sat 1100–1700. Closed Sun and Mon (open Mon in Jul and Aug).*

The Allan Brooks Nature Centre $ *250 Allan Brooks Way; tel: (250) 260-4227; e-mail: info@abnc.ca; www.abnc.ca. Open May–Thanksgiving Tue–Sun 1000–1700.*

the area's most popular museum with authentic store, church and mansion that tells the story through video and highly informed guides. You can follow this up at the **Greater Vernon Museum and Archives** which elaborates on Lord Aberdeen (an early Governor-General) and his involvement in vast orchard plantings. The **Okanagan Science Centre** is new and a big hit with kids. Vernon sits between three spectacular lakes, the Kalamalka, Okanagan and Swan, all of which provide sandy, warm beaches. History buffs can sign up at the Vernon Info Centre for walking tours and photographers love the **Floral Clock in Polson Park**. The 10m powered floral clock is one of only a few in Canada. For a plunge into the dramatic and diverse landscape around Vernon, **The Allan Brooks Nature Centre** has exhibits on everything from climate change to local predators. Lots of hands-on for kids.

Accommodation and food in Vernon

The Castle on the Mountain B&B $$$ *8227 Silver Star Rd; tel: (250) 542-4593; tollfree (800) 667-2229; e-mail: castle@airspeedwireless.ca; www.castleonthemountain.com.* This 4½-star B&B has a great location and view of the lake, lovely rooms and art studio on site.

The Cracked Pot Coffee Emporium $ *2913 30th Ave; tel: (250) 545-6272.* Gourmet coffee and paninis are the speciality.

Harbour Lights B&B $$ *135 Joharon Rd; tel: (250) 549-5117; fax: (250) 549-5162; www.harbourlights.ca.* Panoramic view of the lake, spacious rooms and friendly hosts.

Italian Kitchen Company $$ *2916 30th Ave; tel: (250) 558-7899.* An award-winning Italian menu that has been voted Vernon's best restaurant.

The Vernon Lodge $$ *3914 32nd St; tel: (250) 545-3385, tollfree (800) 663-9400.* A hotel with a real stream, the BX Creek, running through the dining room which is a tropical forest with two-storey-high trees. Restaurant serves Italian-influenced cuisine.

Suggested tour

Total distance: 174km.

Time: 3–4 hours' direct driving time but allow 2–5 days for touring.

Links: The Okanagan Valley connects west to the **Gold Rush Trail** (*see page 140*) from **Kelowna** (*see page 208*) via Hwy 8 and Hwy 1. From there on to **Hope** (*see page 223*) and the Fraser Valley. From **Vernon** (*see page 204*) continuing north, Hwys 97/97A lead to the **Shuswap Lakes** (*see page 160*).

Above
Okanagan Valley fruit stall

Route: After visiting the attractions around **VERNON ❶**, head south on Hwy 97 and follow the signs to **Kalamalka Lake Provincial Park** for wild flowers, unspoiled swimming beaches and excellent bird watching. Kalamalka Lake is called the 'Lake of Many Colours' because of the striking blue-green cast to the water caused by glacial silt.

Detour 1: Head east 17.5km off Hwy 97 for **Silver Star Mountain Resort ❷**, the region's most northerly ski area with 84 runs and a vast area for snowmobiling, cross-country skiing and more. In the summer, the resort turns its chairlift to ferrying visitors up to the summit of the mountain for great views, hiking in alpine meadows and mountain biking. Silver Star features a turn-of-the-century mining town to visit.

Returning to Hwy 97, continue south to **Kelowna ❸** with a turn off at **Winfield** for some wine tasting at the **Gray Monk Estate Winery ❹**. From Kelowna, continue south along Hwy 97 with a stop at the Mariners Reef Waterslides (*tel: (250) 768-5141*), about 1km east of Westbank for anyone with children. Continuing south past Peachland, where alas, there are no peach orchards, to **SUMMERLAND ❺** and its various attractions. This is the place to take a ride on the **Kettle Valley Steam Railway ❻** and to stop at a **viewpoint** overlooking Rattlesnake Island and Squally Point on the east side of the lake 6km past Okanagan Lake Park. Legend has it that Ogopogo, the sea serpent, lives in an underwater cave just off the point and has been sighted here. All along this route and heading south, stands overflowing with fruits and vegetables are everywhere. Just north of **PENTICTON ❼**, photographers should look west for a series of hoodoos formed 10,000 years ago as glaciers retreated.

Detour 2: At **Kaleden**, take White Lake Rd, 9km from Kaleden Junction to the **Dominion Radio Astrophysical Observatory** for a little sci-fi experience (*tel: (250) 497-7916* or *(250) 276-4109; open daily*). This is one of the world's best radio astronomy sites and its visitors' centre explains the use of radio telescopes for gathering astronomical data. White Lake, at the same location, has sand hill cranes, curlews, shrikes and sage thrashers.

From Kaleden, continue south on Hwy 97 to **Okanagan Falls** where there are interesting stops at the **Bassett House and Museum**, a restored residence of the pioneer Bassett family and the **Memorial Rose Garden**. Just south of OK Falls, **Vaseux Lake Provincial Park ❽** is a good place for wildlife with bighorn sheep often on the highway. The Wildlife Centre is at the north end of Vaseux Lake and is one of the best places in North America to see California bighorn sheep. Lots of trails, birdwatching hides (blinds) and about 350 of those sheep. Continue on to **OLIVER ❾** and **OSOYOOS ❿** with lots of stops for seasonal fruit. For a camping and birdwatching experience, drive to **Haynes Point Provincial Park ⓫**.

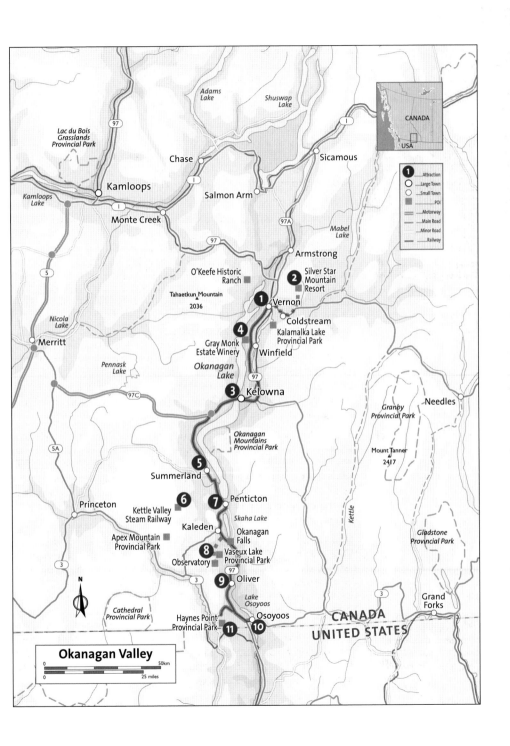

Kelowna

Ratings

Beaches	●●●● ○
Children	●●●● ○
Orchards	●●●● ○
Outdoor activities	●●●● ○
Wineries	●●●● ○
Museums	●●● ○ ○
Nature	●●● ○ ○
Sport	●●● ○ ○

Kelowna proudly announces that its lifestyle is 'the best in Canada' and it presents a convincing list of reasons why this is so. First of all, it sits on Okanagan Lake, a 150km-long stretch of vibrantly clean, clear water surrounded by mountains and wilderness. Coastal and Cascade mountain ranges protect the city from all the coastal rain so summers are hot and dry and winters are mild. What this means is warm water for swimmers who flock to the sandy beaches in the summer and powdery-dry snow for skiers in the winter. The seductive climate is also ideal for all sorts of fruits including grapes, so Kelowna has become the hub of a vast region producing prize-winning wines. While other cities will argue similar virtues, Kelowna has the ultimate prize: a friendly but shy lake monster known as Ogopogo, frequently glimpsed and occasionally photographed. Well, maybe.

ⓘ Kelowna Visitor Information Centre *544 Harvey Ave (Hwy 97); tel: (250) 861-1515, tollfree (800) 663-4345; e-mail: info@tourismkelowna.com; www.tourismkelowna.com. Open daily. Provides information and maps.*

Ⓑ Big White Ski Resort *$$ lies just 55km east of Kelowna; tel: (250) 765-3101, tollfree (800) 663-2772; fax: (250) 491-6122; e-mail: bigwhite@bigwhite.com; www.bigwhite.com*

Sights

Big White Ski Resort

Outside of BC Big White is one of the skiing world's best kept secrets, a ski area that keeps getting accolades as North America's 'best value' or 'best place for families' or even 'one of the best ski resorts in the world'. The reasons for all the hype are many: the mountains here have massive snowfalls of light, dry champagne powder. Combine this with one of the most ambitious development plans in resort development anywhere and you get BC's second largest ski village at much less cost than Whistler/Blackcombe, BC's No 1 resort. The season runs late November–April with an average annual snowfall of over 295in (750cm) spread over 755 groomed acres (305.7ha), 1,325 alpine and gladed acres (536.6ha) and 38 illuminated acres (15.3ha) for night skiing.

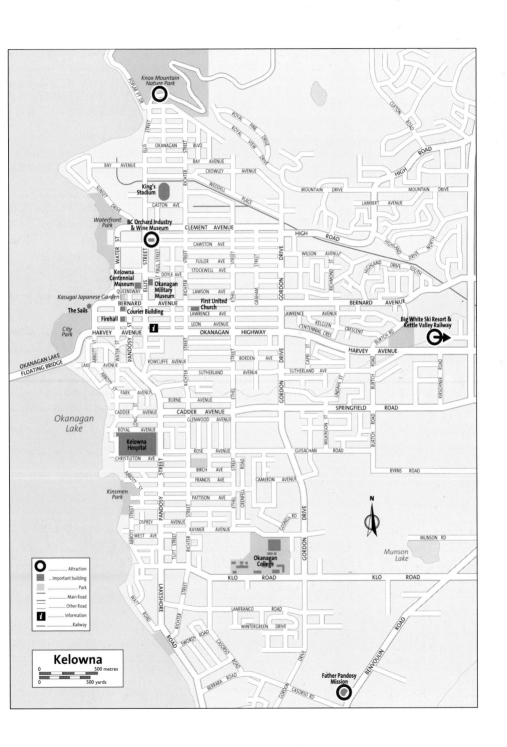

The BC Orchard Industry and Wine Museum *1304 Ellis St; tel: (250) 763-4761; fax: (250) 868-9272; e-mail: laurel@kelownamuseum.ca; www.kelownamuseum.ca. Orchard museum open Mon–Sat 1000–1700; wine museum every day. Donations welcome.*

Father Pandosy Mission $ *3685 Benvoulin Rd; tel: (250) 860-8369. Open Apr–Oct daily.*

Kettle Valley Railway Contact Kelowna Tourism (see page 208) for detailed instructions to the three access points.

The BC Orchard Industry and Wine Museum

Set in a former packing house, this museum provides a good background on Kelowna's early days as a century-old fruit-growing area with lots of photos and hands-on displays. The Wine Museum section has wine-making exhibits, a wine shop and information about touring local wineries.

Father Pandosy Mission

The site of the first European settlement in central British Columbia, founded by Father Charles Pandosy of the Oblate missionaries in 1859. One of the Father's best gifts to the area was the introduction of apple and grape growing to the Okanagan Valley, making him largely responsible for its becoming a major fruit-producing region. Four original log buildings (one a tiny chapel) stand on the 4-acre (1.62ha) site as well as a farmhouse and settler's cabin. All the buildings are furnished as they would have been in the 19th century. The Mission was declared an official heritage site in 1983 following the discovery of Father Pandosy's grave in an abandoned cemetery near his mission.

Kettle Valley Railway

This is not really a railroad anymore but actually a 16km section of abandoned track that once linked Nelson and Hope. The track now

Right
Father Pandosy Mission

Right
Kettle Valley Railway

serves as a dramatic way to see Myra Canyon on mountain bikes, horseback, hiking or on 4x4 adventure tours. There are 18 railway trestles in all, which link the sheer rock walls of the Canyon providing incredible views. There are several ways to access the KVR, but the main three are June Springs, Myra Canyon and Chute Lake. Kelowna has many other hiking trails for all levels including Gallagher's Canyon, Big White Mountain for beginners, Black Knight Mountain, Kelowna Crags and Blue Grouse Mountain for intermediate hikers, and Wild Horse Canyon and Terrace Mountain for advanced hikers.

Orchard tours and agritourism
There are no end of farms in the area to tour, from apples and alpacas to bees and emus, but one of the best is the **Kelowna Land and**

City Park *Extends from the foot of the floating bridge to the large sculpture, The Sails, 1km away.*

The Mission Creek Greenway *An 18km linear trail extending from Lakeshore Rd to Ziprick Rd with access at Lakeshore and Truswell Drives.*

Bill's Honey Farm Vacation $
2910 north, Glenmore Rd; tel: (250) 762-8156. Open May–Sept with tours daily upon prearrangement. Provides honey tasting, birdwatching and canoe trips.

The Geert Maas Sculpture Garden
250 Reynolds Rd; tel: (250) 860-7012; e-mail: maas@geertmaas.org; www.geertmaas.org. Open May–Oct Mon–Sat; varied hours rest of year. Admission by donation.

Kasugai Japanese Garden *1435 Water St; tel: (250) 862-5580; e-mail: ask@kelowna.ca; www.kelowna.ca. Free.*

Kelowna Alpaca Farm $ *2087 Lillooet Crt; tel: (250) 860-5503; e-mail: kelowna.alpaca@shaw.ca; www.kelownaalpaca.com. Call for tours.*

Kelowna Land and Orchard Company $ *3002 Dunster Rd; tel: (250) 763-1091; e-mail: klo@k-l-o.com; www.k-l-o.com. Open daily from Easter–Oct with two tours a day. Call for times.*

Right
Kasugai Japanese Garden

Orchard Company which is the home of the famous Fuji apple that is grown using an old Asian technology in a bag right on the tree. The orchard has operated since 1904 and offers visitors today just about everything you might want to know about apple growing: how for example they get the clever logos 'tattooed' onto the apple. A farm store on the site sells everything from apples (of course) to apple ice cream and a tea house is open for lunch and dinner. There are both self-guided walking tours to the orchard and animal farm or a wagon tour. For a taste of honey, **Bill's Honey Farm** is a working bee farm and the **Kelowna Alpaca Farm** is home to 36 alpacas and their babies. Owner Kelly Cummings welcomes visitors.

Parks and gardens

Kelowna calls itself a walker's paradise with numerous enhanced areas for people who like to stroll. **City Park** that starts from the foot of the floating bridge across Lake Okanagan has a lakeside walkway stretching 1km to the Rotary Marshes at the foot of Knox Mountain. It's paved and a favourite with rollerbladers as well. **The Mission Creek Greenway** is the first children's interpretive trail in BC with signage accompanied by inspired artwork and poetry of local young artists. This 18km linear corridor is a multi-use trail that

Knox Mountain Nature Park *North end of Ellis St.*

Gray Monk *23km from Kelowna at 1055 Camp Rd; tel: (250) 766-3168, tollfree (800) 663-4205; e-mail: mailbox@graymonk.com; www.graymonk.com. Open daily Jul and Aug 0900–2100; Nov–Mar 1100–1700; rest of year 1000–1700; Jan and Feb closed Sundays.*

Mission Hill Winery $ *15km from Kelowna at 1730 Mission Hill Rd; tel: (250) 768-5125, tollfree (800) 957-9911; e-mail: info@missionhillwinery.com; www.missionhillwinery.com. Open daily Apr–Jun 1000–1800; Jul and Aug 0930–1900; Sept–mid-Oct 1000–1800; mid-Oct–Dec 1000–1700.*

Quail's Gate Estate Winery $ *10km from Kelowna at 3303 Boucherie Rd; tel: (250) 769-4451, tollfree (800) 420-9463; e-mail: info@quailsgate.com; www.quailsgate.com. Open summer 1000–1900; winter 1000–1700.*

Summerhill Pyramid Winery $ *20 minutes from Kelowna, 4870 Chute Lake Rd; tel: (250) 764-8000, tollfree (800) 667-3538; e-mail: info@summerhill.bc.ca; www.summerhill.bc.ca. Wine shop open daily 0900–1900. Tours every two hours, starting at 1200.*

accommodates wheelchair users, pedestrians, cyclists and horse riders. Along the way, visitors enjoy ponds, rich foliage such as cottonwoods and aspens, and wildlife such as marmots, mink, skunks, beaver, deer and coyotes. One of the city's loveliest parks is the serene **Kasugai Japanese Garden**, a genuine Oriental garden built as a project between Kelowna and its sister Japanese city. **The Geert Maas Sculpture Garden** is an outdoor 'art park' and the **Knox Mountain Nature Park** draws hikers, picnickers and divers especially to Paul's Tomb where a 7m-long model of Ogopogo lurks 8m below the surface awaiting divers. This is a BC Wildlife Watch viewing site especially for songbirds in the summer.

Winery tours

Since growers in the area began planting quality grapes, local wines have been winning an increasing number of international awards especially for their ice wines. The major showcase for these wines is the Okanagan Wine Festival held each April and in late September, events that have been voted as among the top 100 events in North America several times in recent years. The festival offers upwards of 100 events at venues up and down the Valley including dinners, parades, 'grape stomps' and grape fairs. More than a dozen wineries around Kelowna, the heart of BC's wine country, offer free tours and tastings. **Mission Hill Winery** with its spectacular setting and wide range of activities after a $27million expansion can cater to large groups. You can sit in their outdoor amphitheatre, visit the underground cellar or dine in a state-of-the-art kitchen. **Summerhill Pyramid Winery** is BC's largest producer of sparkling wines and serves excellent lunches featuring Pacific northwestern cuisine between 1000 and 1500 on the Veranda Bistro. **Quail's Gate Estate Winery** is another award-winning winery specialising in ice wines; its Old Vines Patio restaurant is run by Roger Sleiman and serves excellent Pacific Northwestern cuisine from 1100 to dusk. **Gray Monk** owners were pioneers in the 'estate winery' concept and produce a long list of award-winning wines.

Accommodation and food

Kelowna has a good range of hotels, motels, inns and B&Bs from luxury to budget. The city does a good convention business so there can be a rush on rooms at any time and reservations are highly recommended. A good percentage of the properties can be viewed on the Internet before making bookings.

Abbott On the Lake B&B $$ *1986 Abbott St; tel: (250) 762-0221; e-mail: info@abbottonthelake.com; www.abbottonthelake.com.* A heritage Tudor building on the lake filled with antiques. Park-like setting, hot tub and home-cooked breakfast.

At Otella's $$ *42 Altura Rd; tel: (250) 763-4922, tollfree (888) 858-8596; e-mail: info@otellas.com; www.otellas.com.* Lovely 4-bedroom 4¹/₂-star inn on 1 acre (0.405ha) park-like setting with European-trained chef who provides huge gourmet breakfasts. Ask for his home-made chocolate.

De Montreuil Restaurant $$$ *368 Bernard Ave; tel: (250) 860-5508 e-mail: demontreuil@home.com.* This cosy restaurant in downtown Kelowna is known for its regional specialities and its Canadian cuisine.

Edgcombe House B&B $$ *1923 Abbott St; tel: (250) 712-2231; fax: (250) 712-0381; e-mail: edgcombe@silk.net.* Charming English cottage-style home in a heritage neighbourhood near the beach and downtown. Lovely gardens.

Grand Okanagan Resort $$$ *1310 Water St, tel: (250) 763-4500, tollfree (800) 465-4651; fax: (250) 868-5605; e-mail: reserve@ grandokanagan.com; www.grandokanagan.com.* On the lake with a downtown location, this is a 5-star resort with a park, lagoons, recreational facilities, pool and full-service European spa. The resort has several restaurants and coffee shops.

Guisachan House $$–$$$ *1060 Cameron Ave: (250) 862-9368* or *(250) 470-2002; www.worldclasscatering.com.* Located in a BC heritage park that was once the summer home of Lord Aberdeen, a Canadian Governor-General. European cuisine with everything prepared on site. Ask for their special 4-course lunch.

JAKX Neighbourhood Grill $ *203 595 KLO Rd; tel: (250) 763-0773.* A big favourite with locals, it features a menu made from scratch served in healthy portions.

Below
The Sails, Kelowna

The Jammery $ *8038 Hwy 97 north; tel: (250) 766-1139, tollfree (877) 775-5267; e-mail: info@jammery.com; www.jammery.com.* Another local favourite with the added touch of a tour to see some of the delicious jams served being made in what was the Okanagan's first jam factory. Hearty lunches and afternoon tea plus an ice cream parlour featuring specials such as blueberry/amaretto ice cream. The gift shop sells a wide range of speciality jams.

Manteo Resort Waterfront Hotel $$$ *3762 Lakeshore Rd, tel: 860-1031, tollfree (800) 445-5255; e-mail: refresh@manteo.com; www.manteo.com.* Right on the lake with exceptional views, a private beach and marina, spa, cinema and all the facilities of a luxury resort hotel.

The Ridge Restaurant $$–$$$ *3002 Dunster Rd, tel: (250) 712-9404; open for lunch only.* Trendy cuisine using lots of organic fresh produce from the region served in an intimate setting that was once a private home.

Suggested tour

Total distance: 4km.

Time: 1 hour.

Links: From Kelowna, Hwy 97 north connects to **Vernon** (*see page 204*) as well as **Salmon Arm** (*see page 162*). Hwy 97 south links to Penticton (*see page 201*) and **Osoyoos** (*see page 200*).

Route: Heritage walking tour of downtown starting from **The Sails ❶**, a well-known sculptural Kelowna landmark in the **Capozzi Fountain**, follow the path south to the entrance of **City Park ❷** where you will get great views of the lake and see trees imported from different areas around the world. Continue south to the **Okanagan Lake Bridge ❸**, built in 1958 with a 1,300m span. The design of the bridge allows for the rise and fall of lake levels and for high winds through the valley. A new bridge, the William R Bennett Bridge, is slated for completion in 2008. Go back up Harvey Ave northeast to Water St, turn north two blocks for the town's **Firehall** (*1616 Water St*). The original wooden building was replaced in 1924 by the current brick structure. Just up the street, at 1580 Water St, is the **Courier Building** where the town's original newspaper was published. Turn right on Bernard Avenue three blocks to the **First United Church** built in 1909. Backtrack and turn north on Ellis Street to the **Kelowna Centennial Museum** to learn more about the area's first settlers. Stroll over another block to see the **Okanagan Military Museum**. Here you will see historical artefacts that created Okanagan military history. Turn south again and take the path that leads behind City Hall to the serene **Kasugai Japanese Garden ❹** that represents the relationship between Kelowna and her sister city, Kasugai in Japan. A half block east at Pandosy St and Queensway Ave, the Bennett Clock is a carillon clock tower erected in the memory of WAC Bennett, one of BC's longest serving Premiers. The clock tower's seven steps represent the number of terms he was re-elected as Premier, while the 20 spires recognise each year of service as Premier.

Continuing on in your car, head south on Pandosy St taking KLO Rd to Benvoulin Rd and follow it to the intersection of Casorso Rd. Here you will find **FATHER PANDOSY MISSION ❺**, site of Kelowna's first white settlement on Mission Creek. This is a completely refurbished historical mission containing Kelowna's oldest structures. You can also visit **Benvoulin Heritage Church** at 2279 Benvoulin Rd, a Gothic revival-style church that dates back to Kelowna's earliest days. To end the day, take a ride on the **MV *Fintry Queen*** (*www.fintryqueen.com*), a circa 1948 paddle wheeler that still plies the waters of Okanagan Lake and has just undergone a million-dollar restoration. Meals are served on board along with entertainment.

Also worth exploring

Agricultural tours

Dozens of fruit, vegetable and flower markets along with other farming operations welcome visitors to Kelowna. The products offered range from ginseng and lavender to honey and emu meat. A good number are located on Benvoulin, KLO or Casorso roads and Tourism Kelowna will provide complete guides.

The tours available depend on the season, with Blossom Tours taking place during April and May for plums, apples, apricots, cherries, peaches and pears, and harvest tours from early July to mid-September. The **BC ORCHARD INDUSTRY AND WINE MUSEUM** ❻ located in an historic packing house (*1304 Ellis St*) is a good place to see some of the history of fruit production in the area along with artefacts of packing and preserving. There's a gift shop on site as well as a 50ft (15.24m) model railroad. **The Kelowna Land and Orchard Company** ❼ (*3002 Dunster Rd*) is a 140-acre (56.7ha) family-owned historic orchard that welcomes visitors with wagon tours daily during the peak season. The **Gatzke Farm Market** on Hwy 97 in Oyama, just 20 minutes north of Kelowna, overlooks beautiful Kalamalka and Wood lakes and has 52 varieties of fruit trees in its orchard tour along with antique farm implements and a petting zoo. You can watch fresh jam making at **The Jammery** on the way.

Right
MV *Fintry Queen*

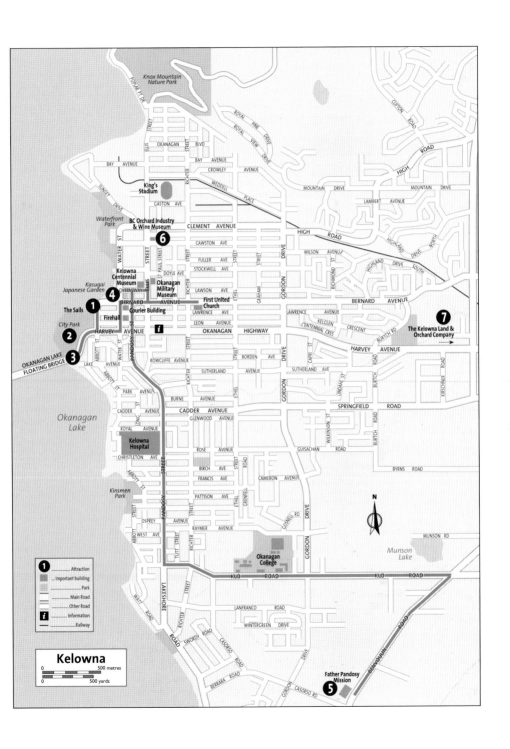

Kelowna

Mighty Fraser Country

Ratings

Children's activities	●●●●●
Gardens	●●●●●
History	●●●●●
Outdoor activities	●●●●●
Parks	●●●●●
Scenery	●●●●●
Beaches	●●●○○
Museums	●●●○○

In 1808, when explorer Simon Fraser guided his canoe through canyons and rapids to the mouth of the brown river that would bear his name, he launched a kind of tidal wave. Within a few years, trading posts sprang up followed by settlers, prospectors, railways and waves of immigrants. At first people came to farm the rich soil but today it's the beauty of the Fraser Valley and the mountains beyond that lures. The Fraser is one of the world's greatest salmon-producing rivers and pulls fishermen from around the world to cast their lines here and in surrounding lakes. Latter-day explorers are keen on other adventures the river and its mountains offer: white-water rafting, skiing, heli-hiking, mountain biking and camping. Near the Fraser, ancient petroglyphs and buried log houses are potent reminders thousands of years old that the river witnessed tenants long before Simon Fraser.

ABBOTSFORD

ℹ Abbotsford Information
Info centre at 34561 Delair Rd; tel: (604) 859-1721, tollfree (888) 332-2229; e-mail: info@ tourismabbotsford.ca; www. tourismabbotsford.ca. Open all year Mon–Fri 0900–1700; daily Jul and Aug.

↪ Old Clayburn Village *Just off Hwy 11 between Abbotsford and Mission.*

Often called 'the hub of the Fraser Valley', Abbotsford is an umbrella city that takes in eight communities and is the centre for a vast area of fertile farms ranging over 357 sq km that include everything from corn mazes and cheese to blueberries and llamas. As North America's second largest producer of raspberries, Abbotsford is called 'the raspberry capital of Canada' but cows, daffodils, kiwi fruit, ostrich and apples are also produced in abundance. The biggest event of the year is North America's best air display, the **Abbotsford International Airshow**, that draws military and civilian precision aerobatics teams, historical and experimental aircraft and stunt flyers from around the world. **Old Clayburn Village** is the site of a 1910 brick manufacturing company and visitors come to see historic brick houses, the schoolhouse, village church and old mill site. The **Clayburn Village Store** with its antiques is a slice of the past and has a charming tea shop with home-baked pastries and sandwiches. Fifteen minutes from

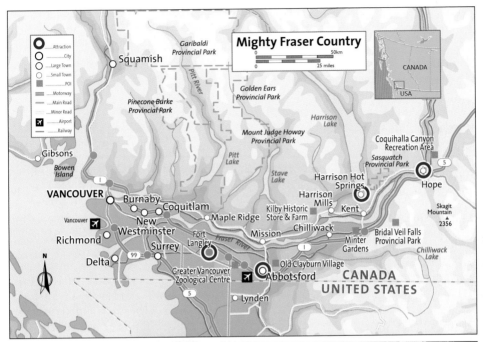

Mighty Fraser Country

Abbotsford International Airshow $ *Held at the Abbotsford Airport on Mount Lehman Rd, 3km south of Hwy I; info from Abbotsford International Airshow Society, 1276 Tower St, Unit 4, Abbotsford V2T 6H5; tel: (604) 852-8511; fax: (604) 852-6093; e-mail: info@abbotsfordairshow.com; www.abbotsfordairshow.com. Second weekend in Aug.*

Greater Vancouver Zoological Centre $ *At the Aldergrove turnoff on Hwy I, 5048 264th St, Aldergrove V4W 1N7; tel: (604) 856-6825; www.gvzoo.com. Open Apr–Sept 0900–1900; Oct–Mar 0900–1600.*

Abbotsford at the Aldergrove exit, the **Greater Vancouver Zoological Centre** has more than 900 animals (200 species) from around the world plus a petting zoo and train rides.

Accommodation and food in Abbotsford

Presto Cucina $$ *103–33640 south Fraser Way; tel: (604) 504-3336.* Excellent pasta, thin-crust pizzas with out of the ordinary toppings and genuine Italian gelato. Don't miss the warm spinach and prosciutto salad.

Restaurant 62 $$ *2001 McCallum Rd; tel: (604) 855-3545; www.restaurant62.ca.* A local gourmet calls this the best restaurant in town.

Clayburn Village Store $ *34810 Clayburn Rd; tel: (604) 853-4020. Open Tue–Sat 0900–1700, Sun 1200–1700.*

Using all fresh Fraser Valley ingredients, meals are prepared by a renowned BC chef. All breads are home-made, good ambience and service. For chocolate lovers, don't miss the truffle dessert.

Sweet Dreams B&B $$ *32288 King Rd; tel: (604) 851-5101; e-mail: info@sweetdreamsbandb.com.* Opened in 2005, has rooms luxuriously furnished with king-sized beds, fireplace, goosedown duvets and all the business amenities.

Taams Resthaven Resort $$ *30061 Townshipline Rd; tel: (604) 856-5687; e-mail: info@resthaven.ca; www.resthaven.ca.* A four-star resort set on 10 acres of lush gardens, koi ponds and natural forest walking trails. Amenities include Jacuzzi tubs, hydro-air massage, saunas, a cinema and library. Only 10 minutes from Abbotsford airport.

FORT LANGLEY

Fort Langley Info Centre *9234 Glover Rd, Langley; tel: (604) 888-1477; e-mail: chamber@langleychamber.com; www.langleychamber.com. Open daily May–Sept.*

Fort Langley National Historic Site $ *23433 Mavis Ave; tel: (604) 513-4777; fax: (604) 513-4788; e-mail: fort.langley@pc.gc.ca; www.pc.gc.ca/fortlangley. Open Mar–Oct daily 1000–1700.*

Paddle Wheeler River Adventures $$ *139–810 Quayside Drive, New Westminster; tel: (604) 525-4465, tollfree (877) 825-1302; fax: (604) 525-5944; www.vancouverpaddlewheeler.com*

The BC Farm Machinery and Agricultural Museum $ *9131 Kings St, Fort Langley; tel: (604) 888-2273; e-mail: bcfarm@vcn.bc.ca; www.bcfarm.com. Open Apr–mid-Oct daily 1000–1600.*

Right Local art gallery in Fort Langley

This rural village is where BC began as a Hudson's Bay Company trading post in 1827 when Europeans started to stake territory in the province. Fort Langley was also a jumping-off point for prospectors heading to the Fraser River gold fields during the late 1850s' rush. The **Fort Langley National Historic Site**, surrounded by a wooden palisade, is a museum today with authentic buildings that provide a glimpse into a pioneering past. In the summer months, costumed staff demonstrate how pelts were traded, blacksmithing, barrel making and pioneer cooking from the mid-19th century. A novel way to reach the Fort is via **Paddle Wheeler River Adventures** who have an old paddle wheeler that drops visitors near the Fort. In Langley nearby, **The BC Farm Machinery and Agricultural Museum** has a large display of 20th-century tractors and threshers, logging and fishing equipment and household furnishings from all over BC, while the **Canadian Museum of Flight** $ *(5333 216 St, tel: (604) 532-0035; e-mail: museum@direct.ca; www.canadianflight.org. Open year round 1000–1600)*

holds one of the largest and most diverse collections of aircraft and other vehicles in Canada.

HARRISON HOT SPRINGS

Harrison Hot Springs Chamber of Commerce *499 Hot Springs Rd; tel: (604) 796-5581; www.harrison.ca. Open May–Oct daily; weekdays rest of the year.*

Harrison Public Hot Pool $ *Harrison Hot Springs Rd and Esplanade Ave. Open daily.*

Kilby Historic Store and Farm $ *215 Kilby Rd, Harrison Mills V0M 1L0; tel: (604) 796-9576; fax: (604) 796-9592; e-mail: info@kilby.ca; www.kilby.ca. Call for current opening hours.*

Minter Gardens $ *52892 Bunker Rd, near Hwy 9, just north of Hwy 1; tel: (604) 794-7191; tollfree (888) MINTERS; fax: (604) 792-8893; e-mail: mail@mintergardens.com; www.mintergardens.com. Open Apr–Oct daily.*

Sasquatch Provincial Park *6.5km beyond Harrison Hotsprings on Rockwell Dr.; tel: (604) 824-2300, tollfree (800) 689-9025; www.env.gov.bc.ca/bcparks*

World Championship Sand Sculpture Competition *PO Box 266, Harrison Hot Springs V0M 1K0; tel: (604) 796-3224; e-mail: info@harrisand.org; www.harrisand.org. Held the second weekend in Sept.*

The tiny resort community of Harrison Hot Springs sits on the edge of Harrison Lake which is 60km long, ringed with sandy beaches and surrounded by mountains. In those mountains, people have reported spotting hairy and elusive humanoids called Sasquatch, legendary creatures related to Bigfoot and Yeti. Sceptics say these reporters may have just stayed in Harrison's equally legendary hot springs too long and were having hallucinations. The first hotel was built here in 1886 to make use of two springs that register at 58°C (136.4°F) and 62°C (143.6°F). Non-guests can use the **Harrison Public Hot Pool**. The mountains around are rich in wildlife and a favourite with rockhounds who can find jade, garnets, agates, fossils and even gold. **Sasquatch Provincial Park** (1,217ha) is a favourite for canoeing, fishing, swimming, hiking, camping and wildlife viewing. Beaver, deer and squirrels are plentiful, along with mountain goats on the Slollicum Bluffs.

The biggest annual event is the **World Championship Sand Sculpture Competition** that draws artists from as far away as Russia and the Netherlands to create masterpieces that are kept on exhibit for a month. Using Harrison as a base, there are a number of short excursions to places like **Minter Gardens**, one of BC's best-known gardens with its mazes, aviaries, Chinese gardens, topiary animals and much more. **Bridal Veil Falls Provincial Park** nearby has a 25m waterfall cascade down a rocky mountain face and strolls through a forest of cedar and fir. For history buffs, **Kilby Historic Store and Farm** is a look at the role the general store played in settlement in BC. Thomas Kilby was a veritable hoarder who saved a vast collection of memorabilia, from eggbeaters to long-gone tinned goods. The hands-on exhibits let you press apples or crank up old wall phones.

Accommodation and food in Harrison Hot Springs

Harrison Hot Springs Resort $$$ *100 Esplanade; tel: (604) 796-2244, tollfree (866) 638-5075; fax: (604) 796-3682; www.harrisonresort.com; e-mail: info@harrisonresort.com.* Newly remodelled spa with a wide range of services.

Rowena's Inn on the River $$$ *14282 Morris Valley Rd, Harrison Mills; tollfree (800) 661-5108; www.rowenasinn.com; e-mail: info@rowenasinn.com.* Intimate luxury inn on 160 acres (64.8ha) with pool, hot tub and excellent dining.

HOPE

Hope Information
Visitor Centre 919
Water St; tel: (604) 869-7322, tollfree (866)
HOPEVIC; fax: (604) 869-2160; e-mail:
destinationhope@telus.net;
www.destination
hopeandbeyond.com.
Open year round.

Memorial Park $
and Japanese
Gardens (free) Downtown
Hope, Memorial Park, 3rd &
Park streets.

Hope Museum $ 919
Water St; tel: (604) 869-7322. Open May–early Sept
daily 0900–1700.

**Coquihalla Canyon
Recreation Area and
Othello Tunnels** 10km
east from Kawkawa Lake.
Open daily but closed if icy
conditions exist.

This little town with its optimistic name nestles against the Cascade Mountains at the point where the Fraser River turns north, a kind of doorway to the Canadian Rockies. Hope is a folksy place known as the Chainsaw Carving Capital because of giant wooden sculptures erected downtown that were carved by local artists. Self-guided walking maps are available from the Hope Information office. **Memorial Park** downtown features 22 stumps carved into animal forms, and next to this the **Japanese Gardens** are dedicated to the Japanese-Canadians placed in the Tashme internment camp during World War II. The **Hope Museum** explains more about the sad history of Japanese-Canadians interred at the camp (24km east) as well as Sto:lo natives and pioneer life in the area. The **Coquihalla Canyon Recreation Area and Othello Tunnels** about 15km east of the town has spectacular gorge scenery that has drawn Hollywood to make films several times including the first *Rambo* flick. The famous Kettle Valley Railroad's Othello Tunnels, blasted out of solid granite 1910–16, were considered one of the world's greatest engineering feats and today are certainly Hope's top attraction. The 2.8km return walk includes four tunnels and dramatic views of the Coquihalla River rushing below. Tunnels and stations are named after both the chief engineer's daughters and Shakespearean characters.

Accommodation and food in Hope

The Blue Moose $ *322 Wallace St; tel: (604) 869-0729; www.bluemoosecafe.com*. Relatively new café with deli-type sandwiches, soups and speciality coffees and live music.

The Home Restaurant $ *665 Old Hope Princeton Way; tel: (604) 869-5558*. Has made a BC magazine's Top Ten list for its home-cooked meals and huge portions; recently opened a second restaurant in Hope.

Quality Inn $ *350 Old Hope Princeton Way, tel: (604) 869-9951, tollfree (800) 359-6279; fax: (604) 869-9421*. On the outskirts, has kitchen, pool and whirlpool sauna.

Rolly's Restaurant $ *888 Fraser Ave; tel: (604) 869-7448*. Family-style cooking and a Hope favourite hangout.

Suggested tour

Total distance: 175km.

Time: Straight driving time from Hope to New Westminster is about 2 hours. Allow 2 hours to half a day for each of Minter Gardens, Harrison Hot Springs and Fort Langley.

Opposite
Bridal Veil Falls

Links: This route links Hope, the Cascade Mountains and the Gold Rush Trail going west to New Westminster.

Route: From **HOPE ❶** follow the Trans-Canada Highway westbound until signs for Hwy 9. Turn north and watch for signs for **Minter Gardens ❷**.

Bridal Veil Falls
Exit 135 from the
Trans-Canada Hwy;
www.env.gov.bc.ca/bcparks/
explore/parkpgs/bridal.html.
Day-use parking fee.

Detour 1: Turn south off Hwy 1 and follow signs to **Bridal Veil Falls ❸**.

Return to Hwy 1. Turn north past Agassiz to **HARRISON HOT SPRINGS ❹**.

Detour 2: Head northeast 6.5km on Rockwell Drive to **Sasquatch Provincial Park ❺**.

Take Hwy 7 going westward to **Harrison Mills ❻** for the **Kilby Historic Store and Farm ❼**. Continue along Hwy 7 for about 35km to **Hatzic Lake** to the right of the highway. Just beyond this, 2.5km before the city of **Mission**, signs will indicate the **Xa:ytem (Hatzic Rock) National Historic Site and Interpretive Centre** *(tel: (604) 820-9725)*. Situated on this site is an immense triangular rock that is sacred to the Sto:lo First Nations people who settled here 9,000 years ago. The cedar **Xa:ytem Longhouse Interpretive Centre** presents the history of both traditional and contemporary Sto:lo people. The historic significance of the rock was discovered just before it was to be destroyed for a planned development. The village that belonged to Sto:lo ancestors was emptied by smallpox in the mid- to late 1800s. Just beyond this, Mission's **Westminster Abbey** is the namesake for the city and now a Benedictine monastery that sits high on a hill overlooking the valley. The Abbey with its 64 stained-glass windows, 12-bell tower and tranquil farm welcomes visitors Monday–Saturday 1330–1600, Sunday 1400–1630. The area's biggest event is the **Mission Annual Powwow** that draws participants from all across North America each year in early July to celebrate native heritage in song, dance and drumming competitions.

Drive through Mission and follow signs leading to the Mission Bridge crossing the Fraser River on Hwy 11 towards **ABBOTSFORD ❽**. Watch for signs indicating the road to the **Clayburn ❾** turnoff on the left. Return to Hwy 11 and continue to Abbotsford where signs will lead you back onto Hwy 1. Follow for 15km and at the **Aldergrove** turnoff (*264th Ave*) exit and follow signs for the **Greater Vancouver Zoological Centre ❿**.

Return to Hwy 1 and continue to the **FORT LANGLEY ⓫** turnoff (*232nd Ave*), following signs to the town and the Fort along Glover Rd. Return to Glover Rd and continue south to Langley for the **Museum Of Flight** and **BC Farm Machinery Museum**.

Return to Hwy 1 and follow to **New Westminster ⓬**. Known as the 'Royal City', New Westminster is older than Vancouver and was once

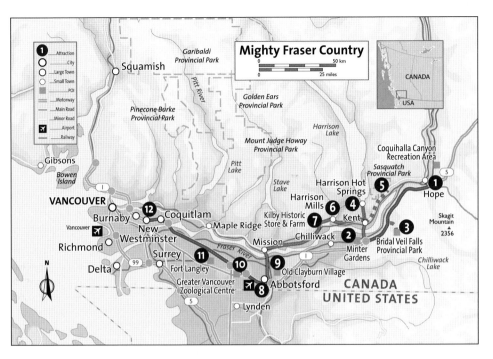

Mighty Fraser Country

a boom town populated by gold prospectors. The city has three interesting museums; the **New Westminster Museum and Archives** *302 Royal Ave; tel: (604) 527-4640*, with artefacts and local history displays; the **Museum of the Royal Westminster Regiment** *530 Queen's Ave; tel: (604) 526-5116; free*, with military artefacts dating back to 1863; and the **SS *Samson V* Maritime Museum** on the Waterfront between the Public Market and the Inn, *tel: (604) 522-6894; donations welcome*. This was the last working sternwheeler on the Fraser River, operating until 1980.

Right
Fort Langley maintains a rural, folksy atmosphere

North Vancouver Island

Ratings

Beaches	●●●●
Children	●●●●
First Nations art	●●●●
Mountains	●●●●
Nature	●●●●
Outdoor activities	●●●●
Scenery	●●●●
Wildlife	●●●

There's a huge immediate difference driving north from the southern parts of Vancouver Island as towns and population thin out dramatically. Less than three per cent of the island's residents live up here, leaving just wilderness to challenge and explore. On the roads, you'll see logging trucks and heavy machinery reflecting the area's traditional history as a timber, mining, milling and fishing base. Now that BC is trying to move beyond its reputation as a resource-based economy, many of the towns are quickly trying to convert to soft-adventure tourism. The north's great assets are its waters and forests with a gold mine of sea mammals cruising up and down the Inside Passage between Vancouver Island and the mainland. For divers and 'watchers', there seems to be no end to the whales because of resident pods that stay year round. This is also a centre for First Nations cultural tourism.

ALERT BAY

ℹ Alert Bay Visitor Centre 116 Fir St; tel: (250) 974-5024, tollfree (877) 974-9911; fax: (250) 974-5026; www.alertbay.ca. Open Mon–Fri year round 0900–1700, daily Jul and Aug 0900–1800.

➜ 'Namgis Burial Ground To the right of the ferry dock. Not open to the public but can be seen clearly from the street.

Located on the beautiful BC Inside Passage, this community blended of native and non-native peoples sits on tiny Cormorant Island just off the coast. Unlike many places, the 'Namgis people of the Kwakwaka'wakw First Nations only moved here in the 1870s from their original home on the Nimpkish River following a church mission and the establishment of a salmon salt plant. Everything in Alert Bay is within walking distance and a good place to start is the **U'mista Cultural Centre**, a building modelled after a traditional Big House. There are excellent ceremonial masks here, ancient baskets and other artefacts confiscated in 1922 after colonial laws banned potlatch ceremonies. The treasures were returned in 1978 after years of dispute. The most visible landmark in town is the Sun Mask at the top of Tall Totem: at 52.7m it held the Guinness record 1972–94 until a taller pole was set up in Victoria. The **'Namgis Burial Ground** has more poles that are oddly haunting in the century-old cemetery.

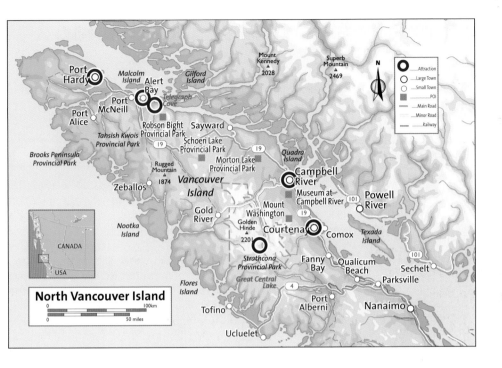

Accommodation and food in Alert Bay

U'mista Cultural Centre $ *Front St north of the ferry landing; tel: (250) 974-5403; fax: (250) 974-5499; e-mail: info@umista.ca; www.umista.org. Open May–Sept daily; rest of the year Mon–Fri. Ask about special tours.*

Deserving Time B&B $$ *400 Pine Rd; (250) 974-2359; e-mail: bookings@deservingtimebnb.com.* Great hospitality, fine ocean view. One of the best.

Janet's Guest House $ *667 Fir St; (250) 974-5947; e-mail: janet@janetsguesthouse.com.* Friendly B&B in a turn-of-the-century restored home.

Nimpkish Hotel Pub & Grill $ *318 Fir St; tel: (250) 974-2324, tollfree (888) NIMPKISH; e-mail: info@nimpkishhotel.com.* The largest hotel and restaurant on the island.

On the Beach $ *tel: (250) 974-5225, tollfree (800) 668-6722; e-mail: seaorca@island.net; www.alertbay.ca.* Panoramic ocean view from deck and comfortable rooms.

CAMPBELL RIVER

Campbell River may have been one of the world's most famous fishing spots years ago but the bloom has somewhat faded from the rose recently. After Roderick Haig-Brown's books on fishing lured such

ⓘ Campbell River Tourism
1235 Shoppers Row, Tyee Plaza; tel: (250) 287-4636; e-mail: visitorinfo@ campbellriverchamber.ca; www.campbellrivertourism.com

☾ Haig-Brown House Education Centre
$ 2250 Campbell River Rd; tel: (250) 286-6646; email: haig.brown@crmuseum.ca; www.haig-brown.bc.ca. Has accommodation in newly restored home of the writer as well as a good library. Seminars and education programmes from end of Feb on environmental issues and gardening.

⊛ HMCS Columbia
Scuba divers should ask at the Info Centre for charters and rentals.

Snorkel with Salmon $$
Tel: (250) 287-2652, tollfree (866) 704-4611; e-mail: info@paradisefound.bc.ca; www.paradisefound.bc.ca. All instruction and equipment supplied.

ⓜ Museum at Campbell River $
470 Island Hwy at the south entrance to town; tel: (250) 287-3103; fax: (250) 286-0109; e-mail: generalinquiries@crmuseum. ca; www.crmuseum.ca. Open Oct–mid-May Tue–Sun 1200–1700; mid-May–Sept daily 1000–1700.

Kwagiulth Museum
Quadra Island, Cape Mudge Village; tel: (250) 285-3733. Open Jun–Sept daily 1000–1630; Oct–May Mon–Sat.

Above
Kayak training

famous fishermen as John Wayne, Bob Hope and Bing Crosby to Campbell River, everyone wanted to come to 'the Salmon Capital of the World'. You can recapture this era in the **Haig-Brown House Education Centre**, the former home and grounds of the conservationist and writer. Tyee salmon are still here but legendary catches such as the 32kg chinook (caught in 1968) are no longer found and the coho and sockeye fisheries are closed. The bigger industry here today is what you can see rather than catch: orcas from a kayak, scuba diving to see Pacific octopus or hikes along forested trails. Campbell River is a hub for most North Island ecotourism so there are scores of charter companies and shops that cater to divers who come to explore sunken ships such as the HMCS *Columbia*. For something totally different, water babies can don wet suits and swim with salmon as they migrate from early July to late October with **Snorkel with Salmon**. In town, the **Museum at Campbell River** tells about early European exploration, pioneer life and First Nations history. Check out the excellent First Nations multimedia presentation. The **Kwagiulth Museum** on Quadra Island is housed in a sea-snail shaped building and holds potlatch artefacts that were seized in 1922 and only returned in 1980.

Accommodation and food in Campbell River

April Point Lodge and Marina $$$ *900 April Point Rd; Quadra Island; tel: (250) 285-2222, tollfree (800) 663-7090; fax: (250) 285-2411; e-mail: info@obmg.com; www.aprilpoint.com.* This legendary lodge is on Quadra Island but caters to a wide range of tours and specialises in fishing. Excellent dining room and sushi bar. Free shuttle to Campbell River.

Chateau Restaurant $$ *3 1170 Island Hwy; tel: (250) 287-4143.* One of the best views in town; steam and seafood menu.

Moxie's Restaurant $ *1360 Island Hwy; tel: (250) 830-1500.* A local favourite, good food and good prices.

Painter's Lodge and Fishing Resort $$$ *1625 McDonald Rd; tel: (250) 286-1102, tollfree (800) 663-7090; fax: (250) 286-0158; e-mail: info@obmg.com; www.painterslodge.com.* Ocean and garden view rooms and dining. Tours can be set up at the hotel.

San Marcos $$ *988 Shoppers Row; tel: (250) 287-7066.* Greek, pizza, seafood and steak, all good.

Town Centre Inn $ *1500 Dogwood St; tel: (250) 287-8866; tollfree: (800) 287-7107; www.towncentreinn.com.* Clean, quiet, well-kept motel.

COURTENAY AND COMOX VALLEY

ⓘ Comox Valley Chamber of Commerce *2040 Cliffe Ave; tel: (250) 334-3234, tollfree (888) 357-4471; fax: (250) 334-4908; e-mail: visitorinfo@comoxvalleychamber.com; www.comoxvalleychamber.com. Open daily.*

ⓘ Courtenay Museum *$ 204 Fourth St.; tel: (250) 334-0686; e-mail: museum@island.net; www.courtenaymuseum.ca. Open May–Sept daily 1000–1700; Oct–Apr Tue–Sat 1000–1700.*

⊛ Mount Washington Ski Area *$$ 25km west of Courtenay, follow signs out of town; tel: (250) 338-1386, tollfree (888) 231-1499; www.mountwashington.ca. Open year round.*

Right
Rainforest flora

The Comox Valley lies in the rain shadow of the Vancouver Island Range and the peaks around offer the best skiing on Vancouver Island. **Mount Washington Ski Area** offers the highest vertical drop on the island, spectacular views, high-speed quad and other chairs plus a ski school, rentals and all the facilities. The Valley also has the most sunshine on the Island along with fertile soil, making the area one of the best agriculturally on Vancouver Island. Today Courtenay is one of Canada's fastest growing urban communities, but 80 million years ago it was a popular stomping ground for giant long-necked elasmosaurs. Fossils of this swimming reptile have been found here, the first of its kind found west of the Rockies. You can see these in the **Courtenay Museum** as well as First Nations artefacts and settlement histories.

PORT HARDY

ⓘ Port Hardy Visitors Centre *7250 Market St; tel: (250) 949-7622; www.ph-chamber.bc.ca. Open winter Mon–Fri 0900–1700; summer Mon–Fri 0830–1800, weekends 0900–1700.*

⊛ Scuba diving *$$ Check in town for centres that take divers out.*

ⓘ Port Hardy Museum and Archives *$ 7110 Market St; tel: (250) 949-8143; e-mail: phmachin@island.net. Open daily in summer.*

Port Hardy has seen better days as a town but it still serves as a supply centre in the north island and is a good base for hiking, fishing and kayaking adventures as well as First Nations cultural experiences. As a **scuba dive centre**, Port Hardy is world famous for its clear waters, coral, white-sided dolphins and wolf eels. A number of soft-adventure operators are based here to take visitors caving, kayaking and animal watching to see grizzly and black bears, Roosevelt elk, orcas, grey whales and humpbacks. There's a good stroll along a paved seaside path to watch for bald eagles and other birds. **The Port Hardy Museum and Archives** gives a glimpse into Kwakwaka'wakw history.

STRATHCONA PROVINCIAL PARK

◑ Canadian Outdoor Leadership Training (COLT) Centre *Contact Strathcona Park Lodge or www.colt.bc.ca*

Strathcona Park Lodge
$–$$ Upper Campbell Lake along Hwy 28, 38km west of Hwy 19; tel: (250) 286-3122; fax: (250) 286-6010; e-mail: info@strathcona.bc.ca; www.strathcona.bc.ca. Open year round.

This roughly triangular park is immense, stretching over 250,000ha of prime wilderness and including Vancouver Island's tallest mountain (Mount Golden Hinde, 2,200m) and Canada's tallest waterfall (Della Falls, 440m). It was BC's first designated provincial park (established 1911) and continues to be a hiker's paradise in alpine meadows with a multitude of small lakes for fishing and canoeing and peaks for skiing. Because of the long separation from the mainland, several animal species such as the Roosevelt elk and the black-tailed deer have evolved differently here. The main centre for ecology is the **Strathcona Park Lodge** which has built an excellent reputation over the years for its wilderness skills programmes, outdoor summer camps and family excursions. The **Canadian Outdoor Leadership Training (COLT) Centre** has a 105-day intensive programme to develop water and land-based outdoor skills and environmental awareness.

TELEGRAPH COVE

🅗 Robson Bight Provincial Park *On the northeast coast, 2km south of Telegraph Cove in Johnstone Strait; www.britishcolumbia.com/parksandtrails. This provincial park is a major whale habitat as well as an ecological reserve protecting rare alpine forests and bogs. Day-use parking fee.*

This town in a teacup (10km off the Island Highway) is about the most photographically picturesque you'll find on Vancouver Island. Telegraph Cove booms in the summer months as a major destination for wilderness seekers, mainly whale watchers who come to see orcas (killer whales) that rub their bellies on the gravel beaches of **Robson Bight**.

Suggested tour

Total distance: 360km.

Time: In driving time allow 6 hours from Parksville to Port Hardy. You could spend weeks here but three days should cover enough adventures.

Links: From Port Hardy, ferry routes lead north to Bella Coola and Prince Rupert (*see page 184*).

Route: Take Hwy 19A from **Parksville ❶** north up island, stopping at **Qualicum Beach ❷**, continuing north if you have time and want ocean views. If short of time, take Hwy 19 west of Qualicum Beach and continue up to **Fanny Bay ❸** which is famous mainly for its excellent oysters. Continue north on Hwy 19.

Detour 1: At COURTENAY ❹ head for **Comox ❺** on 17th Ave for several interesting parks.

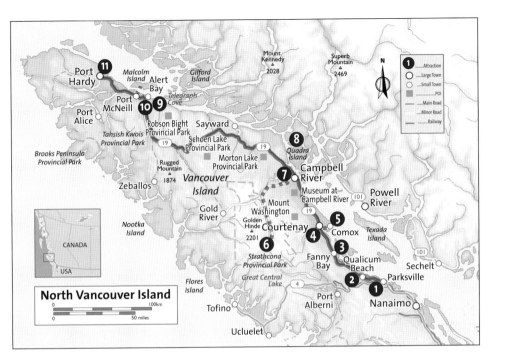

North Vancouver Island
0   100km
0   50 miles

CANADA
USA

Sointula

This fishing village began as an idealistic Finnish co-operative community in 1901 but even after the venture failed, many Finns remained. The museum on the island has artefacts reflecting the fishing and farming roots of the Finnish community.

Detour 2: An access point for **STRATHCONA PROVINCIAL PARK** ⑥ and **Gold River**, 89km west of Campbell River.

Returning to Hwy 19, continue on to **CAMPBELL RIVER** ⑦ to the **Fletcher Challenge Elk Falls Pulp and Paper Mill**, *tel: (250) 287-5594* for free tours during the summer. North of Campbell River, signs indicate the ferry to **Quadra Island** ⑧ and the highly recommended **April Point Lodge** as well as its excellent fishing locations.

Returning to Hwy 19, **Morton Lake Provincial Park** is 1km west of the highway and offers good swimming, fishing and biking. Continuing north, just past Sayward, signs point to **Schoen Lake Provincial Park**, another wilderness park but one requiring a rugged vehicle to reach. Continue on to **TELEGRAPH COVE** ⑨. Just north, the highway passes the **Nimpkish Fish Hatchery**, *tel: (250) 974-9556*, it explains how logging and over-fishing have affected salmon in the area.

East off Hwy 19, take the ferry to **ALERT BAY** ⑩ for its totems and historical sites.

Detour 3: Sointula is on tiny Malcolm Island that can be reached by ferry from Port McNeill and Alert Bay as well. Continue north to **PORT HARDY** ⑪.

South Vancouver Island

Ratings

Food and drink	●●●●●
Beaches	●●●●
Nature	●●●●
Parks	●●●●
Scenery	●●●●
Children	●●●
History	●●●
Wineries	●●●

Until economic conditions and environmental protesters ended large-scale logging, southern Vancouver Island was like a star waiting in the wings. Blessed with a climate so warm and sunny that bananas can actually grow outdoors, it's only been recently that boutique farmers and winemakers have found the proverbial pot of gold. The Cowichan Valley is now heavily dotted with people who have found their calling in specialised food and drink. Although the entire island has spectacular scenery, the provincial parks in the south are easily accessible, some right off the major highways with their virgin forest and ancient petroglyphs. All along the western coastline beaches are steps away from the road for picnicking, tidal pool hunts or hikes summer or winter. Some of the best examples of First Nations tourism have sprung up in this area to provide an enlightened look at the province's original settlers.

CHEMAINUS

ⓘ **Chemainus and District Visitors Centre** 9796 Willow St (across from Waterwheel Park); tel: (250) 246-3944; fax: (250) 246-3251; e-mail: ccoc@islandnet.com; www.chemainus.bc.ca

ⓕ **Waterwheel Park and Chemainus Valley Museum $** in Waterwheel Park in the heart of town.

This is often called 'The Little Town that Did'. When the town's sawmill closed in the early 1980s, Chemainus faced slow extinction until an innovative revitalisation programme was launched by people who loved their town. With so many talented artists in the area, they decided to paint murals telling the town's history on the side of buildings. Local and international artists created 33 murals and 12 statues plus a series of footprints for a self-guided tour of the town. Today, more than 300,000 visitors come every year to photograph the immense murals or take in a production at the professional **Chemainus Theatre** where each season comedies and classics draw in huge crowds. Children will love the **Waterwheel Park** where they can play at being pirates. Nearby is **Chemainus Valley Museum** with its archival documents and artefacts.

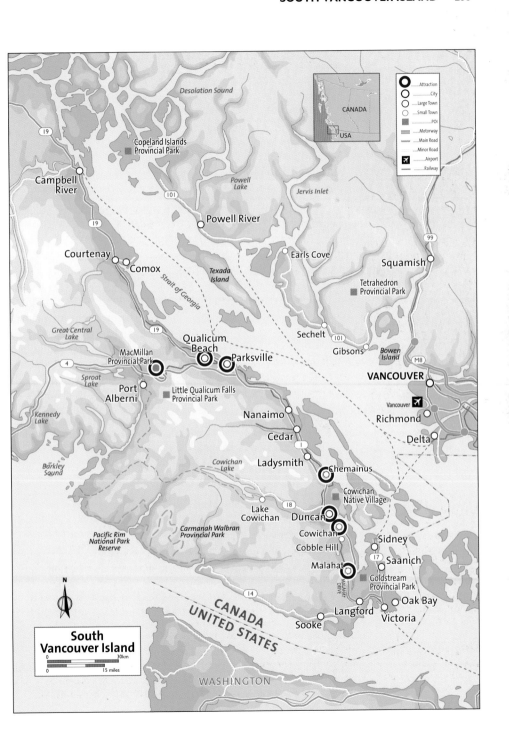

Attraction
City
Large Town
Small Town
POI
Motorway
Main Road
Minor Road
Airport
Railway

CANADA
USA

Desolation Sound

Copeland Islands
Provincial Park

Powell
Lake

Jervis Inlet

19

Powell River

Campbell
River

Courtenay
Comox

Strait of Georgia

Texada
Island

Earls Cove

Squamish

Tetrahedron
Provincial Park

99

19

Great Central
Lake

19

Qualicum
Beach

Sechelt

101

MacMillan
Provincial Park

Parksville

Gibsons

Bowen
Island

M8

4

Sproat
Lake

Port
Alberni

Little Qualicum Falls
Provincial Park

VANCOUVER

Kennedy
Lake

Nanaimo

Vancouver

Richmond

Cedar

Delta

Barkley
Sound

Cowichan
Lake

Ladysmith

Chemainus

Cowichan
Native Village

Lake
Cowichan

18

Duncan

Pacific Rim
National Park
Reserve

Carmanah Walbran
Provincial Park

Cowichan

Sidney

Cobble Hill

Malahat

Saanich

17

Goldstream
Provincial Park

MALAHAT DRIVE

N

14

Langford

Oak Bay

Sooke

Victoria

CANADA
UNITED STATES

South
Vancouver Island

0   30km
0   15 miles

WASHINGTON

○ Chemainus Theatre $$ *Corner of Chemainus Rd and Victoria St; tel: (250) 246-9820 for reservations, tollfree (800) 565-7738; e-mail: info@ chemainustheatre.ca; www.chemainustheatre festival.ca. Offers dinner, theatre and children's shows as well.*

Accommodation and food in Chemainus

A Small World B&B $$ *9866 Willow St; tel: (250) 246-9962; e-mail: stay@asmallworld.ca; www.asmallworld.ca.* John and Lynne Landygo are the hosts at this tastefully decorated B&B that serves great homestyle breakfasts.

Bird Song Cottage B&B $$ *9910 Maple St; tel: (250) 246-9910; fax: (250) 246-2909; e-mail: birdsongcottage@shaw.ca; www. vancouverislandaccommodation.bc.ca.* Spilling over with romance, this lovely B&B is run by a musician and artist and their touch carries through into the charming rooms.

The Dancing Bean Cafe $ *9752A Willow St; tel: (250) 246-5050; www.dancingbean.ca.* Great wraps, panini, sandwiches and salads.

The Willow Street Café $ *9749 Willow St; tel: (250) 246-2434; e-mail: philmich@shaw.ca.* Great muffins and scones; locals love it.

COWICHAN

① Quw'utsun'/ Cowichan Tourism *175 Ingram St, Duncan; tel: (250) 746-1099, tollfree (888) 303-3337; fax: (250) 746-2633; e-mail: tourismcowichan@shaw.ca; www.cowichan.bc.ca*

⑪ Merridale Cider $$ *1230 Merridale Rd, Cobble Hill; tel: (250) 743-4293, tollfree (800) 998-9908; www.merridalecider. com. Call for opening times.*

The name means 'warm land' and the bountiful harvests produced here confirm that it's exactly that: tender and tasty cheeses, ciders and wines. Winemakers here say that there are more hours of sunshine in the Cowichan Valley than anywhere else in Canada and this, coupled with just the right amount of precipitation and glacial deposits of excellent soil, creates perfect vineyard conditions. The best thing to do in this area is follow a map available at Cowichan Tourism and follow the winding roads to sample choice food and drink at boutique farms. **Merridale Cider** welcomes visitors to BC's first estate cidery where you can check out the special fruit that goes into cider in the orchard, chat with cider makers about their craft and walk through the cider making process. **Cherry Point Vineyards** welcomes visitors to try their award-winning Alsatian wines, while **Glenterra Vineyards** (opened in May 2000) has already won prizes for their Pinot Gris. **Hilary's Fine Cheeses** is a Vancouver Island speciality cheese producer with a wide range from Camembert to brushed-rind Tommes and fresh Cheddar curd. Visitors are welcome to taste the European-style full-bodied cheeses.

**Cherry Point
Vineyards $$** *840
Cherry Point Rd, Cobble Hill;
tel: (250) 743-1272; fax:
(250) 743-1059; e-mail:
info@
cherrypointvineyards.com;
www.
cherrypointvineyards.com.
Open daily 1000–1700 for
tastings; tours daily at 1300
or at other times if staff
available.*

Glenterra Vineyards $$
*3897 Cobble Hill Rd, Cobble
Hill; tel: (250) 743-2330;
e-mail:
glenterravineyards@shaw.net.
Open May–Sept daily
1100–1800 for tours and
tastings. Call for winter
hours.*

**Hilary's Fine Cheeses
$$** *1282 Cherry Point Rd,
Cobble Hill; tel: (250) 715-
0563; fax: (250) 715-0564;
e-mail:
hilary@cowichan.com. Open
weekends from mid-Feb;
Apr–Oct daily.*

Right
Merridale Cider

DUNCAN

 **Duncan Visitors
Centre**
*381 Trans-Canada Hwy;
tel: (250) 748-1111; fax:
(250) 746-8222; e-mail:
manager@duncancc.bc.ca;
www.duncancc.bc.ca. In
Overwaitea Centre Mall.
Open Apr–Oct.*

Beginning as a whistle stop for William Duncan's farm in the 1880s, Duncan is now the main centre for the Cowichan Valley's 74,000 residents. It is probably most widely known for the heavy, warm woollen sweaters, mitts, toques and other knitted garments produced by the Cowichan native people who have lived in the area for thousands of years. The **Cowichan Native Village (Quw'utsun Cultural Centre)** presents an excellent up-to-date multimedia presentation blended with stories and dance to tell the story of the

⊕ Quw'utsun' Native Village $ 200
Cowichan Way, immediately after crossing the Cowichan River on Silver Bridge; tel: (250) 746-8119, tollfree (877) 746-8119; fax: (250) 746-4143; e-mail: info@quwutsun.ca; www.quwutsun.ca. Open daily year round May–Sept 0900–1800; Oct–Apr 1000–1700.

Artists $$ For more information on galleries and when to visit contact Cowichan Tourism or www.visit.cowichan.net

BC Forest Museum $ 2892 Drinkwater Rd; tel: (250) 715-1113; fax: (250) 715-1170; e-mail: infobcfdc@shawlink.ca; www.bcforestmuseum.com. Open Jun–Aug 1000–1700; Sept–mid-Oct, Apr & May 1000–1630.

Cowichan people from the beginning of time. Native artists work at the Village, knitting or carving on totem poles and canoes: visitors can try their hand at carving as well. During July and August every Sunday, there's a salmon barbecue done outdoors in the traditional way. Duncan is also home to a number of excellent **artists** and several who have become internationally known. The **BC Forest Museum** tells the story of the BC forest industry with indoor and outdoor exhibits including a small village of pioneers' houses, shops and schoolhouses. Kids will love the narrow-gauge steam train that runs through the 40ha site across a trestle and through a farmstead and logging camp, plus there's lots of hands-on activities such as leaf rubbing.

Accommodation in Duncan

Summer Place Lodge on the River $$$ 5245 Winchester Rd; tel: (250) 715-1222, tollfree (800) 731-1498; fax: (250) 746-0610; e-mail: info@summerplacelodge.com; www.summerplacelodge.com. Luxury B&B set on the banks of the Cowichan River and decorated in 'Canadiana' and antiques.

MACMILLAN PROVINCIAL PARK

⊖ MacMillan Provincial Park At the end of Cameron Lake, 31km west of Parksville. Day-use parking fee.

Cathedral Grove is here with some of the largest Douglas fir trees remaining on Vancouver Island. A parking lot right on the highway leads into the Grove, which has trails that wind through stands of trees as much as 800 years old. This beautiful rainforest is a poignant reminder of what the whole island looked like before logging introduced clear-cutting practices.

MALAHAT DRIVE

⊕ Goldstream Provincial Park Off the Malahat about 20km from Victoria city centre; tel: (250) 478-9414; www.goldstreampark.com

Starting at **Goldstream Provincial Park**, this 16km drive over Malahat Mountain provides glimpses of what looks like Switzerland combined with Norway at times, with magnificent views looking out over Finlayson Arm. Goldstream has great stands of virgin western red cedar forest along with giant maples and Douglas firs. There are old mine shafts from the late 1800s and excellent hikes through arbutus and oak groves. Visitors in the autumn (fall) may catch the annual salmon run (chum, coho and chinook) when the fish spawn here.

Accommodation and food on the Malahat

The Aerie Resort $$$ *600 Ebedora Lane at the Spectacle Lake turnoff on Hwy 1; tel: (250) 743-7115; fax: (250) 743-4766, tollfree (800) 518-1933; e-mail: resort@aerie.bc.ca; www.aerie.bc.ca.* You will swear you've been transformed into an eagle and this is your nest. This luxury hotel with individually designed rooms was ranked No 2 among small hotels in North America and has a dining room with a stunning view of Findlayson Arm. The dining room here is an award winner.

The Prancing Horse Retreat $$ *573 Ebedora Lane, located just below The Aerie (above); tel: (250) 743-9378, tollfree (877) 887-8834; fax: (250) 743-9372; e-mail: stay@prancinghorse.com; www.prancinghorse.com.* This lovely B&B has much the same view as The Aerie but at lower prices. Lovely rooms and excellent breakfast.

PARKSVILLE AND QUALICUM BEACH

🛈 **Parksville Visitors Centre** *1275 E Island Hwy; tel: (250) 248-3631.*

✪ **Little Qualicum Falls** *North off Hwy 4, 4.5km west of Hwy 4A.*

Englishman River Falls *Follow signs at Errington Rd for 9km to the park.*

🛈 **Coombs** *9km west of Parksville on Hwy 4A.* The market is well worth a stop for its fresh produce, baking and hearty restaurant as well as photos of the goats on the roof.

Brant Goose Feeding Area *Just north of Hwy 19/19A junction at Craig's Crossing; tel: (250) 248-4117 for information about programmes.*

Known for its beaches, Parksville is tide-pool heaven when hundreds of hectares of beach are exposed at low tide. Children love to search for tiny trapped sea creatures or build castles in the sand. Parksville is best used as a base to explore **Little Qualicum Falls**, **Englishman River Falls** and **Coombs**. Little Qualicum Falls is a stretch of rainforest and walkways beside both the Upper and Lower falls. There's hiking, swimming, snorkeling and fishing for brown trout in Qualicum River. Englishman River Falls is also a good place to swim, camp and hike by scenic waterfalls and gorges. Coombs is a town of only 840, most famous for its Old Country Market with a herd of goats grazing on the roof. The town grew out of a Salvation Army programme that brought nearly a quarter of a million poor English and Welsh people to settle here and live a simple life. The shores of Parksville and Qualicum Beach are on the Pacific flyway for migratory waterfowl and as many as 20,000 Brant geese stop at the **Brant Goose Feeding Area** to feed each spring en route to the Baja. Many programmes held here include nature talks, bird activities and more.

Accommodation and food in Parksville

Tigh-Na-Mara Resort $$ *1155 Resort Dr.; tel: (250) 248-2072, tollfree (800) 663-7373; e-mail: info@tigh-na-mara.com; www.tigh-na-mara.com.* Cosy solid log cottages with fireplaces tucked into a forest of fir and arbutus trees plus seafront condominiums. Excellent restaurant with Northwest cuisine and fresh seafood.

Above
View over the Malahat

Brother Twelve

BC has always attracted odd characters and bizarre cultists among whom Brother Twelve was legendary. Near Nanaimo, a number of houses were once part of a colony set up by a former English sea captain named Edward Arthur Wilson in the late 1920s. Wilson believed himself to be the '12th brother' of The Great White Lodge that guided the evolution of the human race. After a series of visions, he established a small colony comprising of lonely (and wealthy) followers who gave vast sums of money to share in Brother XII's apocalyptic visions. The colony later moved to Valdes Island and then De Courcy where Wilson stashed away a fortune in jam jars. With the police hot on his heels, Brother Twelve and his strange companion, Madame Zee, disappeared with more than $400,000 in bank notes and gold tucked in the jam jars. Rumour said they went to Switzerland but no one knows for sure.

Suggested tour

Total distance: 213km.

Time: Driving time from the outskirts of Victoria to Parksville and vicinity takes half a day but 4 or 5 days would be necessary to see all the sights in-between.

Links: Continue north up to Port Hardy with a ferry connection to Prince Rupert (*see page 184*). Ferries also go back to the mainland from Nanaimo to Horseshoe Bay.

Route: Follow Hwy 1 north from Victoria past **Thetis Lake Park** to **Goldstream Provincial Park ❶** where the road becomes the **MALAHAT DRIVE ❷**. There are numerous lay-bys on this high-level highway with panoramic views of bays and coastline. The Malahat becomes the Island Highway when it heads into the Cowichan area.

Detour 1: The Shawinigan Lake access road west off Hwy 1 leads to the Lake and to **Memory Island Provincial Park**. This beautiful island was purchased by families who lost their sons in World War II to set up a permanent memorial.

At **Cobble Hill ❸** explore the area's many wineries, cideries and speciality farms with their tasting rooms. Returning to Hwy 1, continue up to **Cowichan Bay ❹** east of Hwy 1 for a walk along the **Hecate Regional Park Footpath** that crosses one of several Cowichan Tribe reserves and offers birdwatching and views of Mount Tzouhalem. Continuing on to DUNCAN, the **Cowichan Native Village ❺** deserves at least a half day for stories, tour, film and barbecue.

Continuing north up Hwy 1, take the signposted cut-off for CHEMAINUS ❻ and the world-famous murals. With a number of quaint tea rooms and restaurants, this is a good place to stop for a rest.

Returning to Hwy 1 for another 10km, **Ladysmith** is worth a quick drive around and a peek at some of the shops. Continuing on Hwy 1, **Petroglyph Provincial Park** is well signposted on the highway and worth a short hike to see the ancient carvings. Nanaimo is a town of more than 70,000 that serves as a supply centre for the area and ferry access to Vancouver. History buffs might check out **The Bastion** on the corner of Bastion and Front Sts for its military archives and artefacts. Hwy 1 becomes Hwy 19 at Nanaimo and continues up to PARKSVILLE ❼.

Detour 2: At Parksville, private boats will take visitors on tours of **Lasqueti Island** and **Jedediah Island Provincial Park** where you will see rich marine life and mammals along with a host of birds. This is prime ocean kayaking terrain as well.

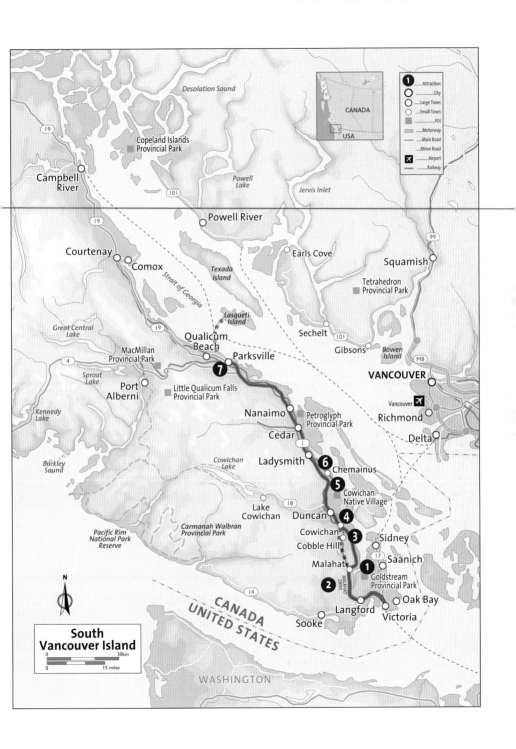

South
Vancouver Island

Attraction
City
Large Town
Small Town
POI
Motorway
Main Road
Minor Road
Airport
Railway

Desolation Sound

CANADA
USA

Copeland Islands
Provincial Park

Campbell
River

Powell
Lake

Jervis Inlet

Powell River

Courtenay
Comox

Texada
Island

Earls Cove

Squamish

Tetrahedron
Provincial Park

Great Central
Lake

Strait of Georgia

Lasqueti
Island

Sechelt

MacMillan
Provincial Park

Qualicum
Beach
Parksville

Gibsons   Bowen
Island

VANCOUVER

Sproat
Lake

Port
Alberni

Little Qualicum Falls
Provincial Park

Vancouver

Richmond

Kennedy
Lake

Nanaimo

Petroglyph
Provincial Park

Delta

Barkley
Sound

Cedar

Cowichan
Lake

Ladysmith

Chemainus

Cowichan
Native Village

Lake
Cowichan

Duncan

Cowichan

Sidney

Saanich

Pacific Rim
National Park
Reserve

Carmanah Walbran
Provincial Park

Cobble Hill

Malahat

Goldstream
Provincial Park

MALAHAT DRIVE

CANADA
UNITED STATES

Sooke

Langford

Oak Bay

Victoria

WASHINGTON

0   30km
0   15 miles

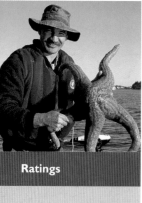

The Wild West Coast

Ratings

Beaches	●●●●
National parks	●●●●
Nature	●●●●
Outdoor activities	●●●●
Scenery	●●●●
Walking	●●●●
Wildlife	●●●●

It takes some driving: but haven't we been told that the best things in life don't come easily? The scenery is unmatchable anywhere, 'drop dead gorgeous' as they would say here. The West Coast Trail is one of life's great adventures for the fit and hardy, but even soft-adventure seekers find all they could want on the West Coast: kayaking or canoeing through the Broken Group Islands or watching whales from a Zodiac. It's a superb place to see marine life, especially great whales, and some of the world's best scuba diving can be found here. The crystal-clear water holds anemones in every shade of the rainbow, the world's largest octopuses and ancient shipwrecks. Beaches here are not for swimming but for walking in summer and in winter too when the wild, wild storms hit with fury. The Pacific Coast is simply a world in itself.

BAMFIELD

 Bamfield Chamber of Commerce
Town centre; tel: (250) 728-3006; e-mail: info@bamfieldchamber.com; www.bamfieldchamber.com

West Coast Trail $
For permits, information and fees, call after 1 Mar for upcoming season; *tel: (604) 663-6000, tollfree (800) 663-6000 or (250) 387-1642 (outside Canada and US); www.ucluelet.net*

This tiny seaside village is best known as the starting point of the 77-km long **West Coast Trail** but it's also a destination for fishermen, kayakers, scuba divers and whale and bear watchers. In the summer months, the government wharves are filled with boats heading out to catch halibut, cod and salmon; or ferrying visitors to the prime viewing grounds for orcas, sea lions and whales. Salmon fishing causes the local population of 338 to jump dramatically in the summer with sports fishermen and kayakers, who use Bamfield as a launching spot for tours of the **Broken Group Islands** (*see page 245*), an archipelago in Barkley Sound. Bamfield looks off-the-beaten-track but visitors can brave an unpaved road from Port Alberni or take either a boat or float plane.

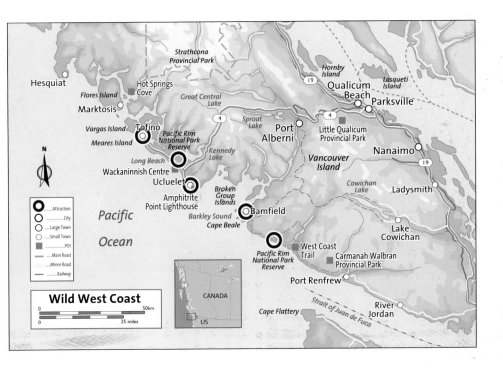

Map legend:
- ◎ ....Attraction
- ○ ....City
- ○ ....Large Town
- ○ ....Small Town
- ■ ....POI
- ─ ....Main Road
- ─ ....Minor Road
- ─ ....Railway

Wild West Coast

0 ————————————— 50km

0 ————————————— 25 miles

PACIFIC RIM NATIONAL PARK RESERVE

The Wickaninnish Centre $$ *At the end of Long Beach Rd, beyond Park headquarters. Open daily late spring to autumn (fall).*

This is the umbrella for three parks and a goodly amount of ocean: the West Coast Trail (*see page 245*), the Broken Group Islands (*see page 245*) and Long Beach, which runs between Ucluelet and Tofino. This is a vast park (130km long and covering 84,642ha) that was created to preserve wild things in a terrain of beaches, rainforests, bogs and rocky headlands. Long Beach was for years a Vancouver Island secret until a paved road replaced the dirt track linking Port Alberni and the coast. Today, visitors stream into the area but beaches are still not overcrowded and it's possible to find a deserted cove or lonely stretch of sand. The Wickaninnish Centre has observation decks with telescopes for looking out to sea. Inside there are exhibits and murals plus films to bring an insight into the local ecology.

Right
The wild west coast,
Wickaninnish Inn, Tofino

Opposite
Tofino beach

TOFINO

ⓘ Tofino-Long Beach Chamber of Commerce *Campbell St; tel: (250) 725-3414; fax: (250) 725-3296; e-mail: info@tourismtofino.com; www.tourismtofino.com. Open Jul and Aug daily; weekends May, Jun & Sept.*

ⓖ Eagle Aerie Gallery *$$ 350 Campbell St; tel: (250) 725-3235.*

Hot Springs Cove $$$ While the bathing is free, the boat or plane rides are not. Contact Remote Passages Marine Excursions; *tel: (250) 725-3330, tollfree (800) 666-9833; fax: (250) 725-3380; e-mail: tofino@ remotepassages.com; www.remotepassages.com.* Offers kayaking, whale watching, Hot Springs Cove and other adventures.

Tucked into a vast rainforest, Tofino is not only the gateway to Clayoquot Sound but also the jumping off spot for a score of adventures. Aboriginal people have lived in the area for more than 2,000 years: a timeline shared by a cedar tree that sprouted on nearby Meares Island 20 centuries ago. This village on the edge of a continent has a long history of logging and fishing that still continues, tempered nowadays by a powerful cadre of environmentalists. When the BC Government decided to log Clayoquot Sound in 1993, it sparked Canada's largest civil disobedience action. Clayoquot is the largest expanse of old-growth temperate rainforest left in North America and the international protest saved the Sound.

There's a hike along a boardwalk through the ancient cedar and hemlock forests on **Meares Island** where you'll see trees that were alive before the Roman Empire fell. The island is larger than Hong Kong or Bermuda and it was one of the numerous places saved (for now) from the chainsaw. From Tofino, there are whale watching and wildlife tours, sea-kayaking adventures, First Nations cultural tours and fishing. One of the most unusual is **Hot Springs Cove** where steaming 50°C (122°F) water percolates from the ground and flows over a waterfall through a series of pools to the sea. You can bathe in these natural pools in exquisite scenery. Fans of First Nations art will find the works of Roy Vickers, one of Canada's most successful aboriginal artists, at the **Eagle Aerie Gallery** with its traditional longhouse façade.

Accommodation and food in Tofino

Meares Island numerous boating and kayaking tours available by operators in Tofino.

Breakers Delicatessen $ *430 Campbell St; tel: (250) 725-2558; e-mail: tdixon@island.net; www.breakersdeli.com.* Great healthy breakfasts and lunches at low prices.

The Common Loaf Bake Shop $ *180 First St, tel: (250) 725-3915.* A local hangout, especially on rainy days with great baking, breads and sandwiches.

Middle Beach Lodge $$ *400 MacKenzie Beach Rd; tel: (250) 725-2900; fax: (250) 725-2901; e-mail: lodge@middlebeach.com; www. middlebeach.com.* Rustic ocean-front lodges and cabins on the Pacific Ocean with fireplaces and hot tubs. Good for families.

Pointe Restaurant $$$ *at the Wickaninnish Inn (see below).* Extraordinary view from the dining room with a menu to match.

Schooner Restaurant $–$$ *331 Campbell St; tel: (250) 725-3444; e-mail: schooner@seaviewcable.net; www.schoonerrestaurant.com.* A favourite with locals, good ambience and excellent seafood and healthy dishes.

Wickaninnish Inn $$$ *Osprey Lane at Chesterman Beach, tel: (250) 725-3100; tollfree: (800) 333-4604; fax: (250) 725-3100; e-mail: wick@wickinn.com; www.wickinn.com.* The luxury and quality of this Inn comes as a surprise with one of the finest restaurants on Vancouver Island and a luxuriously newly renovated spa, the Ancient Cedars.

Below
Whale watching

UCLUELET

ⓘ Ucluelet Chamber of Commerce
At the foot of Government Wharf on Main St;
tel: (250) 726-4641; e-mail:
info@ucluetinfo.com;
www.ucluetinfo.com.
Open daily in the summer;
rest of the year Mon–Fri.

➋ Amphitrite Point Lighthouse
On the southern tip of Ucluth Peninsula.

⑪ Broken Group Islands $$
Various outfitters such as Majestic Ocean Kayaking,
1167 Helen Rd;
tel: (250) 726-2868 or (800) 889-7644;
e-mail: majestic@ oceankayaking.com;
www.oceankayaking.com

◖ Canadian Princess Resort $$
1943 Peninsula Rd; tel: (250) 726-7771, tollfree (800) 633-7090;
www.canadianprincess.com.
Sleep on a ship or in chalets with tour facilities right on the resort property.

Perched on the tip of a peninsula at the edge of Barkley Sound, Ucluelet faces the ocean with a great rainforest at its back. These woods are filled with trails including the 2km Wild Pacific Trail that starts near **Amphitrite Point Lighthouse**. This was built in 1905 and it's the best spot around for viewing sunsets or migrating grey whales in the summer and storms in the winter. Two of the most popular trips out of Ucluelet are bear-watching adventures in a guided canoe and kayaking in the **Broken Group Islands**. He-Tin-Kis Park is a boardwalk trail through old growth cedar and spruce forest along a rugged shoreline with views to the Pacific Ocean. In town, the **Canadian Princess** is an historic West Coast steamship built in 1932 that's been converted into a hotel, lounge and restaurant.

The West Coast Trail

This world-famous, 5–10-day, 77km trek from Bamfield to Port Renfrew is a test of endurance but offers so many rewards in stunning scenery and adventures that fans of the hike rave about it. The trail was first established in 1907 to create an 'escape route' for survivors of shipwrecks along the coast (known as the Graveyard of the Pacific). The path was so difficult however that some shipwreck victims might have considered jumping back into the water. It's more groomed now but hikers should be fit, well-prepared with all the necessary gear (such as excellent footwear) and have the required permits. Parks Canada only allows 60 hikers to start each day. The trail can be slippery with lots of rain, waterfalls, tricky slopes, streams, bogs and blisters. If you have strong legs and a bit of experience, this is a journey of soul-enhancing bliss you'll never forget.

Suggested tour

Total distance: 42km from Ucluelet to Tofino.

Time: Varies depending on the number of adventures chosen. Allow a full day (travel time and relaxing) for boat or plane trips to Hot Springs Cove. Hikers should allow 5–7 days depending on experience.

Links: Returning from Vancouver Island's west coast via Hwy 4, continue north from **Parksville** (*see page 237*) on Hwy 19 to **Port Hardy** (*see page 229*) and the ferry to **Prince Rupert** (*see page 184*) or south to Nanaimo to catch BC Ferries back to **Vancouver** (*see page 268*).

Route: Most visitors will drive to **UCLUELET ❶** and **TOFINO ❷** north from Victoria along Hwy 1 to Nanaimo, Hwy 19 to Parksville and then Hwy 4 west, approximately 320km and 4–5 hours' driving time.

Detour 1: With a base in Tofino, depending on the season, take one of the whale-watching or marine-watching Zodiac trips offshore. Kayaking trips to **Meares Island ❸** will take about 4 hours including hiking time on the island. For **Hot Springs Cove ❹** trips, allow a half to full day.

Driving south on Hwy 4, watch for the sign for **Chesterman Beach** for good walks and shell hunting. Returning to Hwy 4, continue south to the turnoff for **Radar Hill** (18km from Tofino). This was built by the US as part of the Distant Early Warning system in the 1950s and is used today as an excellent viewpoint. About 2km down the road, a sign will indicate **Long Beach ❺**, an ideal spot summer or winter for strolls along the surf-pounded beach. The **Wickaninnish Centre ❻** is at the end of Long Beach Rd just beyond the park headquarters. At the **Ucluelet–Tofino–Port Alberni** junction, turn west 8km for Ucluelet.

Detour 2: Ucluelet is a base for a variety of adventure trips including bear watching, whale watching or kayaking trips to **The Broken Islands ❼**.

Right
Ucluelet harbour

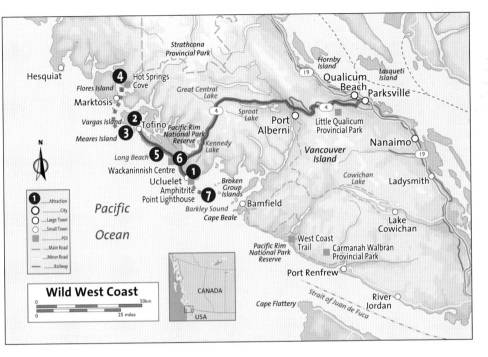

Strathcona
Provincial Park

Hornby
Island

Hesquiat

Lasqueti
Island

4 Hot Springs
Cove

Flores Island

Great Central
Lake

Qualicum
Beach

Parksville

Marktosis

2 Tofino
Pacific Rim
National Park
Reserve

Sproat
Lake

Port
Alberni

Little Qualicum
Provincial Park

Vargas Island

3

Meares Island

N

Kennedy
Lake

Nanaimo

Vancouver
Island

Long Beach

5

6

Wackaninnish Centre

1

Broken
Group
Islands

Cowichan
Lake

Ladysmith

Ucluelet

Amphitrite
Point Lighthouse

7

Barkley Sound

Bamfield

Lake
Cowichan

1 Attraction

Cape Beale

Pacific

City

Large Town

Pacific Rim
National Park
Reserve

West Coast
Trail

Carmanah Walbran
Provincial Park

Small Town

POI

Ocean

Main Road

Minor Road

Port Renfrew

Railway

Wild West Coast

CANADA

River
Jordan

0   50km

Strait of Juan de Fuca

Cape Flattery

0   25 miles

USA

Right
Bald eagle, the Wild West
Coast

Victoria

Ratings

Food and drink	●●●●●
Gardens	●●●●●
Museums	●●●●●
Art	●●●●○
History	●●●●○
Outdoor activities	●●●●○
Parks	●●●●○
Shopping	●●●○○

Once upon a time, Victoria was 'more English than the English', a kind of fantasy created by British immigrants who wanted to reproduce a half-remembered home. Like a lot of tags, the impression that Victoria is a little bit of England seems to linger on despite the city's contemporary hip scene. People still come expecting afternoon tea, but they find following Victoria's Ale Trail a lot more fun. They'll take in the museums and history but find themselves surprised at the talent in local theatres and the *au courant* flavour of Victoria's restaurants. The city seems to always have one festival or another going on – music, wine or food – and everything from hot jazz to hillbilly pours out of nightclubs and bars. If you insist on believing in myths, Victorians will introduce you to 'Caddy', a legendary local sea monster sighted here and there for more than a century.

Arriving and departing

ⓘ Tourism Victoria Visitor Info Centre
812 Wharf St; tel: (250) 953-2033; e-mail: info@tourismvictoria.com; www.tourismvictoria.com. Open daily.

🚢 BC Ferries *1112 Fort St; tel: (250) 386-3431, tollfree (888) 223-3779; fax: (250) 381-5452; www.bcferries.com*

By air: Victoria International Airport (*www.victoriaairport.com*) is served by Air Canada (JAZZ), Horizon, Westjet, Pacific Coastal and Airspeed Aviation. Flights take about 35 minutes from Vancouver. West Coast Air and Harbour Air provide 35-minute harbour-to-harbour service from downtown Vancouver to downtown Victoria several times a day. Taxis $$$ to downtown Victoria, or the **Airporter Bus** $$ *tel: (250) 386-2525, tollfree (877) 386-2525*, with coach service every 30 minutes, or BC **Transit** $ *tel: (250) 382-6161.*

By sea: BC Ferries have regular ferries between Tsawwassen on the mainland (1 hour from downtown Vancouver) and Swartz Bay at the north end of the Saanich Peninsula (about 45 minutes by car from downtown Victoria). **Pacific Coach Lines** *tel: (604) 662-7575, tollfree (800) 661-1725; www.pacificcoach.com* have buses from Vancouver's

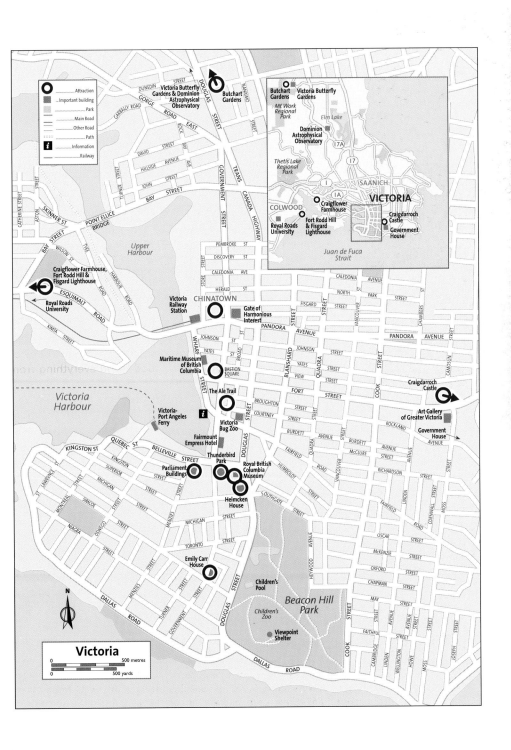

Harbour Air *tel: (604) 274-1277, tollfree (800) 665-0212; www.harbour-air.com. Flights to Victoria, Nanaimo and Gulf Islands.*

Victoria International Airport *Willingdon Rd off Hwy 17, Sidney, tel: (250) 953-7500; www.victoriaairport.com. 25km from downtown Victoria.*

West Coast Air *tel: (604) 606-6800, tollfree (800) 347-2222; e-mail: info@westcoastair.com; www.westcoastair.com for schedules.*

Main Terminal via ferry to downtown Victoria. From Washington State several ferries come into Victoria. **Black Ball Transport** *tel: (250) 386-2202* has service from Port Angeles. The **Victoria Clipper** *tel: (250) 382-8100, tollfree (800) 888-2535; www.victoriaclipper.com* has daily catamaran service from Seattle. **Victoria San Juan Cruises** *tel: (800) 443-4552; www.whales.com* has daily service May–October with dinner on the return. **Washington State Ferries** *tel: (250) 656-1831; www.wsdot.wa.gov/ferries* has one sailing daily to Sidney from Anacortes.

Getting around

Downtown Victoria is compact and so walking is the best way to explore (*see Walking tours, page 254*). For sights further out, **BC Transit** *tel: (250) 382-6161; www.transitbc.com* provides frequent service all through the city with special discount passes available through Tourism Victoria Visitor Info Centre. **Victoria Harbour Ferries** *tel: (250) 708-0201; www.harbourferry.com* serve the Inner Harbour with various stops and a harbour tour.

Driving in the inner city can be difficult because of one-way streets, traffic and limited street parking so the best advice is park and walk. Limits at meters are strictly enforced with fines so parking garages are advised unless you are certain you can return on time. Read the meters carefully for hours when coins are required. Downtown traffic is usually heavy most of the day but lighter in outlying areas except for rush hour (0730–0900 and 1500–1800).

Right
The Empress Hotel

Right
Butchart Gardens

Sights

⟳ **Bastion Square**
Wharf St between
Yates and Fort Sts. Open
daily.

The Ale Trail

By all means do have cucumber sandwiches and tea at The Empress in the afternoon but join youthful Victorians too in a self-guided tour as they sample some of the best brews you'll taste. Following on the heels of 'boutique wineries', beer connoisseurs have set up a string of brew pubs serving beverages you won't even recognise as beer. Some of the brew pubs have as many as 40 different beers that range from porters, lagers and ales to ginseng and yeasty wheat brews. Some of the pubs on the tour are: Spinnakers Brew Pub *308 Catherine St; tel: (250) 386-2739; www.spinnakers.com*; Hugo's Grill and Brewhouse *625 Courtney St; tel: (250) 920-4846; www.hugoslounge.com*; Vancouver Island Brewery *2330 Government St; tel: (250) 361-0007; www.vanislandbrewery.com*; Canoe Brew Club *450 Swift St; tel: (250) 361-1940; www.canoebrewpub.com*; and Swans Brew Pub *506 Pandora Ave; tel: (250) 361-3310; www.swanshotel.com*. Beer, they all say, is Victoria's latest 'culture'.

The wonderful world of whales

You can watch whales in many places, but in BC the experience becomes almost a personal 'close encounter' as massive killer whales (orcas) frolic, leap and breach only metres away from your boat. Victoria and Vancouver Island are the best of all places to view migrating and resident whales in their natural surroundings throughout the seasons, and even visitors get to know resident pods. Numerous tour operators take whale watchers out from Victoria (and other parts of Vancouver Island), and most are successful most of the time. The best time to see migrating grey whales is during March and April, with February to October the best season in Clayoquot and Barkley Sounds. 'Resident' orcas (those that live in local waters) are best viewed from May to November when they are at their feeding grounds.

⊙ Chinatown *between Herald, Government, Pandora and Store streets.*

🛈 Butchart Gardens *$$$ 21km north of downtown Victoria, 800 Benvenuto Ave; tel: (250) 652-5256, tollfree (866) 652-4422; www.butchartgardens.com. Open year round. There is also an excellent dining room; reservations required.*

Craigdarroch Castle $ *1050 Joan Crescent (off Fort St); tel: (250) 592-5323; fax: (250) 592-1099; e-mail: info@thecastle.ca; www.craigdarrochcastle.com. Open daily.*

Bastion Square

This was the spot Sir James Douglas, Victoria's first colonial governor, selected for the Hudson's Bay Company trading post with gaol and courthouse to follow. Today the buildings all belong to funky boutiques and restaurants.

Butchart Gardens

It's just about the most famous garden in Canada and never fails to please no matter what the season. This stunning 50-acre (20.25ha) garden has been drawing fans from around the world since it was shaped out of a limestone quarry in 1904. The flowers are planted in theme gardens – Japanese, Italian or sunken – with fountains, streams and winding pathways. There are musicians and entertainers in the afternoons and everything is illuminated at night with fireworks displays during July and August. The Christmas displays are a special draw.

Chinatown

When labourers were brought to Canada to build the Canadian Pacific Railway in the 19th century, many of them settled in Victoria where Chinese who had come as gold prospectors had already set up a small community. It's the oldest and most historically intact Chinatown in Canada. The entrance is through an ornate **Gate of Harmonious Interest** made of ceramic tiles and leads to **Fan Tan Alley**, the narrowest street in the country, once filled with gambling houses and opium dens.

Craigdarroch Castle

When the wealthiest man in British Columbia decided to build his wife a house, only a castle would do. Coal baron Robert Dunsmuir

Right
Craigdarroch Castle

Craigflower Farmhouse $
110 Island Hwy, Admiral Rd at Hwy 1A; tel: (250) 479-8053. Open daily.

Emily Carr House $
207 Government St; tel: (250) 383-5843; e-mail: ecarr@island.net; www.emilycarr.com. Open Mid-May–mid-Oct daily; rest of the year by arrangement.

Fort Rodd Hill and Fisgard Lighthouse $
603 Fort Rodd Hill Rd; tel: (250) 478-5849; www.fisgardlighthouse.com. Open daily Mar–Oct 1000–1730; Nov–Feb 0900–1630. The lighthouse is accessible from the beach area at the Hill.

Helmcken House $
10 Elliot St; tel: (250) 356-7226, tollfree (888) 447-7077. Open May–Oct.

Parliament Buildings
501 Belleville St; tel: (250) 387-3046. Visitors can watch politicians scrap when the House is in session.

ordered a 39-room stone mansion but died in 1889 before it was completed; Mrs Dunsmuir lived at Craigdarroch until 1908. The house is now a museum displaying what life for the very rich was like in the late-19th century. Floors are intricate woodwork, windows are exquisite stained glass and the furnishings lavish Victorian. If you climb the 87 steps to the top of Castle Tower, you're rewarded with a great view of the city, the Strait of Juan de Fuca and the Olympic Mountains.

Craigflower Farmhouse
When Victoria was founded in 1843 by the Hudson's Bay Fur Trading Company, this farmstead was its most successful enterprise. Guides in period costume will take you on a tour of the colonial furnishings as well as the gardens and orchards.

Emily Carr House
This is where Emily Carr, one of Canada's most famous and loved authors and artists, was born (see page 255).

Fort Rodd Hill and Fisgard Lighthouse
This fortress set in 44 acres (17.82ha) of wild-flower meadows and rocky bluffs was originally conceived to defend Victoria and the Esquimalt naval base in the late-19th century. Victoria was then headquarters for the Royal Navy's Pacific Squadron and required massive fortifications including command posts, underground magazines and related buildings. After two world wars (when it was fully staffed), Fort Rodd Hill was in 1962 designated a national historic site and is considered one of the best preserved 19th-century forts in the world. Fisgard Lighthouse was built in 1862 and was the first permanent lighthouse on Canada's West Coast.

Helmcken House
Built in 1852, this is the oldest house in Victoria and holds the furniture and memories of a pioneer doctor and statesman named John Sebastian Helmcken. An audio tour of the house explains his life, his 19th-century medical tools and the times.

Parliament Buildings
The massive stone Parliament Buildings brooding over Victoria's harbour were designed by a 25-year-old architect named Francis Rattenbury who went on to put his stamp on much of the city including The Empress Hotel and Crystal Garden. His personal life was less impressive. Rattenbury divorced his wife and married a scandalous, cigarette-smoking 'new woman' 30 years younger than him who caused scandals all over town. The architect was murdered in England by his wife's lover in 1934. Statues of prominent 19th-century figures such as Sir James Douglas and Sir Matthew Baille Begbie surround the building. At night, the buildings are lit up by lights outlining the solid Victorian architecture.

Royal British Columbia Museum
$$ 675 Belleville St; tel: (250) 356-7226, tollfree (888) 447-7977; www.royalbcmuseum.bc.ca. Open daily 0900–1700; closed Christmas and New Year's Day.

Thunderbird Park $
Belleville and Douglas Sts; tel: (250) 356-7226. Open daily.

Royal British Columbia Museum

It's routinely rated as one of the best museum/research centres in the world for both its permanent collection and its highly praised special exhibitions. These exhibits creatively blend live performers, interactive sets, models and historic materials so appealing that everyone from tots to seniors gets involved. Some of the highlights are: the frontier town with its cobblestone streets, silent movie house and Chinatown; a nostalgic 20th-century gallery; and a natural history gallery with life-like dioramas of the last Ice Age and a submarine journey to the depths of the ocean. The First Nations exhibits are creatively presented and beautifully lit with a genuine Kwakwaka'wakw longhouse, masks and scenes from the daily life of Canada's first people. A six-storey-tall IMAX screen plays the latest and best National Geographic films several times a day. There are also first rate special exhibits such as a recent one on the Titanic.

Thunderbird Park

This is another example of how BC aboriginal peoples are teaching new generations a sense of pride in traditional culture. When the totems in this park next to the museum began to deteriorate with time

and weather, the choice was to pull them down or find some way of replacing them. Mungo Martin, then chief of the Kwakwaka'wakw band who was restoring totem poles at the university, found young people and began to teach them the lost art of totem making. The original poles have been taken inside the museum but many of those carved by Martin and his group in the 1950s are now in the park. In the summer months, you can watch carvers at work.

Walking tours

Well-laid-out Victoria with its concentrated attractions is perfect for walkers on their own, but to discover all the local secrets and stories, a guided walk is a treat. Every other Sunday a well-known local historian guides people past places where odd things happened and tells entertaining stories about Victoria's most colourful characters. Another weekly tour takes people through old cemeteries to learn about the city's history, and 2-hour walking tours in the summer explore the many ghosts and haunted houses of Victoria.

Walking tours $
For Neighbourhood Discovery Walks, tel: (250) 384-6698 for times and places; for Cemetery Tours, tel: (250) 598-8870; for haunted tours, tel: (250) 726-4224; e-mail: discoverthepast@telus.net; www.discoverthepast.com. No reservations needed.

Emily Carr: an independent spirit

She was one of those gifted 19th-century women unfortunately born before her time. Today, her talent would bring her a legion of fans: in her day, she was called an eccentric and her genius decried as 'unseemly'. Born in 1871 in Carr House, she studied art in San Francisco and quickly developed her distinctive style. Following a year in France, she found a vigorous post-impressionist style with which to convey the wild beauty of Vancouver Island and vanishing native life. Despite the strength and beauty of her paintings and writings, she was forced to open a boarding house in Victoria to survive. It wasn't until she was 57 and travelled east to meet The Group of Seven that her work began to get critical recognition. After a heart attack in 1937, she devoted her time to writing and today is known for both her books and her art.

Accommodation and food

Blighty Bistro $$ *2006 Oak Bay Ave; tel: (250) 592-5111.* This former fish 'n' chip shop now serves delicious homestyle cooking in a bohemian atmosphere. Try their splendid chicken in filo.

Brasserie L'école $$ *1715 Government St; tel: (250) 475-6260; www.lecole.ca.* The love child of an award-winning chef and accomplished sommelier, this is classic bistro-style cuisine that is based on local ingredients. Food is simple but hearty in an informal atmosphere.

Café Brio $$ *944 Fort St; tel: (250) 383-0009; www.cafe-brio.com.* Italian but promoting Vancouver Island cuisine with a nice outdoor patio and salon art on the walls. Try the Saltspring goat cheese, duck confit and the hearts of romaine salad.

Fairholme Manor $$ *638 Rockland Place; tel: (250) 298-3240, tollfree (877) 511-3322; www.fairholmemanor.com.* Luxury accommodation near the ocean, in a recently restored 110-year-old Italianate mansion near the gardens of Government House in lush Rockland district. Rooms are charming and food excellent.

The Fairmont Empress $$$ *721 Government St; tel: (250) 384-8111, tollfree (800) 441-1414; www.fairmont.com/empress.* Restored to its turn-of-the-century beauty, the Empress is a Victoria legend and almost a destination in itself. Sitting in regal splendour on Victoria's Inner Harbour, this hotel has seen the famous and the royal as well as the humble over its long history. Tea at the Empress is a century-old tradition.

Hernande'z Taqueria $ *735 Yates; tel: (250) 386-1662.* Great authentic Mexican and Latin American food, and a great experience (don't forget to ask for the owner's comical tips on how to transport and eat your takeaway). All tortillas are home-made and the tacos are divine.

Opposite
Totem pole, detail

Marina Restaurant $$ *1327 Beach Dr.; tel: (250) 598-8555.* Some of the best sushi in Victoria and an extensive menu of seafood and pastas. Also views onto Oak Bay marina.

Millstream Llama Farm B&B $$ *355 Atkins Rd; tel: (250) 744-6420, tollfree (866) 849-3938; fax: (250) 478-9194; e-mail:mail@millstreamllamas.com; www.millstreamllamas.com.* For something totally different, this B&B in the country only 15 minutes from downtown Victoria offers quiet and a 6-acre (2.43ha) llama farm. Take the llamas for a walk or just enjoy the countryside.

Niche $$$ *225 Quebec St; tel: (250) 388-4255; www.nichedining.com.* A remake of a dining room featuring fine French food, Niche combines contemporary design with the old charm of a building in historic James Bay. Menu is west coast, seasonal and local, and draws praise from everyone.

The Noodle Box $ *818 Douglas St; tel: (250) 384-1314.* Starting as a street vendor serving Southeast Asian noodles in classic white Chinese-style boxes, this is now a bonafide restaurant. A local favourite.

The Oswego Hotel $$–$$$ *500 Oswego St; tel: (877) 767-9346; www.oswegovictoria.com.* This newly opened hotel offers an eclectic mix of both contemporary design and West Coast at its best, in soothing earth tones. Spa packages are favourites, there's a bar and bistro, meeting rooms and a range of accommodation from studios to one- and two-bedrooms to penthouse suites.

Sanuk Infusion $$ *625 Courtney St; tel: (250) 920-4844; www.sanukinfusion.com.* This is a bit of east-meeting-west as a hip Pan-Asian restaurant nestles in with the excellent Magnolia boutique hotel and spa. Headed by Chef Patrick Lynch, who has a formidable list of culinary credits, Sanuk has a menu that is creative and innovative Thai using the best of local ingredients.

Sidney Pier Hotel & Spa $$–$$$ *9805 Seaport Place, Sidney; tel: (250) 655-9445; www.sidneypier.com.* A retreat outside the bustling city, this convenient hotel is 25 minutes north of Victoria, five minutes from the international airport, and steps from Butchart Gardens, wineries and farms in the area. Upscale and boutique, guest rooms all have ocean and mountain views and there are a host of amenities including an in-house bakery, European-style café, full-service spa and more.

Swan's Hotel $$ *506 Pandora Ave; tel: (250) 361-3310, tollfree (800) 668-7926; e-mail: swanshotel@swanshotel.com; www.swanshotel.com.* Restored 1913 heritage buildings with 30 spacious suites and penthouse all fully equipped and right in downtown Victoria. Good restaurant and brew pub.

Right
A mammoth at the Royal
British Columbia Museum

Suggested walking tour of downtown area

Total distance: 16km.

Time: Allow 3 hours with stops.

Links: Victoria connects with the **Gulf Islands** (*see page 260*) via ferry from Swartz Bay and north via Hwy 1 to the **Cowichan Valley** (*see page 234*).

Route: Starting at **BASTION SQUARE** ❶ check out **The Maritime Museum of British Columbia** for a look at seadogs and seafarers.

Detour: Heading away from downtown along Wharf Street, turn right on Johnson Street and then left on Government Street to reach **CHINATOWN** and **Fan Tan Alley**.

Return via Wharf Street towards the Inner Harbour, and for the kids the **Victoria Bug Zoo** is filled with creepy crawlies and lots of bug information. Continue on Wharf Street to the **Fairmont Empress Hotel** ❷, the majestic grande dame of the city, opened in 1908. Afternoon tea here is an old (but high-priced) tradition, if that's your thing. The Inner Harbour is alive with activity day and evening and a good place to pick up a horse-drawn carriage or pedal-carriage.

Across the street **THE ROYAL BC MUSEUM** ❸ is an absolute must and you could spend an entire day here quite easily if you have the time. Try not to miss the IMAX theatre presentations. Leaving the museum, to the left of the building you'll find **THUNDERBIRD PARK** ❹ with its impressive totem poles, and to the right **HELMCKEN HOUSE** ❺, the

➋ **Beacon Hill Park**
East of Douglas St,
south of Southgate St.

oldest house in Victoria along with the tiny 19th-century **St Ann's Schoolhouse.**

Return to Belleville Street and walk west to the **PARLIAMENT BUILDINGS ❻** for a stroll through the groomed lawns and flower gardens and also to sit in on one of the combative sessions of the House if it happens to be sitting. Retrace your steps to Douglas Street and head south via Southgate Street to the spacious lawns of **BEACON HILL PARK ❼**. You can watch the water birds on the many ponds, stop at the petting zoo or enjoy a match at the cricket pitch.

From here, continue towards the water at the bottom of the park to Dallas Rd; cross the road and the park where Victorians enjoy walking their dogs to pick up the **Shore Trail Walk ❽**. This can be a short easy stroll or you can follow the coast all the way to **Clover Point.**

At the foot of Government Street, backtrack north to spend a little time in the **EMILY CARR HOUSE ❾**.

Driving tour (see inset map)

Starting downtown, take Government Street north and then turn west on Gorge Road (1A), continuing until you reach Ocean Boulevard. Turn south and follow Ocean Boulevard to reach **FORT RODD HILL** National Historic Park. **Royal Roads University**, BC's famous military college, is just west of here. Return to the Island Highway going north until it intersects with Hwy 1 and follow this east to McKenzie Road, which leads to Hwy 17 going north. Follow 17 to Keating Cross Road and turn west for **BUTCHART GARDENS** with a stop at the **Victoria Butterfly Gardens** on the way to see a wondrous display of colourful creatures.

Returning via Benvenuto turn south onto the West Saanich Road (17A) and follow to Observatory Road to visit the **Dominion Astrophysical Observatory** where the public is invited for free tours and Saturday night gazing at the heavens, April–October. Continue south on 17A and follow this, turning east on McKenzie Avenue (it becomes Sinclair Rd) and then south on Beach Drive. Follow scenic Beach Drive to Oak Bay Village for a stop at the **Ottavio Italian Bakery and Delicatessen** for great sandwiches and gelato, or at the **White Heather Tea Room** for late lunch or afternoon tea. Owner Agnes Campbell, a fiery, red-haired Scot with a distinctive laugh, is an added pleasure.

Continue along Beach Drive to Stannard Avenue and turn north to reach **Government House** facing on Rockland Avenue. After a stroll through the gardens, take Joan Avenue from the front of the house and follow it north to **CRAIGDARROCH CASTLE**. Follow Joan Avenue to Fort Street and return to downtown Victoria.

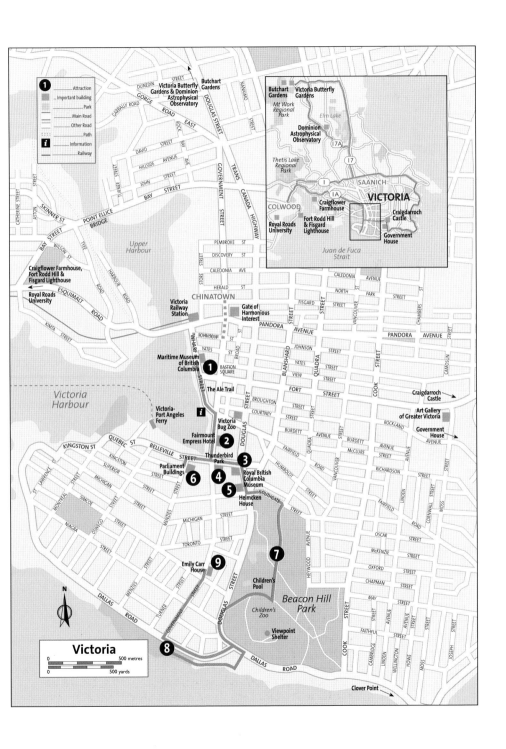

Victoria

The Gulf Islands

Ratings

Art and craft	●●●●●
Nature	●●●●●
Outdoor activities	●●●●●
Parks	●●●●●
Scenery	●●●●●
Coastal villages	●●●●○
Wildlife	●●●●○
Beaches	●●●○○

This archipelago of 200 plus islands lies in the rain shadow of the Vancouver Island mountain range, creating an idyllic climate with low rainfall. Most of the islands are small and uninhabited and have no ferry access, but five of the southern group are home to almost 12,000 permanent residents. These are like miniature countries with unique histories and personalities. Like islanders everywhere, Gulf Islanders are colourful and controversial with a good sprinkling of celebrities and activists. They set their own pace and value such things as quality of life, organic food, art and crafts, as do visitors who come for the weekend markets. The islands have stunning views, white crushed shell beaches, protected forest and pastoral valleys tucked between mountains and forests. The coastline with its cliffs, bays and coves draws sea kayakers and hikers as well as fishermen on day trips from the mainland.

GALIANO ISLAND

ⓘ Galiano Chamber of Commerce/ Travel Info Centre *2590 Sturdies Bay Rd; tel: (250) 539-2233; www.galianoisland.com. Open Jul and Aug daily; weekends rest of the year.*

♻ Ferries from both the mainland and Vancouver Island arrive on Galiano at Sturdies Bay.

Go Galiano Island Shuttle *Tel: (250) 539-0202. Operates from the Sturdies Bay Ferry.*

Galiano's destiny was determined by its geography: since most of the island was unsuitable for farming it attracted artsy and environmentally progressive settlers, followed by tourists with a passion for the outdoors. This narrow, hilly island stretches over 57sq km with a population of about 1,000, most of them involved in arts and crafts or tourism. With less than 60cm of rainfall a year, Galiano is the driest of the islands which makes it perfect for a multitude of sporting activities such as the best-organised mountain bike trail system in the Gulf Islands and a coastline ideal for hiking, kayaking, canoeing, scuba diving and fishing. There are seven parks on the island where visitors can spin-cast for salmon, hike or train binoculars on migrating birds. **Bellhouse Provincial Park** lures photographers with bizarre eroded limestone formations and its dramatic setting overlooking Active Pass. **Bluffs Park** has spectacular views of marine

⊘ Bellhouse
Provincial Park *is*
on the southside of Sturdies
Bay at Burrill Point. **Galiano**
Bluffs Park *is on Bluff Rd*
above Active Pass.
Montague Harbour
Marine Provincial Park
is 10km northwest of
Sturdies Bay at Montague
Harbour. **Bodega Ridge**
Nature Preserve *can be*
reached via Cook Rd at the
northwest end of Galiano.

life, seabirds and eagles, while **Montague Harbour Marine Provincial Park** is known for its ground white shell beaches and enormous Indian middens. **Bodega Ridge Nature Preserve** is part of a new national park and has well-developed hiking trails through grasslands and old-growth Douglas fir forest and along the waterfront. Sturdies Bay is the main commercial centre with several stores, a petrol (gas) station, restaurants, ferry terminal, info centre and lodge. The island has no transportation system but the Go Galiano Island Shuttle provides tours and taxi service. Shops in town will rent mountain bikes, canoes and kayaks and the island has numerous excellent B&Bs and inns. **Dionisio Point Provincial Park** at the end of the island is only accessible by boat.

MAYNE ISLAND

ⓘ Mayne Island
Information and
Chamber of Commerce
www.mayneislandchamber.ca

What you find strongest among the 900 residents on Mayne Island (21sq km) is a powerful sense of community and a pride in the island's history. They'll point out for example that they have BC's oldest continuously operating hotel, the **Springwater Lodge**, built in the 1890s with 'a million-dollar sunset view' from the hotel's massive deck. Food here is hearty and affordable. **Miner's Bay**, the

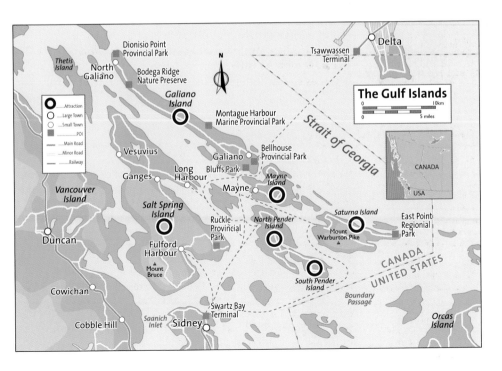

Ferries dock at Village Bay; reservations for vehicles from Tsawwassen are recommended in the week and required on weekends.

Active Pass Lighthouse on *Georgina Point.* Also **Georgina Point Heritage Park.** **Mount Parke** *is off Fernhill Rd but ask a local for directions.*

The Government Dock at Horton Bay has freshly caught fish and shellfish seasonally; boats also come into the Government Dock in Miner's Bay usually on Fri & Sat.

Mayne Island Museum $ *Opposite the community centre off Fernhill Rd. Open daily in the summer 1000–1700; winter Sat 1300–1600.*

Springwater Lodge $ *C-27 Miner's Bay, Mayne Island; tel: (250) 539-5521; www.springwaterlodge.com.* Good hearty food with the best fish and chips on the island. The cabins, right on the beach, are the best bargain on the Gulf Islands.

main village, looks over Active Pass and is really just a collection of funky little stores and good art and crafts shops. During the Fraser River gold rush in 1858, miners would stop here as a halfway point when they rowed across Georgia Strait from Victoria to the mainland. There are no provincial parks on Mayne Island but as hunting is not allowed deer can usually be seen calmly grazing on local front lawns. A summer farmers' market has just started for fresh produce and freshly caught seafood is available in season at the **Government Dock.** Best attractions for visitors are the **Mayne Island Museum,** formerly the local gaol, **Active Pass Lighthouse** and the stunning view across the Strait from **Mount Parke.** There are a number of pleasant beaches and the **Georgina Point Heritage Park** is a good place to check out a wide range of birds and some of the 250 varieties of wild flowers. Good photo op: the **St Mary Magdalene Church** overlooking Miner's Bay.

Right
Relax and take in the Gulf Islands Scenery

NORTH AND SOUTH PENDER ISLANDS

ℹ Pender Island Information *2332 Otter Bay Rd, North Pender; tel: (250) 629-6541; e-mail: travel@ penderislandchamber.com; www.penderislandchamber. com or www.gulfislands.net. Located 800m from the ferry terminal. Open Jun–Sept daily.*

⛴ Ferries *pull in at Otter Bay in North Pender.*

↪ Mount Norman and **Beaumont Marine Park** *from Canal Rd linking the Penders to Ainsley Rd, then follow signs to the parking lot.*

⌂ The Driftwood Centre *Bedwell Harbour and Razor Point roads. Hosts the Saturday farmers' market.*

People refer to them just as 'the Penders' but they're actually two islands connected by a one-lane wooden bridge across a narrow canal dug in 1903 to facilitate ship travel in the Gulf Islands. There are around 2,200 full-time inhabitants who have set up a surprising number of amenities (mostly on the North island) but there's no town in the combined 34sq km islands. **The Driftwood Centre** serves as a hub for post office, bank, petrol (gas) station, groceries etc., but most visitors hit the many hiking trails or head to the island's 20 lovely beaches. **Mount Norman** (217m) on South Pender has a great overall view of the Gulf Islands as does **George Hill** on the north end. The 40-minute **Beaumont Marine Park** trail begins at the same spot as Mount Norman and is well worth the effort. There's a white shell beach here and the marine park is one of the Gulf Islands' most popular. The Penders have numerous small speciality farms that provide produce, cheeses and much more for a thriving weekend market that runs mid-May–1 September.

SALT SPRING ISLAND

ℹ Salt Spring Island Visitor Info Centre *121 Lower Ganges Rd, Ganges, tel: (250) 537-5252; e-mail: chamber@ssisland.com; www.saltspringtourism.com. Open daily 1100–1500 (summer 1000–1600).*

⛴ Ferries *run from Tsawwassen to Long Harbour, from Swartz Bay on Vancouver Island to Fulford Harbour and from Crofton to Vesuvius Bay. There is also a Harbour Air seaplane service from Vancouver.*

Salt Spring Island has attracted people wanting to get away from it all ever since nine African-Americans became the island's first settlers in 1857 after purchasing their freedom. Today, it's the most populated of the Gulf Islands and home to internationally known celebrities such as Robert Bateman and Robin Williams, fine craftspeople, boutique farmers and retirees who are passionate about quality of life. The biggest draw is the **Saturday Market** where you can find the most creative crafts imaginable, fresh produce, artistic birdhouses, preserves and live entertainment that draws people from everywhere. The **Studio Tour** is almost as famous; this is a self-guided tour (maps available from Salt Spring Tourism) to 36 artist studios indicated by a sign with a sheep. The island actually raises a lot of sheep to produce famous Salt Spring Island lamb and wool for the **Gulf Islands Spinning Mill**. Mohair goats, llamas and alpaca are also raised on the island and the mill spins these into products available for purchase. **Ganges**, which is not only the island's main village but also the largest community in the Gulf Islands, has shops that reflect the exacting tastes of the islanders: excellent bakeries, delis and galleries plus of

**◯ Ruckle Provincial
    Park** *can be reached
via Beaver Point Rd.* **Mount
Maxwell** *is southwest of
Ganges taking Cranberry Rd
to Maxwell Rd.* **Mount
Bruce** *is reached from
Fulford Harbour, left onto
Isabella Point Rd and then
via narrow and rough
Musgrave Rd.*

**◯ Salt Spring
    Cheese Company**
*285 Reynolds Rd;
tel: (250) 653-2300.*

**◯ Akerman
    Museum $**
*2501 Fulford–Ganges Rd,
near the ferry; tel: (250)
653-4228. Open by
appointment.*

**Gulf Islands Spinning
Mill $$**
*351A Rainbow Rd, Ganges;
tel: (250) 537-4895. Regular
tours variable summer hours
or by appointment.*

Saturday Market $
*Centennial Park, Ganges.
Open first Sat in Apr–last Sat
in Oct.*

Studio Tour $
*Tel: (250) 537-9476. The
artist studio tour is self-
guided. Obtain maps and
hours at Salt Spring Info
Centre.*

course the Saturday Market. Don't miss the **Salt Spring Cheese Company** for the best cheeses in the islands (and maybe BC!). A glimpse of the island's interesting history can be found in **Akerman Museum** that has First Nations and early settlers' artefacts. Salt Spring has dozens of lakes with fine fishing for bass or trout and numerous parks with **Ruckle Provincial Park** the largest. At 486ha, this is the largest in the Gulf Islands and embraces a working sheep farm, forest and open fields above a rocky shoreline. Smaller **Mount Maxwell Provincial Park** has a breathtaking view of the islands as does **Mount Bruce**, the highest point in the Gulf Islands and a popular jumping off point for hang-gliders. Several endangered plants and butterflies can be found here.

Right
Dining out, Salt Spring style

SATURNA ISLAND

ℹ **Saturna Island Information**
There is no office on the island but people at the Lighthouse Pub and at the island's two stores can provide guidance. There is also a website:
www.saturnatourism.com

⛴ **Ferries** to Saturna are caught from Mayne Island and dock at Lyall Harbour Government Wharf.

↪ **East Point Regional Park** Follow East Point Rd. **Mount Warburton Pike** Can be reached via Staples Rd in the western section of the island.

🏨 **Saturna Island Vineyard and Winery $$** Tel: (250) 539-5139, (250) 539-3521 or tollfree (877) 918-3388; e-mail: wine@saturnavineyards.com; www.saturnavineyards.com. 60 acres (24.3ha) of vines under cultivation in four vineyards and produces a range of award-winning white and red wines. Free tours and tastings.

Although Saturna is the closest island to the mainland, it's ironically the least accessible since there are no direct ferries. There's no town, no pharmacy, no bank, few B&Bs, no public campsites and you're requested to take your rubbish home with you. What it does have is a **vineyard and winery** with a good bistro, a totally unspoiled quality and some of the most beautiful scenery on the Islands. There's a view from the top of **Mount Warburton Pike** (490m) that will simply knock your socks off: and you may also catch a glimpse of wild goats that hang around the Pike. There are only around 315 inhabitants (give or take) on the island but they're an interesting bunch: from a member of the Canadian Senate to tarot card readers and Japanese *raku* potters. Visitors, whether for the day or longer, come to hike, cycle, kayak, fish or take nature walks. **East Point Regional Park** has a lighthouse built in 1888 that looks towards the Canada/US border from the most easterly point in the Gulf Islands as well as a stretch of strange sandstone formations. This is one of the best places in the Islands to see killer whales in the summer, and spincasting for salmon is excellent, as is bird and mammal watching. You can see seals, sea lions and an endless list of seabirds. The biggest island event is the Canada Day Lamb Barbecue that draws people from all over BC.

Accommodation and food

There are a couple of excellent hotels with international rating and first-class inns and B&Bs plus most islands have budget accommodation and camping facilities. Restaurants vary from pub food to gourmet dining.

Blue Vista Resort $–$$ S-8, C-19, RR1, 563 Arbutus Drive, Mayne Island; tel: (250) 539-2463, tollfree (877) 535-2424; e-mail: bluevista@bluevistaresort.com; www.bluevistaresort.com. Eight comfortable, self-contained studios, one- and two-bedroom cottages for people who want to explore the beauty of Mayne.

Bodega Ridge $–$$ 120 Manatee Rd, Box 115, Galiano; tel: (250) 539-2677; e-mail: info@bodegaridge.com; www.bodegaridge.com. Year-round destination, perfect for people who love the outdoors. Accommodation is in well-kept, modern cabins with three bedrooms, TV, DVD, BBQ and other amenities. The cabins are pet friendly.

Canadian Gulf Islands Reservations tel: (250) 539-9984; e-mail: reservations@gulfislandsreservations.com; www.gulfislandsreservations.com. Provides free bookings and availability information for over 100 of the best B&Bs, inns and cottages on all the Gulf Islands, as well as island hopping packages on Galiano, Salt Spring, Mayne, Pender and more.

Hastings House $$$ *160 Upper Ganges Rd, Salt Spring Island; tel: (250) 537-2362 or (800) 661-9255; fax: (250) 537-5333; e-mail: info@hastingshouse.com; www.hastingshouse.com*. This award-winning Relais and Chateaux country house hotel on a 25-acre seaside estate is as good as it gets. Beautiful individual rooms and a dining room that changes its menu daily and serves some of the best food on the islands.

House Piccolo $$$ *108 Hereford Ave, Salt Spring Island; tel: (250) 537-1844; e-mail: housepiccolo@shaw.ca; www.housepiccolo.com*. Known for its great wine list and European cuisine in an intimate setting.

Oceanwood Country Inn $$$ *630 Dinner Bay Rd, Mayne Island; tel: (250) 539-5074; fax: (250) 539-3002; e-mail: oceanwood@gulfislands.com; www.oceanwood.com*. Another country hotel run with loads of grace and style with the best cuisine on Mayne Island served in a waterfront dining room with a spectacular view. Menus change daily with fresh garden ingredients blended into the Pacific Northwest style accompanied by award-winning West Coast wines.

Poet's Cove $$$ *9801 Spalding Rd, South Pender Island; tel: (250) 629-2100, tollfree (888) 512-7638; e-mail: reservations@poetscove.com; www. poetscove.com*. One of the newer and most luxurious resorts in the Gulf Islands with 15 cottages, nine villas, a 22-room lodge and a host of features such as a world-class spa, marina and elegant restaurant.

Sahhali Serenity Inn $$$ *5915 Pirates Rd, Pender Island; tel: (250) 629-3756, tollfree (888) 724-4254; e-mail: sahhali@islandnet.com; www.pender-island-bedandbreakfast.com*. Sits on 10 acres (4.05ha) surrounded by gnarled Garry oaks, ancient firs and arbutus trees. The inn has lovely rooms with fireplaces, ocean views and jacuzzis.

Below
Gulf Islands' sunset

Saturna Lodge and Restaurant $$$ *130 Payne Rd; tel: (250) 539-2254 or (250) 769-0360; fax: (250) 539-3091; e-mail: innkeeper@saturna.ca; www.saturna.ca; open Mar–Oct*. Country inn overlooking Boot Cove with seven charming rooms and an excellent restaurant presided over by Shawn Fitzgerald, a Red Seal chef, with an extensive wine list.

Woodstone Country Inn $$ *Georgeson Bay Rd, Galiano Island; tel: (250) 539-2022, tollfree (888) 339-2022; fax: (250) 539-5198; e-mail: info@woodstoneinn.com; www.woodstoneinn.com*. Has 12 spacious guest rooms tastefully furnished in antiques and wicker with fireplaces in many of the rooms. Excellent dining room.

Suggested tour

Time: This will vary widely depending on how many islands are visited and the time of the year (more ferries operate in the summer months). A good routing is from Tsawwassen to **GALIANO** ❶, a 1-hour trip, then to **MAYNE** ❷ for 20 minutes more. There are connecting ferries between Mayne and **SATURNA** ❸, then from Mayne to **PENDER** ❹ and **SALT SPRING** ❺ with the run around 20–30 minutes between the islands. There are direct Tsawwassen to Salt Spring Island ferries without the stops. While you can cover a lot in one day on each island, allow at least 2 or 3 on Salt Spring Island.

Links: BC Ferries from Tsawwassen, the mainland BC link to the Gulf Islands. From Vancouver Island, ferries operate to Fulford Harbour from Swartz Bay and from Crofton to Vesuvius Bay on Salt Spring Island: a 20-minute ferry trip.

Route: For visitors with the time, the most direct route would be from Tsawwassen to Galiano and then Mayne with a side tour to Saturna. From Mayne to Pender and then to Salt Spring Island. If you just have the time for a couple of islands, Salt Spring is a must for the famous market, hiking and some art tours, with perhaps either Galiano or Saturna for hiking and kayaking.

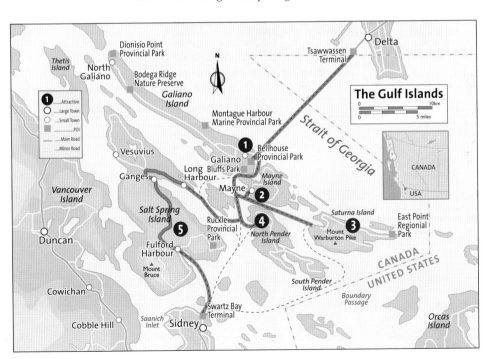

Vancouver

Ratings

Beaches	●●●●●
Food	●●●●●
Outdoor activities	●●●●●
Scenery	●●●●●
Entertainment	●●●●
Children	●●●●
Gardens	●●●●
Shopping	●●●●

Vancouver is a little like the Sleeping Beauty, blessed at birth by nature with only a tiny curse: winter rain. It sits on a point wrapped by high mountains and surrounded by ocean, remains brilliantly green all year round and enjoys the warmest year-round climate in Canada. Because of its youth, clever city planners drew on experience and bestowed upon the city splendid Stanley Park right downtown along with abundant gardens everywhere. In the spring, downtown streets explode with colour as plum and cherry trees turn Vancouver pink. In the summer, everyone flocks to beaches that wrap around the extensive shoreline, and in the winter three ski mountains are a short city bus ride away. With the city's cosmopolitan population, restaurants run the gamut, serving the freshest seafoods, meats and produce from local farms. Vancouverites love the outdoors and their beloved city in equal measure.

Arriving and departing

❶ Tourism Vancouver *Plaza level, 200 Burrard St; tel: (604) 683-2000; www.tourismvancouver.com or e-mail: info@tourismvancouver.com; www.hellobc.com. Open mid-May–Labour Day daily 0830–1900; rest of the year Mon–Sat 0830–1700.*

By air: Most flights arrive via **Vancouver International Airport** (YVR), 3211 *Grant McDonachie Way, Richmond, tel: (604) 207-7077; www.yvr.ca*, about 23km south of downtown off Hwy 99, with **Abbotsford** as a secondary airport. Many international carriers have non-stop flights to Vancouver and numerous smaller airlines service BC. **Taxis** from the airport to the city take 25 minutes and cost around $25–$30; the **Airporter Bus** *tel: (604) 946-8866, tollfree (800) 668-3141; e-mail: yvrairporter@vttgroup.com; www.yvrairporter.com*, is $13.50 one way and $21 round trip. Limos and car hire are also available.

By rail: Via Rail *1150 Station St; tel: (604) 640-3741, tollfree (888) 842-7245; www.viarail.ca* is Canada's national passenger rail service with trains between Vancouver and Toronto. **Amtrak** *tel: (800) USARail; www.amtrak.com* has daily trains between Seattle and Vancouver.

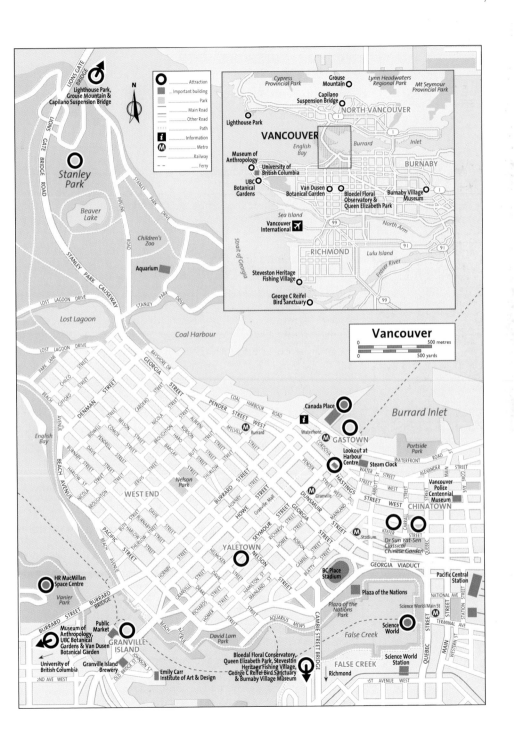

Legend

- ○ Attraction
- ■ Important building
- Park
- Main Road
- Other Road
- Path
- **i** Information
- **M** Metro
- Railway
- -- Ferry

N

Lighthouse Park, Grouse Mountain & Capilano Suspension Bridge

Stanley Park

Beaver Lake

Children's Zoo

Aquarium

Lost Lagoon

Lost Lagoon Drive

Coal Harbour

Cypress Provincial Park
Grouse Mountain ○
Lynn Headwaters Regional Park
Mt Seymour Provincial Park
Capilano Suspension Bridge
NORTH VANCOUVER

Lighthouse Park ○

VANCOUVER
English Bay
Burrard
Inlet

Museum of Anthropology ○
University of British Columbia ■

BURNABY

UBC Botanical Gardens ○
Van Dusen Botanical Garden ○
Bloedel Floral Observatory & Queen Elizabeth Park ○
Burnaby Village Museum ○

Sea Island

Vancouver International ✈

North Arm

RICHMOND
Lulu Island

Strait of Georgia

Steveston Heritage Fishing Village ○

Fraser River

George C Reifel Bird Sanctuary ○

Vancouver

| 0 | | 500 metres |
| 0 | | 500 yards |

Canada Place ○

Burrard Inlet

Waterfront **M** Burrard
GASTOWN
Portside Park
Lookout at Harbour Centre
Steam Clock
WATERFRONT ROAD

WEST END
Nelson Park
Granville Mall

Vancouver Police Centennial Museum
CHINATOWN

HR MacMillan Space Centre
Vanier Park

DUNSMUIR
Granville **M**

Dr Sun Yat-Sen Classical Chinese Garden
GEORGIA VIADUCT

YALETOWN

BC Place Stadium
Pacific Central Station

Plaza of the Nations
Plaza of the Nations Park

Science World/Main St **M**

Museum of Anthropology, UBC Botanical Gardens & Van Dusen Botanical Garden

Public Market
GRANVILLE ISLAND

University of British Columbia
Granville Island Brewery
Emily Carr Institute of Art & Design

David Lam Park

Science World

False Creek

Science World Station

FALSE CREEK

Bloedel Floral Conservatory, Queen Elizabeth Park, Steveston Heritage Fishing Village, George C Reifel Bird Sanctuary & Burnaby Village Museum
↓ Richmond

English Bay

Rocky Mountaineer Vacations *1755 Cottrell St; tel: (604) 606-7245, tollfree (877) 460-3200; www.rockymountaineer.com* has a luxury 2-day ride through the best of Rocky Mountain scenery and several new routes. (*See Train Travel, pages 170–9.*)

By sea: BC Ferries *tel: (250) 386-3431, tollfree (888) 223-3779; www.bcferries.com* have numerous ferries arriving from Nanaimo and Swartz Bay on Vancouver Island to Horseshoe Bay and Tsawwassen. Vancouver has also become a highly popular cruise ship destination with most ships departing from Canada Place but others arriving in from US ports.

By land: Hwy 99 extends from the Canada/US border at Blaine to Vancouver. Hwy 1 is the Trans-Canada Highway spanning the width of Canada. Greyhound is the major bus line that connects Vancouver with many cities in Canada and the US.

Getting around

Unlike some cities, Vancouver doesn't have freeways leading into the city so traffic tends to move more slowly downtown. You can get by without a car in the downtown core since everything is within walking distance and parking can be expensive. **BC Transit** has a good system of buses, trolleys, the **West Coast Express** and an elevated rail system called **SkyTrain**, plus the **SeaBus** going across to North and West Vancouver. In False Creek the little **Aquabus** takes people from downtown over to Granville Island.

Aside from coping with one-way streets, driving is practical around Vancouver although left-turn lanes are not frequent, streets can be narrow with parking on the kerbs and traffic is often heavy during the day. Metered parking is available but can cost as much as $12 per hour in the downtown core. Car parks accept either coins or credit cards.

Sights

ⓘ **Bloedel Floral**
Conservatory and
Queen Elizabeth Park $
33rd Ave and Cambie St;
tel: (604) 257-8584. Open
Oct–Mar daily 1000–1700;
Apr–Sept Mon–Fri
0900–2000, Sat and Sun
1000–2100.

Beaches
Beaches are plentiful and crowded in the summer with swimmers, sun bathers and volleyball nets. They curve in an arc from English Bay around Stanley Park and from Kitsilano to Wreck Beach (the unofficial nudist beach) near the University of British Columbia (UBC). Less crowded in the winter, the beaches are great for walking and beachcombing.

Bloedel Floral Conservatory and Queen Elizabeth Park
Spread over Vancouver's Little Mountain, this is a good place to come if only for a panoramic view of the city. But there's more. The park is

Burnaby Village Museum $ 6501 Deer Lake Ave; tel: (604) 293-6500 or 293-6501; www. burnabyvillagemuseum.ca. Open May–Aug 1100–1630; special hours at Christmas.

Canada Place On the harbour between Burrard and Howe Sts.

second only to Stanley Park in size and it's filled with visitors year round, particularly bridal parties posing for pictures. The Conservatory has more than 500 species of plants with an emphasis on exotic plants, and birds that fly around your head as you wander along circular paths. The nearby Arboretum has almost all the trees native to Canada plus some exotic specimens from other countries.

Burnaby Village Museum

This 4ha village is a recreation of life in 1920s Burnaby, and has 30 full-scale buildings manned by costumed interpreters who bring the village to life. The blacksmith hammers at his forge, the school-marm tells kids about life in a one-room school, and the ice-cream shop dispenses huge cones. Kids adore the genuine vintage carousel that spins them around at a good clip.

Canada Place

Like the Sydney Opera House, the sails on the roof of Canada Place have become a symbol for Vancouver. This is a multi-use building: it's a convention centre, ship terminal, hotel site and IMAX cinema. All summer long there will be at least a couple of ships docked alongside. This is a photographic 'must' for visitors.

Below
Canada Place from Stanley Park

Capilano Suspension Bridge $$
3735 Capilano Rd;
tel: (604) 985-7474;
www.capbridge.com. Open
everyday except Christmas
Day; 0830 to dusk in
summer, 0900–1700 in
winter.

Dr Sun Yat-Sen Classical Chinese Garden $
578 Carrall St; tel: (604) 662-3207; e-mail:
sunyatsen@telus.net; www.vancouverchinesegarden.com

Capilano Suspension Bridge

This is the longest and highest suspended footbridge in the world spanning 137m across the Capilano River canyon at a height of 70m. The original bridge was built in 1889 for men logging on the other side of the chasm but it was opened to the public later by a widow lonely for company who charged 10¢ to cross to the quiet forest on the other side. This is Vancouver's oldest tourist attraction and home to a 'first' in North America – Treetops. This new attraction offers a squirrel's-eye-view of a thriving coastal rainforest via a series of elevated suspension bridges that link the tops of majestic Douglas firs, some as high as 100 feet above the forest floor.

Right
Capilano Suspension Bridge

Below
Chinatown market stall

Chinatown

There's a real feel of authenticity here with even street signs marked with Chinese characters. Vancouver's Chinatown is the third-largest in North America and filled with people daily shopping for vegetables, strange dried fish, ducks hanging in glass cases, or having breakfast in numerable restaurants. During the summer, there's a great night market that captures the colour and excitement in the area and this has done a lot to revitalise Chinatown. If you can make it here for Chinese New Year or the Moon Festival, you're in for a special treat.

Dr Sun Yat-Sen Classical Chinese Garden

This authentic Ming Dynasty garden is the first of its kind to be built anywhere in the world, including China, since 1492. For authenticity, most of the materials and traditional construction tools were imported from Suzhou, China's foremost garden city. There is such a gentleness and serenity in this tranquil oasis, it's hard to believe bustling Chinatown is just beyond the gate. All through the garden Taoist principles of yin and yang appear in numerous ways: rugged and hard balanced by soft and flowing; dark balanced by light. This is a place to slip into for rest and tranquillity.

Gastown $–$$$
along Water St between Columbia and East Cordova Sts.

George C Reifel Bird Sanctuary $
Westham Island, Richmond, near the airport; tel: (604) 946-6980; www.reifelbirdsanctuary.com

Granville Island $–$$$
On the south side of False Creek beneath the Granville Bridge. Open daily. The Aquabus leaves for the Island from the foot of Hornby St.

Grouse Mountain $$
6400 Nancy Greene Way, North Vancouver; tel: (604) 980-9311; www.grousemountain.com. Skyride leaves every 15 minutes 0900–2200 daily.

HR MacMillan Space Centre $$ *1160 Chestnut St, Vancouver; tel: (604) 738-7827; e-mail: info@spacecentre.ca; www. hrmacmillanspacecentre.com. Open Tue–Sun 1000–1700.*

Lighthouse Park
Off Marine Drive at Beacon Lane, between West Vancouver and Horseshoe Bay.

Gastown

This is where Vancouver began when a loquacious publican named John 'Gassy Jack' Deighton set up a saw horse with a barrel of whisky and thereby became the city's first businessman. There's a statue to **Gassy Jack** at the corner of Water and Carrall Sts to honour Vancouver's disreputable City Founder. The area now caters mainly to tourists, particularly those off the cruise ships, but there are some good restaurants and pubs. Don't miss the **steam clock** that blows its top on the quarter-hour and makes a wonderful photographic memento of Gastown.

George C Reifel Migratory Bird Sanctuary

This is a mecca for naturalists from around the world who come for the migratory birds and those that over-winter in this internationally recognised 360ha bird sanctuary. Buy an inexpensive package of birdseed and you'll have flocks around you.

Granville Island

Until the 1960s when a new sense of civic beauty and pride began, this is where tons of metal products and industrial pollutants were manufactured. It was all cleaned up and transformed into an immensely popular centre for live theatre, markets, speciality boutiques and galleries. **Emily Carr School of Art and Design** is here along with many workshops where potters, glass blowers and designers work at their crafts. It's a place to come to shop for fresh produce, seafood and much more in the **Granville Market**, to dine at one of the restaurants, visit the **Granville Island Brewery** or stay at the Island's Boatel.

Grouse Mountain

Take the 125-passenger Skyride to the top of the mountain for a spectacular view on a clear day or to hike the trails around the 1,242m summit. This aerial tramway is the largest built in North America and it whisks you from the base to the chalet 1,100m above sea level. In the summer a short helicopter ride offers a bird's-eye view, there's a restaurant, a film on Grouse Mountain a couple of rescued grizzly cubs and lots of sporting activities such as paragliding. In the winter, Grouse is the closest ski area to downtown.

The HR MacMillan Space Centre

Children from the age of four upwards will adore this interactive journey into space, including computers that let kids turn themselves into aliens. The emphasis is on interaction, and kids will be thoroughly drawn in by hosts who introduce life in a space station, rockets and space life in general. The Virtual Voyages Simulator is a special thrill for kids over 1m tall – a chance to travel without leaving planet Earth. The Planetarium also has interactive shows.

Lighthouse Park

This park is in West Vancouver and covers 75ha of rainforest. Some of the largest Douglas firs in Vancouver are here, many estimated to be

Lookout at Harbour Centre $$
555 west Hastings St; tel: (604) 689-0421; www.vancouverlookout.com. For restaurant patrons the elevator ride is free. Open 0830–2230 daily.

Museum of Anthropology $
6393 northwest Marine Dr.; tel: (604) 822-5087; e-mail: info@moa.ubc.ca; www.moa.ubc.ca. Open mid-May–Labour Day daily 1000–1700, Tue until 2100; rest of the year closed Mon, open Wed–Sun 1100–1700, Tue until 2100.

Science World $$
1455 Quebec St near Main St at the east end of False Creek; tel: (604) 443-7440; www.scienceworld.bc.ca. Open daily 1000–1800.

Stanley Park Follow Georgia St away from the city centre going northwest until you see the park entrance. www.seestanleypark.com. For the **Aquarium $$** tel: (604) 659-3474; www.vanaqua.org. Open daily.

Right
Science World's geodesic dome

more than 500 years old. Trails run through the park with some leading to the Lighthouse at **Point Atkinson**, built in 1912.

Lookout at Harbour Centre

This looks a bit like a flying saucer sitting on top of a high-rise, but glass elevators will whizz you up 50 storeys for a panoramic view of the city that's hard to beat. On a clear day you can actually see all the way to Vancouver Island. Tickets are good all day so you can come back to see the city at night. There's a revolving restaurant up at the top as well.

Museum of Anthropology

The museum, inspired by West Coast aboriginal longhouses, holds one of the world's finest collections of First Nations art and artefacts with both modern and antique totem poles, masks and much more. Outside, there's a life-size model of a Haida village and many modern totem poles.

Science World

This geodesic dome began life as an Expo '86 pavilion and was transformed into a $50 million science museum with lots of hands-on

displays explaining science and the natural world for kids and kids-at-heart. There's lots of interactive exhibits, live performances and special events. Don't miss the opportunity to see what your child will look like as an adult!

Stanley Park

This park lies deep in the heart of Vancouver, and of Vancouverites; a place where as a child you ride the **Miniature Train** through the forest and as an adult return for 1,001 pleasures. In winter 2006 a near-hurricane levelled many of the trees in the park's 405ha, leaving gaps in the former impenetrable density, but most trails are open again and the park is healing. The beaches, totem poles, cricket pitches, rose gardens and famous seawall are in full swing again, and professional guides on **horse-drawn tours** now add the storm to their list of

**ⓘ Steveston
Heritage Fishing
Village $** *Southwest corner
of Richmond, 8km off Hwy
99 along Steveston Hwy tel:
(604) 275-9452;
www.steveston.bc.ca*

Talaysay Tours $$$
*Tel: (604) 628-8555, tollfree
(800) 605-4643; e-mail:
candace@talaysaytours.com;
www.talaysaytours.com*

**UBC Botanical
Gardens $**
*University of British
Columbia, southwest Marine
Dr.; tel: (604) 822-9666;
www.ubcbotanicalgarden.org.
Open daily mid-Mar–mid-Oct
1000–1800.*

**Van Dusen Botanical
Garden $**
*5251 Oak St at 37th Ave;
tel: (604) 878-9274; www.
city.vancouver.bc.ca/parks/
parks/vandusen. Open daily.*

Yaletown *Runs from False
Creek to Burrard St on the
northwest and Georgia St on
the northeast.*

Below
Cruise ship sails under Lion's
Gate Bridge

favourite stories such as Deadman's Island and Girl in Wetsuit. The former zoo is gone but the revitalised **Vancouver Aquarium** more than makes up for it. Displays such as the room with jellyfish are a knockout, and everywhere you go in the aquarium clever designers have created interactive displays that wow kids. There are numerous feeding and activity shows with dolphins, belugas and otters that are informative and funny. Underwater windows provide a rare close-up glimpse of the enormous but gentle belugas. Ask at the Aquarium about their special 'Sleeping with the Whales' programme, when guests can bunk down in sleeping bags beside the whales.

Steveston Heritage Fishing Village
Back in the late 1800s, when this was a thriving fishing village, more than 10,000 people lived here and worked a series of canneries. Today, Steveston is still the largest commercial fishing harbour in Canada but it also attracts artists and photographers who come for the rustic buildings, museums, galleries and restaurants. You can buy fresh fish and shellfish right off the boats here.

Talaysay Tours
These kayaking tours led by anthropologist and kayak guide Candace Campo combine an intimate exploration of the coastline with local history, legends and stories of the Shishalh First Nations people on BC's Sunshine Coast.

UBC Botanical Gardens
This is really five gardens in one, making up one of the oldest and finest botanical gardens in Canada. The Asian Garden has a range from magnolias to rare blue Himalayan poppies, the Native Garden displays more than 3,500 indigenous plants, the Alpine Garden thrives on imported soil and rare mountain plants from around the world, the Physick Garden re-creates a 16th-century monastic herb garden and the Food Garden is a lesson in efficient planting, all on a hectare. Also at UBC is the Nitobe Memorial Garden, a gentle stroll in a traditional Japanese garden.

Van Dusen Botanical Garden
This vast collection of small gardens was once a Vancouver golf course. Within the 22ha of gardens there are many rare and international species, topiaries, an Elizabethan hedge maze, lakes and children's gardens.

Yaletown
City planners come from around the world to admire the skill used in redeveloping this part of Vancouver from its former self as a rowdy warehouse area. At one time, Yaletown boasted more saloons per acre than anywhere in the world; today it's filled with galleries, fashionable furnishing shops, architects, designers and filmmakers. It's also a centre for some of the city's most trendy restaurants.

Accommodation and food

Vancouver has the full range of hotels: from the ultra luxurious with spectacular views to quaint and folksy but easy on the purse plus all the familiar chain hotels – Marriott, Four Seasons, PanPacific, Holiday Inn etc. Rates are considerably higher in the summer at many hotels and inns.

Eating out in Vancouver is a genuine pleasure with so many different ethnic restaurants from which to choose in every price range. Vancouver has seen a huge explosion of places to eat out since the wildly successful Expo '86 and the influx of thousands of immigrants, particularly from Hong Kong. As a result of this immigration, Vancouver has been blessed with some of the finest Chinese restaurants (and Hong Kong chefs) in the world.

Buchan Hotel $ *1906 Haro St; tel: (604) 685-5354, tollfree (800) 668-6654; e-mail: mail@buchanhotel.com; www.buchanhotel.com.* Basic clean rooms on a tree-lined street one block from Stanley Park. One of the best downtown bargains. Vancouver's first non-smoking hotel.

C $$$ *2 1600 Howe St; tel: (604) 681-1164; www.crestaurant.com.* Wonderful and exotic seafood, Zen-like surroundings and a great view of False Creek and Granville Island. This restaurant gets high praise from everyone.

The Cannery Seafood House $$ *2205 Commissioner St; tel: (604) 254-9606, tollfree (877) 254-9606; www.canneryseafood.com.* A long-time award-winning Vancouver favourite for seafood. Try the house speciality Salmon Wellington.

Diva at the Met $$$ *645 Howe St; tel: (604) 602-7788; www.metropolitan.com.* Innovative and contemporary cuisine that is as tasty as it is beautiful. The Alaska Black Cod here is sinfully good.

English Bay Inn $$ *1968 Comox St; tel: (604) 683-8002, tollfree (866) 683-8002; e-mail: stay@englishbayinn.com; www.englishbayinn.com.* A romantic and cosy inn just minutes away from Stanley Park and English Bay.

Fairmont Hotel Vancouver $$$ *900 west Georgia St; tel: (604) 684-3131; www.fairmont.com/hotelvancouver.* This is Vancouver's trademark hotel with its famous peaked green rooftops. Renovated many times and worth its price in comfort and convenience.

Go Fish $ *1505 W 1st Ave; tel: (604) 730-5040.* Fans say this is the best fish and chips in Vancouver. By Fisherman's Wharf.

Listel Vancouver $$$ *1300 Robson St; tel: (604) 684-8461, tollfree (800) 663-5491; e-mail: moreinfo@listel-vancouver.com; www.listel-vancouver.com.* Intimate hotel right in the heart of the lively Robson shopping district. Rooms beautifully decorated featuring choice First Nation's works of art and jazz.

Opposite
Van Dusen Botanical Gardens

Above
Vancouver Fountain

Lord Stanley Suites On the Park $$ *1889 Alberni St; tel: (604) 688-9299, tollfree (888) 767-7829; e-mail: info@lordstanley.com; www.lordstanley.com.* All-suites boutique hotel ideal for extended stay visitors.

Meinhardt Fine Foods $$ *3002 Granville St; tel: (604) 732-4405; www.meinhardt.com.* This is the best equipped food store in town; also offers an excellent deli for dining in at a counter or taking out for a picnic.

Nu $$ *1661 Granville St; tel: (604) 646-4668.* Sophisticated, delicious dining, great atmosphere.

'O Canada' House $$ *1114 Barclay St; tel: (604) 688-0555, tollfree (877) 688-1114; www.ocanadahouse.com; e-mail: info@ocanadahouse.com.* A beautifully restored 1897 Victorian home in the West End.

Opus Hotel $$$ *322 Davie St; tel: (604) 642-6787, tollfree (866) 642-6787; e-mail: info@opushotel.com; www.opushotel.com.* Strikingly modern but with traditionally gracious service. Considered one of Vancouver's hottest 'hangout' places and truly one of the city's best kept secrets.

Shao Lin Noodle Restaurant $ *548 west Broadway; tel: (604) 873-1816.* In addition to great noodle dishes and Dim sum treats, you get to watch noodle makers spinning and stretching the noodles before your eyes.

Sophie's Cosmic Café $ *2095 west 4th Ave; tel: (604) 732-6810.* This funky diner in Kitsilano has good hearty food with lots of vegetarian dishes. Famous for its breakfasts.

Sun Sui Wah Seafood Restaurant $–$$ *3888 Main St; tel: (604) 872-8822.* Ask anyone about his or her favourite Chinese restaurant in Vancouver and this usually comes up. Great creative Cantonese cooking at reasonable prices. Another restaurant in Richmond.

Tojo's $$$ *1133 W Broadway; tel: (604) 872-8050.* About as good as Japanese food gets.

Vij's $$–$$$ *1480 W 11th Ave; tel: (604) 736-6664.* The best Indian food in Vancouver, and maybe Canada.

Wedgewood Hotel $$$ *845 Hornby St; tel: (604) 689-7777, tollfree (800) 663-0666; e-mail: info@wedgewoodhotel.com; www.wedgewoodhotel. com.* Considered Vancouver's leading intimate boutique hotel, the Wedgewood does everything right from its fireplace-lit bar, elegant spa to superb award-winning restaurant, Bacchus.

West End Guest House $$ *1362 Haro St; tel: (604) 681-2889, tollfree (888) 546-3327; e-mail: info@westendguesthouse.com; www. westendguesthouse.com.* A hot-pink Victorian inn with antiques and terrific service.

West Restaurant $$$ *2881 Granville St (at 13th); tel: (604) 738-8938; e-mail: info@westrestaurant.com; www.westrestaurant.com.* Voted

Restaurant of the Year in 2007, West is one of those miraculous blends of highly creative food that tastes down-home delicious.

Suggested walking tour

Total distance: 16km.

Time: About 3 hours for the walking but could stretch to 8 with stops in Yaletown and on Granville Island.

Links: This city tour links with ferry routes to Vancouver Island from Horseshoe Bay via Hwy 1 westbound and to the Fraser Valley eastbound. From **Hope** (*see page 223*) Hwy 3 goes through the Cascade Mountains to **Osoyoos** (*see page 200*), the starting point for a journey through the Okanagan Valley.

Route: Starting at **CANADA PLACE** ❶, head east down Cordova Street West. Turn right on Seymour Street for **THE LOOKOUT AT HARBOUR CENTRE** ❷ for a ride up to an eagle's view of the city. Return to Cordova Street and veer left on Water Street as this is the start of **GASTOWN** ❸ where Vancouver souvenirs of every sort can be bought or you can just hang around the **steam-powered clock** at Water and Cambie Streets until it puffs out billowing white clouds. Anyone interested in historical architecture should note **Gaoler's Mews** at 12 Water Street and the **Byrnes Block** on the corner of Water and Carrall Streets.

Detour 1: Continuing east along Cordova Street brings you into Vancouver's Skid Row, not the best place to walk around alone. If you have a companion though you might check out the **Vancouver Police Centennial Museum** at Cordova St and Gore Ave just east of Main Street. This museum has a fascinating collection from the city's more notorious crimes including the famous Babes in the Wood murder.

Walk south on Carrall Street until it hits Pender Street and you will see the entrance to the **DR SUN YAT-SEN CLASSICAL CHINESE GARDEN** ❹. This serene oasis is worth half a day just for time to rest and contemplate. The free public park next door is also designed as a Chinese garden. A short path through the park will take you to Columbia Street where on the left you find the entrance to the **Chinese Cultural Centre Museum and Archives**, the first museum in Canada dedicated to Chinese-Canadian history. Return to Pender Street and continue east into **CHINATOWN** ❺ where there is good shopping for both eastern and western cooking, and kitchen wares at **Ming Wo Cookware**, 23 East Pender St. For a vast selection of teas, visit **Ten Ren Tea and Ginseng** at 500 Main Street, and for ceramics and furniture **Yeu Hua Handicrafts Limited** at 173 East Pender Street.

Following Main Street south, turn right at the **SkyTrain** station and walk towards the huge geodesic dome that is **SCIENCE WORLD** ❻. If you have kids from three up, you'll have to drag them away from here. You can pick up the start of the grand Seawall Trail here and continue by foot around False Creek to Pacific Boulevard and cross to Maitland. This is **YALETOWN** ❽, a perfect area for browsing or having lunch in one of the area's many funky restaurants.

Detour 2: Catch the **Aquabus** at the dock at the foot of Hornby Street for **GRANVILLE ISLAND** ❼ where you can spend a couple of hours sampling the excellent foods at the Granville Market, watch street performers, visit artists in their studios or just throw chips to the seagulls.

Head down to Beach Avenue via Hornby Street to pick up the Seawall Trail. The Seawall Trail on almost any day of the year will be alive with walkers, cyclists and rollerbladers, mostly Vancouverites who enjoy this easy road to fitness. It's a beautiful trail that hugs the shoreline for 10km winding past **English Bay** ❾. The trail goes past several beaches, under the **Lion's Gate Bridge** and by the rock on which **Girl in Wetsuit** sits, Vancouver's answer to Copenhagen's Little Mermaid. The walk offers excellent photo opportunities across **Coal Harbour** ❿ over to **CANADA PLACE** and the city.

Coming back to the entrance of the park, continue north to the park's **rose garden** and then under a viaduct to **Lost Lagoon** ⓫.

What to do on a rainy day

It's rumoured that Vancouverites are actually the ones who spread the myth that it rains in Vancouver all the time: but when it does, here's what to do. You can head out to the Stanley Park Aquarium and even spend the night in your sleeping bag by the belugas on special dates. Visit the Bloedel Conservatory in Queen Elizabeth Park for tropical heat and flowers. Enjoy a tranquil tea in the Bacchus Lounge of the Wedgewood Hotel on Hornby Street. Take an X-Tour where the actual scenes were shot for some of the 118 X Files episodes filmed in Vancouver. Visit the Vancouver Public Library with its Roman Colosseum design to catch up on your reading. Buy a 'brolly' or have one custom-made in The Umbrella Shop, 1106 West Broadway, then head out to Lighthouse Park for a wilderness walk in the rain with Manfred Scholermann, Rockwood Adventures, tel: (604) 980-7749; www.rockwoodadventures.com

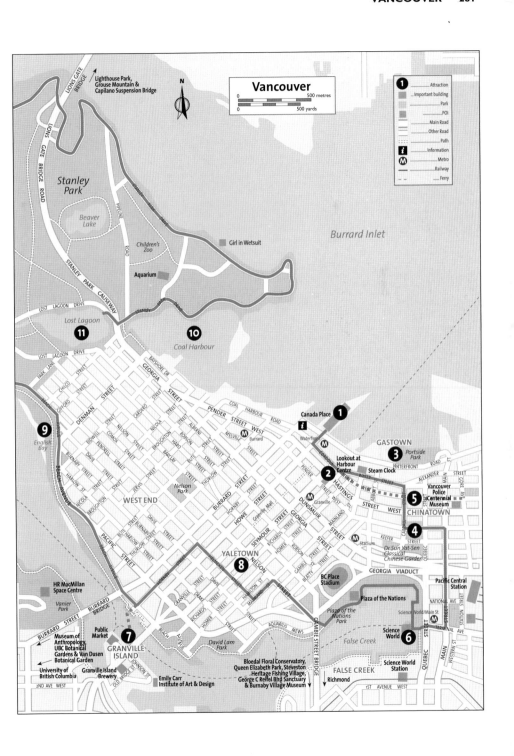

Vancouver

Lighthouse Park,
Grouse Mountain &
Capilano Suspension Bridge

N

0   500 metres
0   500 yards

1 ....Attraction
........Important building
............Park
............POI
............Main Road
............Other Road
............Path
i ....Information
M ....Metro
............Railway
............Ferry

Stanley
Park

Beaver
Lake

Children's
Zoo

Girl in Wetsuit

Aquarium

Burrard Inlet

LIONS GATE
BRIDGE

LIONS GATE BRIDGE ROAD

STANLEY PARK CAUSEWAY

PIPE LINE ROAD

LOST LAGOON DRIVE

Lost Lagoon

11

10

Coal Harbour

LOST LAGOON DRIVE

BAYSHORE DR

PARK LANE

CHILCO STREET

GIFFORD

GEORGIA STREET

COAL HARBOUR ROAD

PENDER STREET WEST

Canada Place **1**

i

GASTOWN

3 Portside
Park

Waterfront

M
Burrard

MELVILLE STREET

ALBERNI STREET

ROBSON STREET

HARO STREET

BARCLAY STREET

NELSON STREET

COMOX STREET

PENDRELL STREET

DAVIE STREET

BURNABY STREET

HARWOOD ST

NICOLA STREET

JERVIS STREET

BROUGHTON STREET

THURLOW STREET

BURRARD STREET

HORNBY STREET

HOWE STREET

Granville Mall

SEYMOUR STREET

RICHARDS STREET

HOMER STREET

HAMILTON STREET

MAINLAND STREET

CAMBIE STREET

BEATTY STREET

ABBOTT STREET

CARRALL ST

MAIN STREET

COLUMBIA STREET

QUEBEC STREET

GORE AVE

DUNLEVY AVE

JACKSON AVE

DENMAN STREET

BIDWELL STREET

CARDERO STREET

NICOLA STREET

THURLOW STREET

BUTE STREET

Nelson
Park

M
Granville

BURRARD STREET

GEORGIA STREET

DUNSMUIR STREET

PENDER STREET

HASTINGS STREET WEST

WATER STREET

Steam Clock

Lookout at
Harbour
Centre

2

ALEXANDER STREET

POWELL STREET

CORDOVA STREET

Vancouver
Police
Centennial
Museum **5**

CHINATOWN

KEEFER STREET

PENDER STREET

4

Dr Sun Yat-Sen
Classical
Chinese Garden

GEORGIA VIADUCT

English
Bay

9

PACIFIC STREET

DAVIE STREET

BEACH AVENUE

HARO STREET

NICOLA STREET

BROUGHTON STREET

BUTE STREET

HARLOW STREET

THURLOW STREET

WEST END

BURRARD STREET

HOWE STREET

HORNBY STREET

NELSON STREET

HELMCKEN STREET

DAVIE STREET

SEYMOUR STREET

RICHARDS STREET

HOMER STREET

MAINLAND STREET

CAMBIE STREET

BEATTY STREET

M
Stadium

M
Yaletown

YALETOWN

8

BC Place
Stadium

Pacific Central
Station

NATIONAL AVE

TERMINAL AVE

STATION STREET

MAIN STREET

WESTERN ST

QUEBEC STREET

GORE AVE

HR MacMillan
Space Centre

Vanier
Park

BURRARD BRIDGE

BURRARD STREET

PACIFIC STREET

GRANVILLE STREET

HOWE STREET

SEYMOUR STREET

RICHARDS STREET

HOMER STREET

MAINLAND STREET

DRAKE STREET

DAVIE STREET

BEACH

PACIFIC BOULEVARD

CAMBIE STREET BRIDGE

Plaza of the Nations

Plaza of the
Nations
Park

Science World/Main St

False Creek

Science
World **6**

M
Science World/Main St

Museum of
Anthropology,
UBC Botanical
Gardens & Van Dusen
Botanical Garden

University of
British Columbia

Public
Market

7

GRANVILLE
ISLAND

Granville Island
Brewery

Emily Carr
Institute of Art & Design

OLD BRIDGE STREET

JOHNSTON ST

ALDER ST

David Lam
Park

AQUARIUS MEWS

Bloedal Floral Conservatory,
Queen Elizabeth Park, Steveston
Heritage Fishing Village,
George C Reifel Bird Sanctuary
& Burnaby Village Museum ▼

Richmond

FALSE CREEK

Science World
Station

M

2ND AVE WEST

1ST AVENUE WEST

Acknowledgements

The authors and publishers would like to thank the following people and organisations for their assistance during the preparation of this book: the spirit, inspiration and dedication of Patrick and Peggy Telfer; Mona Gauvreau and Carla Moesman of pr works; Maria Crump, Travel Alberta; Cindy Burr and Mika Ryan, Tourism British Columbia; Marla Daniels, Edmonton Tourism; Danielle Oberle, Calgary Convention and Visitors Bureau; Kimberley Lyall, Alberta South Tourism Destination Region; Delta Lodge at Kananaskis; Lisa Kiehl, Fairmont Palliser Hotel; Panorama Mountain Village; Ramada Hotel, Lethbridge; Anastasia Martin-Stilwell, Fairmont Jasper Park Lodge, Jasper; André and George Schwarz, Post Hotel, Lake Louise; Nora Weber, BC Rail; Monica Ott, Okanagan Wine Train; Deirdre Campbell; Grace and Karl Sands, Amethyst Inn at Regent's Park; The Prancing Horse; WKL Communications; Chris Higgins, Seasmoke Communications; Markus Griesser, The Aerie; Laura Serena, Tourism Vancouver; Josette Whist, Stump Lake; Beverley Dragseth, Pacific Wilderness Railway; Ali Macaraeg, VIA Rail, Vancouver; Janice Greenwood, Rocky Mountaineer Railtours.

Project management: Cambridge Publishing Management Limited
Project editor: Karen Beaulah
Series design: Fox Design
Cover design: Liz Lyons Design
Layout: Cambridge Publishing Management Limited
Map work: PCGraphics (UK) Ltd
Repro and image setting: PDQ Digital Media Solutions Ltd/
Cambridge Publishing Management Limited
Printed and bound in India by: Replika Press Pvt Ltd

We would also like to thank the following for the photographs used in this book, to whom the copyright in the following photographs belong:

Bob Swift/Alberta Heritage Exposition: page 72
Candace Meyer/BC Rail: page 170
Cariboo Chilcotin Coast Tourism Association/Thomas Drasclauskis: page 147
BC Ferries: pages 180, 185, 186
Fred Gebhart: page 187
Karen Beaulah: page 277
Kootenay Rockies Tourism: page 118
Merridale Cider: page 235
Medicine River Wildlife Rehabilitation Centre: page 79
Pictures Colour Library: pages 51, 156, 173, 174
Royal BC Museum: page 257
Spectrum Colour Library: page 46
Sundance Guest Ranch: page 195
Donald L Telfer: pages 3, 6, 7, 13, 14 (top), 19, 21, 38, 40, 41, 44, 50, 52, 55, 56, 59, 62, 64, 65, 67, 70, 74, 77, 81 (both), 84, 88, 89 (both), 90, 91, 94, 97, 98, 99, 102, 104, 107, 108, 109, 112, 115, 121, 124, 126, 127, 129, 132, 134, 140, 143, 144, 145, 146, 148, 160, 163, 165 (both), 271
Tim Thompson: pages 12, 14 (bottom), 29, 86, 155, 275
Don Weixl (www.donweixl.com): pages 167, 200, 204, 206, 211
Helena Zukowski: pages 17, 22, 42, 54, 117, 122, 135, 150, 177, 183, 190, 193, 194, 197, 198, 203, 208, 210, 212, 214, 216, 218, 219, 220, 222, 225, 226, 228, 229, 232, 237, 240, 242, 243, 244, 246, 247, 248, 250, 251, 252, 254, 260, 262, 264, 266, 268, 272 (both), 274, 278

Feedback form

We're committed to providing the very best up-to-date information in our travel guides and constantly strive to make them as useful as they can be. You can help us to improve future editions by letting us have your feedback. Just take a few minutes to complete and return this form to us. And, as an extra 'thank you' from Thomas Cook Publishing, you'll be automatically entered into our exciting prize draw.

When did you buy this book? ....
....

Where did you buy it? (Please give town/city and, if possible, name of retailer)
....
....

When did you/do you intend to travel in the Canadian Rockies?...
....

For how long (approx.)? ....

How many people in your party? ....

Which cities, national parks and other locations did you/do you intend mainly to visit?
....
....
....
....

Did you/will you:
❏ Make all your travel arrangements independently?
❏ Travel on a fly-drive package?
Please give brief details: ....
....

Did you/do you intend to use this book:
❏ For planning your trip?   ❏ Both?
❏ During the trip itself?

Did you/do you intend also to purchase any of the following travel publications for your trip?
Thomas Cook *Travellers: Vancouver and BC* ....
A road map/atlas (please specify) ....
Other guidebooks (please specify) ....

Have you used any other Thomas Cook guidebooks in the past? If so, which?

....

....

Please rate the following features of *Drive Around Canadian Rockies* for their value to you (circle VU for 'very useful', U for 'useful', NU for 'little or no use'):

The *Travel facts* section on pages 14–21	VU	U	NU
The *Driver's guide* section on pages 22–7	VU	U	NU
The *Highlights* on pages 36–7	VU	U	NU
The recommended driving routes throughout the book	VU	U	NU
Information on towns and cities, national parks, etc.	VU	U	NU
The maps of towns and cities, parks, etc.	VU	U	NU

Please use this space to tell us about any features that in your opinion could be changed, improved, or added in future editions of the book, or any other comments you would like to make concerning the book:

....

....

....

....

....

....

....

Your age category: ❏ 21–30   ❏ 31–40   ❏ 41–50   ❏ over 50

Your name: Mr/Mrs/Miss/Ms ....

(First name or initials) ....

(Last name) ....

Your full address: (Please include postal or zip code)

....

....

....

....

Your daytime telephone number: ....

Please detach this page and send it to: Drive Around Series Editor, Thomas Cook Publishing, PO Box 227, The Thomas Cook Business Park, 9 Coningsby Road, Peterborough PE3 8SB.

Alternatively, you can e-mail us at: *books@thomascook.com*